W&C Women and Culture Series

The Women and Culture Series is dedicated to books that illuminate the lives, roles, achievements, and status of women, past or present.

Gold Diggers and Silver Miners

GOLD DIGGERS &

PROSTITUTION AND SOCIAL LIFE

The University of Michigan Press *Ann Arbor*

Marion S. Goldman

SILVER MINERS

ON THE COMSTOCK LODE

For Paul and Michael

2001   2000   1999   1998   10   9   8   7

Library of Congress Cataloging in Publication Data

Goldman, Marion S.
  Gold diggers and silver miners.

  (Women and culture series)
  Bibliography: p.
  Includes index.
   1. Prostitution—Nevada—Virginia City—History—
19th century.   2. Miners—Nevada—Virginia City—
History—19th century.   3. Comstock Lode (Nev.)—
History—19th century.   I. Title.   II. Series.
HQ146.V55G64   979.3'56   81-11474
                    AACR2
ISBN 0-472-06332-4 (pbk.)

Preface

LIKE MOST OF the men and women who traveled to the Comstock Lode searching for riches in the nineteenth century, I had almost no idea of what Nevada was like when I moved there. After my husband was appointed an Assistant Professor of Sociology at the University of Nevada at Reno, I went along for the ride, determined to complete my special field and language examinations and write my dissertation in the sociology of deviance for the University of Chicago.

One sunny August morning in 1970 we loaded up a U-Haul, hitched it to our Volkswagen, and left Hyde Park to seek our fortune in the West. Somewhere near Des Moines I opened a bon voyage present from a close woman friend, a copy of Kate Millett's newly published *Sexual Politics*. By the second day of the trip we were crossing the Rockies and I was quoting appropriate passages at Paul, wondering why I had ever agreed to "stand by my man." When we arrived in Reno, my mood did not improve at all.

I had come with the strange idea that northern Nevada probably resembled northern California. After all, Reno is a mere ten miles from the California border, and ten years ago it was possible to drive to Berkeley in less than four hours. I was decidedly wrong, for Reno was like nowhere I had ever lived before. The university was less than six blocks from the downtown casino strip which was topped off by four fifteen-foot-high plaster and neon show girls mounted on the roof of the Prima Donna Club. There were slot machines everywhere—in restaurants, in supermarkets, in the psychology department (where several faculty members studied risk taking). Women were called "girls," or "gals," or "broads," and I had suddenly been transformed from a reasonably successful graduate student with my own identity into Mrs. Paul Goldman, wife of the new sociology professor.

My consciousness of women's subordination was raised in a remarkably short time when I was stuck in a desert city and treated as a faculty spouse more interested in supermarkets than social theory. My situation began to change, however, as I joined six remarkable women who had formed a group to discuss the personal and political dimensions of feminism. Several faculty members in sociology also appreciated my difficult position, and they made it possible for me to teach part time and encouraged me to begin my dissertation research.

Both the women in the group and academic colleagues suggested that prostitution was a natural topic because of my interest in the sociology of deviance and the sociology of sex roles. Nevada offered a unique field setting for that research, since it is the only state where prostitution is legally tolerated as a local option in all but two counties. Like gambling, organized sexual commerce is a visible part of everyday life in the Silver State and once I became interested in sexual commerce I found information about it everywhere.

Even though prostitution was illegal in Reno, major casinos and hotels had call girls available to high rollers, and Mustang Bridge Brothel was close by in another county. Revenue from prostitution was important to a number of rural counties, a point which the town fathers of Searchlight emphasized in the early seventies when a brothel owner decided to add on a new wing. The renovation made Searchlight's most important business illegal, for the addition violated a statute prohibiting houses of prostitution within four hundred yards of a school or church. Naturally, the mayor and city council relocated the school.

The Searchlight story reached local newspapers, and I heard many other private tales from people aware of my interest in prostitution. A man from Winnemucca remembered a minister who preached against the local brothel until he was finally run out of town by merchants refusing to sell him food, gas, or other necessities. In Fallon the sheriff's wife threw a Molotov cocktail at a brothel, and she was arrested and brought to trial. She was placed on probation rather than jailed only because she promised never to do it again. More than a dozen people told me about their experiences growing up in small Nevada towns where brothels were as central to community life as churches. I was soon convinced that prostitution was an integral part of life in Nevada, rooted in the state's unusual social organization and colorful history.

At the same time that I was learning about current sexual commerce in Nevada, I began to explore its history in early mining camps and boomtowns. The forty-minute drive up the Geiger Grade took me from Reno to Virginia City, the greatest, richest mining city in nineteenth-century America, and I discovered why many people loved Nevada. The journey took me from the tawdry glitter of casino row to a city of a hundred years ago, preserved in the clear mountain air and scented by juniper and sagebrush. Rickety tourist traps full of slot machines and hideous antique reproductions dominated the main street; but down the mountain below there were abandoned mines, cottages over a century old, and the remains of a Chinese settlement where it was still possible to dig in the dirt and find fragments of the blue and white pottery its inhabitants had used. A few splendid stone and brick mansions remained on the slope above C Street along with Piper's Opera House, the Miners' Union Hall, and the Storey County courthouse.

The ornate courthouse, built after the Great Fire of 1875, contained hundreds of uncataloged items relevant to Comstock prostitution. I found county commissioners' reports, maps, assessment records, and rare probate records with detailed lists of prostitutes' possessions. I waded into the courthouse documents and also began to visit the university library's unique Special Collections which had nearly complete bound volumes of the *Virginia City Territorial Enterprise,* manuscript census records, and the private, bawdy diaries of a Comstock newspaper editor. The wealth of resources from the Comstock proved to be more interesting to me than modern materials, because the extreme case of prostitution on the Lode could be explored in terms of its relationship to the community as a whole and its impact on the lives of customers, respectable women, and prostitutes.

By the summer of 1973, when my husband and I left Nevada to join the faculty at the University of Oregon, I had gathered all of the data for my dissertation, but my work on this book had only just begun. Scholars throughout the world were turning their attention to feminist issues and developing a new body of knowledge about women, culture, and society which added theoretical dimensions to my initial research, making it necessary for me to ask more questions. After receiving my degree, I went back to the archives for information about the texture of prostitutes' and other Comstock women's daily lives and for additional demographic materials as well. The long process of research and writing was made much easier because students and faculty involved with the Center for the Sociological Study of Women at the University of Oregon provided me with both encouragement and spirited criticism.

My work was also enriched by a number of informants who took the trouble to show me something of modern prostitution. They included streetwalkers, call girls, exotic dancers, and even the great-grandson of a Comstock prostitute and pimp. My graduate advisor had no idea how appropriate his comments were when I first outlined my tentative research proposal and he said, "Even if you don't get enough data for a thesis, you'll be able to make terrific dinner party conversation."

This book represents almost a decade of physical, emotional, and intellectual journeys which I could only undertake because of the direction provided by the feminist community and the support offered by so many colleagues and friends. I benefited from the special expertise generously supplied by a number of individuals who took the time to help during various stages of this project.

This book could not have been written without the assistance of staff members of the Special Collections of the Library of the University of Nevada at Reno, the Nevada Historical Society, and the National Archives. I am also indebted to Barbara Kosydar, Lynn Shy, and Vicki Van Nortwick who not only typed the manuscript but also proved to be invaluable editors and critics.

Discussions with Carl Backman and Neal Ferguson helped me clarify my ideas and frame my research, and Thom Pilkington and Erica Stone offered me unique introductions to various aspects of the fast life. Many people read drafts at different stages and provided careful, detailed criticism. I would especially like to thank Tom Brady, Arlene Daniels, Mimi Johnson, George Kjaer, Barbara Pope, Barry Schwartz, and Jerry Skolnick.

The six feminist scholars who evaluated my original manuscript for the Alice and Edith Hamilton Prize Competition were outstanding readers who painstakingly pointed out ways to revise and strengthen my work. The very existence of a prize dedicated to two pathbreaking women has inspired me, and I am grateful to the University of Michigan Press and to Carol Mitchell for offering me a rare combination of editorial guidance and academic autonomy. I did not always learn as well as I might have from my many teachers or take full advantage of their generously given criticisms, and the flaws in my work are of course my own.

Finally, I would like to thank my husband Paul for helping me make the best of life in the wild west and sustaining me throughout this enterprise. He graciously aided me with my computer work, suggested research questions, and read draft after draft, assimilating more information about the Comstock than he could possibly want or need to know. His dear friendship and warm support happily contradicted some of my central assumptions about sexism, and this book is dedicated to him and to our son Michael.

Contents

Introduction

First came the miners to work in the mine.
Then came the ladies who lived on the line.
Old Mining Camp Ballad

"TRUE SHE WAS a woman of easy virtue. Yet hundreds in this city had cause to bless her name for her many acts of kindness and charity. That woman probably had more real friends than any other."[1]

This praise was bestowed upon a frontier prostitute, Julia Bulette, after her brutal murder in 1867. Like other prostitutes on the Comstock Lode in northwestern Nevada, Julia lived under harsh conditions of discriminatory criminal justice and routine social stigma, but after her death she was honored and gradually transformed into a folk heroine. Julia was an extraordinary woman who combined economic acumen with charity work. She provided customers with companionship as well as sex and aided in the construction of minimal civic order in Virginia City, but she neither lived in luxury nor ruled the community as some of her latter-day biographers suggested.[2]

An introduction to Julia Bulette is a good introduction to this book, for her life and exaggerated legend touch on its three central goals. The first goal is to bury gracefully the legend of the frontier prostitute. Although the decline of western movies and television shows and the rise of feminist scholarship have diluted some of the legend's power, it is still very much alive in Ely, Nevada, and Tulsa, Oklahoma, and points in between. The second goal is to describe the lives of prostitutes and other women on the mining frontier as clearly and accurately as possible, reconstructing a history which is often distorted or buried. The final goal is to use material from the extreme case of the Comstock to sketch some theoretical considerations for future students of sexual commerce.

The Prostitute's Legend

Harlot heroines from Matt Dillon's Kitty to Bob Dylan's Lily continue to capture people's imaginations. Julia, Lola Montez, Belle Cora, and Mattie Silks are among the many real prostitutes whose often painful lives underwent a strange alchemical process from which they emerged as golden women.[3] The idealized frontier prostitute had a number of attributes: (1) beauty, (2) wealth, (3) luxurious surroundings, (4) adoring male companions, (5) envious female rivals, and (6) eventual mobility into respectable affluence. No known frontier prostitute achieved this ideal and only a very few approached it; yet it has come to typify the women who worked on the line. Consider this description of Julia Bulette, accompanied by a photograph of a gorgeous Creole:

She brought airs and graces where comparative barbarism had reigned and the miners accorded her an homage that elsewhere would have been the prerogative of a great lady.

When she occupied a special loge in Macguire's (theater), screened from the general view but an object of universal interest, diamonds sparkled at her throat and ears. . . . The wives of the Comstock were not only morally outraged; they were consumed with embittered jealousy.

Julia's Palace might well have been called "Julia's bank," for her ever expanding business, which by the middle sixties showed tangibly in a neat row of white clapboard cottages with red lights over the door after dark, was making her wealthy even by Comstock standards.[4]

Julia was actually a rather plain Englishwoman in her mid-thirties who came from New Orleans to the Lode in 1861 or 1862 when there were few respectable women. She nursed the sick and injured and donated money to Volunteer Engine Company No. 1, but she received little public thanks until her death. Her house was no mansion, but was instead a two-room cottage without a kitchen or indoor plumbing. She had been seriously ill for several months prior to her death, and her medical and funeral expenses were not covered by her estate.[5]

Over the past hundred years, Julia's beauty, youth, riches, and friends have increased beyond recognition, as have those of other famous frontier prostitutes. The genesis of the frontier prostitute's legend and the reasons for its continued appeal merit books in themselves. Those topics, however, are too interesting to ignore entirely, and some attention to them makes it easier to get beyond popular preconceptions and onto the Comstock.

The legend of the frontier prostitute in American fiction can be a nearly perfect fantasy for men and also for women, allowing both sexes to project their own somewhat different wishes onto a shared image. For men, the fantasy includes the prostitute and often her consort as well. In this couple the prostitute is less the ideal woman than the ideal foil. She is socially skilled, sexually experienced, rich, and beautiful; but she is also calculating and manipulative. This vision of the frontier prostitute rests on an almost classic ambivalence toward women.[6] *Bonanza Queen*, a popular novel about the Comstock, sums up this image in its hero's thoughts:

Kitty cared. It was in her voice, her bearing, her defeated eyes. Looking at her narrowly he wondered how old she was. Twenty-five perhaps. Not a great age to have clawed and ripped her way to line control in Virginia [City]. Canny, beautiful, and in her own fashion a square dealer. . . . Women he mused were the devil.[7]

Whether he was a lawman or an outlaw, the consort was able to see through the prostitute's ruses, meet her on his own terms, and temporarily tame her. His friendship with her added to his stature as a maverick willing to ignore social conventions for his own values. While he may have tried to uplift her or he may have taken her as she was, the consort would never take a prostitute's money. Another recent western novel makes it clear that the consort was also a square dealer in his own fashion, and a sensitive one at that:

Clay had always gone apart . . . one who had looked into vast distances with an impatience that pulled him almost physically to be off. . . . Like Leila, Clay had heard laughter where there was none, had listened to music where no songs were sung. The music and laughter were wild and sirenlike, and maybe a little obscene. But there were tears behind them.[8]

Idealized consorts differed as much from actual customers as legendary prostitutes did from their real counterparts. Alf Doten, the Comstock's most illustrious resident journalist, kept an astonishing diary which is by far the best available private chronicle of daily life on the Lode, and it includes notes on his activities in the bawdy districts. During the first two years he lived on the Comstock, Alf visited prostitutes several times a week, but while he had two or three favorites, Alf never became deeply attached to any of them. Although he could be charming, in his later years Alf was a bully and a drunkard whose ambivalence toward women approached misogyny.[9]

Much of the legend's fascination stems from its characters' independence. The prostitute is as free as her consort, and this freedom makes her attractive to women. The idealized frontier prostitute was among the few "whole" women of the late nineteenth century, possessing both the stereotypic good woman's kindness and warmth and the bad woman's sensuality and vigor. She epitomized feminine strivings for adventure and autonomy at a time when most women were constricted by economic discrimination and custom. The imaginary prostitute could have everything, as she earned a good living and achieved friendship and a modicum of fame by affirming her own sexuality.

The attractive portrait of the loose woman as independent woman is flawed by its lack of fit with reality. The legendary prostitute freely chose to enter the fast life, while her real counterpart was usually forced into prostitution by economic want and destructive sexual relationships. While the harlot heroine lived in luxury, surrounded by adoring friends, the actual prostitute lived in near poverty surrounded by degradation, disease, and violence.

Today's high-priced call girl complements yesterday's romantic adventuress, and both of their legends legitimate the existing distribution of economic and sexual power, permitting respectable people to forget an unpleasant reality and substitute titillating fantasies. Those fantasies are probably as widely believed by academics as they are by other people, and no apologist for prostitution is more blatant than Kingsley Davis, author of the landmark article on the sociology of prostitution who wrote, "From a purely economic point of view, prostitution comes perilously near getting something for nothing."[10] No working prostitute could forget the obvious costs of her rent, police bribes, clothes, doctors' bills, contraceptives, and abortions, as well as the incalculable costs to her body and spirit.

The pervasive fantasy of prostitution and the fear of it must influence scholars, for we are members of our own culture. While most earlier works on prostitution were biased by assumptions that it was an individual woman's choice or problem, this work reflects my own biases toward a sociological perspective shaped by the second wave of American feminism.[11] It is impossible to dismiss psychological explanations entirely, but they alone cannot account for the ways in which sexual commerce is integrated into the fabric of social life. Similarly, psychological factors alone cannot explain the persistence of the harlot heroine's legend.

The legend is grounded in a time and place that brought together the extremes of American social life, and it survives because of the ways in which history is recorded, preserved, and transmitted. The Comstock Lode is an excellent place to begin a search for the frontier prostitute because it was the greatest boomtown of the post-Civil War mining frontier. Now it is familiar only to Nevada history enthusiasts and visitors seeking respite from the Reno casinos, but a hundred years ago it was a household word. Major newspapers across the United States and Europe carried stories about the silver strikes and the community built on them. Residents self-consciously saved scraps of their history and chronicled their daily lives, convinced that their community would become an enduring metropolis. Thus, some unusual documents have been preserved from a unique, albeit brief, situation in which prostitution was a central part of social life.

The Comstock Lode

The current Comstock is a curious mixture of tourist traps, exploratory mining ventures, and counterculture havens located in the high north-western Nevada desert amid magnificent natural vistas and the scents of desert sage and low-growing juniper. Yet, only a century ago the streets were packed with people who jostled each other going to work, shopping, or carousing, and the air was filled with noise from mines and ore mills, dust from teams of horses galloping through town, and shouts from saloons and brothels.

Virginia City and Gold Hill formed the Comstock Lode—the quintessential American boomtown perched on a mountain of silver. In prosperous periods the two communities were almost contiguous, but during major mining depressions they shrank back from each other and the omnibus lines connecting them were usually discontinued. Despite their separate incorporation, each community was always dependent upon the other, and they will be treated as a unit of sister cities in this book.

In 1860, the Comstock was a rude collection of shanties, but by 1873 it had become a bustling center of more than twenty thousand people.[12] The community typified the frontier phenomenon because of its rapid growth and enormous wealth from the mining of silver ore, and because only twenty years marked its rise and final decline. During that brief period, however, people came to the Lode prepared to found a lasting metropolis and they used brick and stone to erect elaborate buildings testifying to their hopes. They created a social organization far more complex than that of a temporary mining camp, as intricate stratification patterns developed to reflect differences in class, race, and sex.

Although the Comstock sprang up in the isolated high desert, its economic and social patterns were intimately bound to all postbellum America. Ore from the mines fueled the Union cause during the Civil

War and later helped generate the national surge of industrialization in the later sixties and seventies. Influential residents tried to make the Comstock resemble San Francisco, Chicago, or other metropolitan centers, and, while life on the Lode was often quite different from life in those cities, its fundamental shape was similar.

The Comstock could scarcely be called a typical city or an average one, but its very excesses reveal something about the social organization of more sedate communities. The blatant boosterism, wild speculation, ethnic variety, and rampant commercial vice characteristic of the Comstock were present to some degree in every mid-nineteenth-century American city. Some conditions of life on the Lode surely crossed the invisible boundary separating the "normal" from the "deviant" in the United States, but most of that was an exuberant extension of general social trends in an era of rapid industrialization and urbanization.

An extraordinary dearth of women on the Comstock somewhat distorted all relations between the sexes. The scarcity combined with the community's sudden growth and fluid social structure to produce an unusual situation in which prostitution developed freely. In 1875 at least one woman in twelve was a prostitute, and an intricate body of local laws and customs regulated life in the vice districts. But while prostitution on the Comstock was extreme in its size and impact, its form and functions differed little from commercial vice in other American cities.[13]

The relative absence of structural constraints on the Comstock permitted prostitution to flower more fully than it could in other places. Prostitution on the Lode clearly exhibited some of the central features of sexual commerce in the United States, making obvious some of the social relationships hidden in more complex, ambiguous contexts. It came close to resembling a Weberian ideal type, displaying the essential logic and meaning of American sexual commerce.[14] Although Comstock prostitution was extraordinary, it illuminates the central features of prostitution in America, just as a distorted magnifying mirror ultimately clarifies an image.

Questions of Research

Some miners rushed to the Comstock with little more than the clothes on their back, while more affluent people brought trunks or whole freight wagons of goods. However, no one came to the frontier with more cognitive and emotional baggage than social researchers seeking to reconstruct the past. The scholar's baggage includes many half-articulated assumptions about human nature and social structure, as well as methodological problems of understanding subjective meanings and the biased transmission of historical materials.

Difficulties in understanding the subjective meaning of action plague social scientists. There are often disjunctions between people's attitudes and their behavior—between their inner and outer social worlds.[15] Moreover, the same activities can have vastly different meanings depending on where and when they occurred. Participants in the Comstock boom years spoke the same language, lived in many of the same houses, and did some of the same work as the people who live there now. However, enormous changes in social time and technology separate the generations as much as the years.

In the sixties and seventies almost all people on the Lode organized their lives around the silver mines' schedules.[16] Everything from store hours to mealtimes to brothel timetables depended upon whether the mines were in full operation around the clock, on daily schedules, or partially or completely shut down. The variable number of working hours and their spread were very different from the regulated times most of us now take for granted. They were the result of the community's isolation and dependence on one labor-intensive industry with minimal labor organization.

The technological advances in transportation also created enormous gaps between nineteenth- and twentieth-century social time. Today it takes less than five hours to drive from San Francisco to Virginia City, but in 1862 the average trip took more than a day.[17] Similarly, cleaning a parlor or washing clothes took far more time a century ago, and both the nature and social definitions of housework have altered along with its technology.[18] Activities have changed as technology has changed the time and social meanings which people invest in them. Historical research demands attention to differences in the structure of activities and the social meanings attached to them in order to develop a closer approximation of subjective understanding.

There is no set method for comprehending subjective reality, but the best way to get close to that subjectivity is to find as much information as possible, weighing whether it is intentional or unintentional.[19] Intentional sources are meant to be public, and the individuals who created them did so with conscious motives, while unintentional sources often yield different information because they were not shaped by conscious standards of social desirability. It is sometimes difficult to distinguish intentionality. For example, most people writing private diaries were aware of their descendants' judgments and newspaper reporters may have successfully presented absolute, unembellished facts. Moreover, some intentional sources provide unintentional information. Thus, Comstock newspaper advertisements for sexual tonics inadvertently revealed common assumptions about the nature of sexuality and disease.

While there is no absolute classification of sources, it is still possible to define information as more or less purposive. Usually less intentional sources are more accurate because they were not consciously constructed to change minds or images. Those sources also furnish most information about people who could not write about themselves because of lack of literacy or time. The lives of workers, children, ordinary wives, and prostitutes must often be pieced together through dry census data, probate records, and other public documents recording the bare facts of their existence.

The finite data available make it necessary to study the past in an atmosphere of scarcity, using whatever information survives.[20] This study used every important primary and secondary source of data from the Comstock boom years, including every extant issue of the *Territorial Enterprise* published from 1860 through 1880, manuscript census materials, legislative records, city directories, probates, private diaries, and even the ruins of shanty towns. All of those sources had to be used, because prostitutes wrote little and most of what they did write disappeared.

In 1870, 20 percent of the United States population over ten years of age could neither read nor write and literacy was a valued, scarce resource.[21] The traditional historical focus on great men and great events in the nineteenth century reflects the distribution of literacy, as well as the denial of full political participation to women of all classes. Traditional historical orientations also reflect the hard fact that the ruling class (of men) was the most important class in terms of its power to affect the rest of society. Nevertheless, people of every class shaped their own social worlds, and some aspects of social organization and the texture of everyday life can only be understood in terms of the underclasses. The variety of sources on Comstock prostitution allows it to be placed in the context of the wider community and viewed through the eyes of many different kinds of people.

Much of what can be discovered about sexual commerce on the mining frontier comes from observers such as census enumerators determined to record every resident of the Lode or local aldermen bent on regulating the social evil. Their public documents had good chances for survival because they were often duplicated and placed in "fire proof" containers.[22] Those dry documents contain remarkable details about who prostitutes were and how they lived, making it possible to reconstruct a history buried by legends of glamorous ladies with hearts of gold. Most Comstock prostitutes were ordinary women with the courage to endure and sometimes thrive under circumstances which were at once bizarre and mundane.

The organization of chapters in this book is based on implicit theoretical assumptions about prostitution in the United States from after the Civil War through the twentieth century. It is organized in terms of my belief that there is a fundamental interdependence and similarity between the "normal" and the "deviant" in American society, and prostitution cannot be separated from other social institutions. Thus, chapters are organized from an examination of the wider community context of prostitution to a discussion of the organization and dynamics of prostitution itself.

The first chapter will introduce readers to the general physical, economic, and social contours of Virginia City and Gold Hill as background for a discussion of the specific characteristics of the labor force and population generating demand for prostitutes. The second chapter examines women's roles in the family and in public voluntary associations, describing the differences and functional complementarity of prostitution and marriage. Sexual commerce can only be understood in terms of wider economic and social arrangements, particularly as they relate to the general place of women in society, and these chapters are necessary background for the following section on prostitution. The next four chapters will focus on prostitutes themselves. First there will be a description of who prostitutes were and how they lived, offering general information about their ages, ethnicity and race, and marital status. The next chapter will examine the intricate pattern of stratification within prostitution using case studies of individual women to illuminate the process of daily life in various strata. The fifth chapter will describe the different roles men played as essential partners in sexual barter. The final chapter in this section deals with occupational hazards common to prostitution, including faulty birth control, venereal disease, drug abuse, and violence.

Even though the same social force shaped the lives of prostitutes and ladies, the two groups were separated from one another by competition for scarce status resources and by a complex body of local customs and laws. Chapter 7 will explore the sexual ideology and social patterns controlling all feminine sexuality on the Lode. The definition of prostitutes as deviant human beings not only legitimated respectable women's status, but also contributed to the social solidarity and clarification of behavioral rules for everyone within the respectable community. Thus, prostitution served general social functions for the Comstock as a whole.

Prostitution involves the complex intersection of sexual status and social class with both structural and social-psychological dimensions. The last chapter will draw information from the extreme case of prostitution on the Comstock to examine some general theoretical issues concerning sexual commerce and the social control of sexuality. It will not present a full theory of prostitution, but will instead sketch some theoretical directions. The case of the Comstock Lode suggests that economic considerations were of primary importance in generating and sustaining a supply of female prostitutes, but that men's motives as customers can best be understood in terms of their socially structured psychic needs.

In searching for alternatives to the painted ladies of the prostitute's legend and the silent hero who allegedly accompanied her, I found real people who were far more exciting than those characters. Some of them were distasteful and a few of them were downright bad, but all of them made me aware of the enormous possibilities in the social history of outcasts and renegades.

1
Material Life on the Comstock Lode

For the work I'm too lazy
And beggin's too low,
Train robbin's too dangerous
So to gamblin' I'll go.
Traditional Folksong

THIS CHAPTER WILL discuss material life on the Comstock Lode as part of the social context in which prostitution was embedded. The simple physical setting of the Comstock will be described first, in order to provide readers with a meaningful visual image of the mining frontier. After that the specific nature of the labor force and the economy will be examined, because those social arrangements were fundamental in shaping both the supply and the demand for sexual commerce. Comstock prostitution flourished in the boom-or-bust atmosphere of a community extraordinarily dependent on the single economic base of silver mining. Many of the men and women who came to the Lode were rootless, violent, and hungry for sudden wealth; but their volatility was tempered and ordered by relatively clear patterns of economic and social organization.

Virginia City squatted precariously on the eastern slope of Mount Davidson in northwestern Nevada, and a steep divide separated it from Gold Hill which nestled to the city's southwest. Although Gold Hill had its own small main district of churches, shops, and saloons, its residents depended upon Virginia for much of their social life, and it was essentially a working-class suburb of Virginia City, primarily populated by miners and their families.

The people of Gold Hill successfully resisted civic incorporation with their dominant sister city, arguing that the two cities were separated by clear social and physical boundaries. Virginia City had "gorgeous saloons," melodeons, and an array of other diversions necessitating more police, sewage, and street maintenance. Gold Hill did not need those public services, and therefore its residents did not wish to be as heavily taxed as those in the neighboring community.[1] The sister cities shared a Board of County Commissioners, but retained separate municipal governments. Formal civic separation, however, did not obscure the cities' fundamental interdependence. Gold Hill housed many of the Comstock's workers and Virginia City clothed, fed, and amused them. Sociologically, the two communities were one—the Comstock—and they will be so treated in this study.

Deserts and mountains isolated the Comstock from the rest of the United States, but the community's enormous underground wealth encouraged the development of freight and transport connections. Most supplies came over the Sierras in freight wagons drawn by teams of horses, until the Virginia and Truckee Railroad was completed in 1870. During peak seasons there was an almost unbroken line of wagons over the one-hundred-mile stretch from Placerville, California, to Virginia City. From 1863 to 1869, yearly freight transported from California to the Comstock ranged from forty-five thousand to seventy-five thousand tons.[2] Passengers came too, and a businessman could leave San Francisco at 4:00 P.M. to arrive in Virginia City by 10:00 P.M. the next day, traveling at an average of eight and one-third miles an hour. The demand for stage coaches was so great that one of several successful companies had seventy-five coaches, thirty drivers, and 268 horses. When there was a bonanza period, every traveler appeared destined for the Comstock, and the *Alta Californian* described the road between Placerville and Virginia City as the Far West's "main street."[3]

High grade silver ore was first discovered on the Lode in 1859, and by mid-1860 Virginia City boasted fifteen stone houses and dozens of tents and shanties constructed of cardboard and canvas. Less than five years later the city contained scores of fine houses and an ordered, although far from orderly, street plan. At the height of the first boom, Mark Twain, the Lode's most famous booster, described the "Queen of the Comstock":

The "city" of Virginia roosted royally midway up the steep side of Mount Davidson, seven thousand two hundred feet above the level of the sea, and in the clear Nevada atmosphere was visible for a distance of fifty miles! It claimed a population of fifteen to eighteen thousand, and all day half of this little army swarmed the streets like bees, and the other half swarmed among the drifts and tunnels of the "Comstock," hundreds of feet down in the earth directly under those same streets. Often we felt our chairs jar, and heard the faint boom of a blast in the bowels of the earth under the office.

The mountainside was so steep that the entire town had a slant to it like a roof. Each street was a terrace, and from each to the next street below the descent was forty or fifty feet. The fronts of the houses were level with the streets they faced, but their rear first floors were propped on lofty stilts; a man could stand at a rear first-floor window of a C Street house and look down the chimneys of the houses below him facing D Street. . . .[4]

Like other cities spawned by ore strikes, the Comstock had unique economic and cultural features differentiating it from long-established communities. Denver and San Francisco never fully recovered from the spirit of their first boom years, and if the Comstock had survived as a city, it would have retained a frontier flavor. The frontier veneer, however, overlaid patterns of urban life associated with metropolitan areas in other parts of the country. The Comstock possessed the classic attributes of urban situations in terms of its relatively large size, high density, and cultural heterogeneity.[5]

The Comstock as an Urban Situation

Virginia City was a rude collection of shanties housing about 500 people in 1860. One year later the city claimed 3,284 residents. Close to 25,000 people lived on the Comstock at the peak of the Big Bonanza of 1873, but by 1875 the population of Storey County had tapered off to 19,528. Final decline began in 1880, when there were only 16,115 residents of the county and by 1900, only 3,673 people resided there. During the twenty boom years, the Comstock's size made it metropolitan in comparison to most other communities in the country, for in 1870 the U.S. Census Bureau formally defined communities of 8,000 or more as possessing urban populations.[6]

Virginia City was fundamentally urban in its high density as well as its size. It was a compact city, and anyone who dared could easily walk its span in spite of the steep streets. The terrain, people's desire to be close to the mines, and their need for cheap, quickly built housing all contributed to high density. In 1875, the 19,528 people in Storey County crowded into 4,185 closely packed dwellings. The *Enterprise* commented "Virginia City has worse houses, higher rents, narrower stairs, and poorer lighted streets than any other city of so much wealth in the world."[7]

Another commentator, Louise M. Palmer, a mine superintendent's wife, apologized for housing conditions:

You are surprised that Mrs. _____, who wore such magnificent diamonds last night, should live in so small and plain a house. But the fact is the house is their own. None but wealthy companies build grand houses here. Persons are not

judged by the places they live in. Ladies may envy me for living in the stone
mansion of the Great Bamboozle Company, but nevertheless, they are not
ashamed to receive me in their cloth and paper dwellings.[8]

Affluent people usually lived up the mountain above the main commercial district on C Street, while working-class residences and lodging
houses sprawled below C, edging west and south toward Gold Hill.
Virginia City's small area and disorderly development impeded the strict
segregation of residential and commercial districts common to long-
established cities; and until reconstruction after the Great Fire of 1875,
the major streets, B, C, and D, contained a crazy quilt of commercial
enterprises, municipal buildings, bawdy establishments, lodging houses
and private homes. Despite the mixture, however, there was noticeable
residential segregation on the basis of the ethnic, racial, and class
heterogeneity which gave the Comstock its truly urban ethos.

A separate Chinatown sprang up on the city's northwest because of
racism and a discriminatory city ordinance allowing any number of white
citizens to petition the Virginia board of aldermen to remove an Asian
residence or business from their neighborhood.[9] Random violence and
social custom also kept Paiute Indians on the outskirts of town, where
about one hundred of them occupied a squalid encampment. Even after
the Great Fire of 1875 they received no charity and they were depicted as
"broken-hearted onlookers of relief distribution."[10] Blacks faced far less
discrimination because there were fewer than one hundred of them on
the Comstock and because the Lode was overwhelmingly pro-Union
during the Civil War. Most blacks, however, worked at service occupations, lived in their own enclave in Virginia City, sent their children to
private schools, and attended an African Methodist Episcopal Church.
There was less prejudice against blacks than against other people of
color, but there was still some visible racism.[11]

The most obvious patterns of residential segregation reflected racial
distinctions, but other people who shared ethnicity chose to live near one
another. There was an Irish district known as Little Tipperary and a
Cornish neighborhood in Gold Hill. German merchants, managers, and
professionals clustered together on South A Street in Virginia City. In
1870 and 1875 about half (49 and 51 percent respectively) of the people
on the Comstock were foreign-born, while that was true of only 35
percent of the people in Boston and only 36 percent of those in St.
Louis.[12] Local celebrations included a banquet on the Quatorze Juillet, a
St. Patrick's Day Parade, and a Mexican Independence Day festival.

Throughout the great boom years of the seventies Virginia City's
Piper's Opera House was the best theater between Chicago and San

Francisco. In 1879, Virginia City housed 131 saloons, twenty-eight restaurants, twenty hotels, four banks, and four breweries.[13] C Street, the principal commercial thoroughfare, literally teemed with pedestrians. Loungers jostled ladies on their way to buy produce or dry goods, and stock speculators hurrying to the telegraph office dodged express wagons. On warm evenings there was even more confusion.

During the summer, men who have for sale all manner of quack nostrums, men with all kinds of notions for sale, street-shows, beggars, singers, men with electrical machines, apparatus for testing the strength of the lungs, and a thousand other similar things, flock to Virginia City. Of evenings, when torches of these parties of peddlers, showmen, and quack doctors are all lighted and all are in full cry, a great fair seems to be under headway in the principal street of the town—there is a perfect Babel of cries and harangues.[14]

Beneath the roar of wagons and voices there was a steady hum from the mines as hoisting engines vibrated and underground ore trains creaked. At the peak of each new boom some mines had three consecutive eight-hour shifts and their machinery could be heard throughout the night as well as during the day. The Comstock was built on silver ore, both figuratively and literally. An underground city of square-set timbered shafts lay beneath the Comstock and the surrounding countryside. There were six important ore bodies on the Lode and twenty-five major mines, including the Consolidated Virginia and California Mines which produced an unbelievable $105,157,490 from 1873 to 1882.[15]

The Shape of the Population

The Comstock's population was in constant flux, depending on the condition of the mines. In- and out-migration were so frequent, that "just visiting" was an accurate synonym for most people's residency.[16] The Lode was a community of permanent transients, many of whom flocked to each new minor ore strike but came back home to the silver mines. Newspapers listed arriving stage coach and rail passengers, and a sample of passenger lists drawn from the years 1871, 1875, 1876, and 1879 produced an estimate that one hundred twenty-seven thousand people arrived on the Comstock during the 1870s.[17] Of course many of those listed were regular commuters, but other, unreported individuals came by wagon, horseback, or on foot, so the number of actual new arrivals was probably very high. Another indication of population instability was a list of 140 men's names drawn from the 1870 census. Only 43 of them appeared in the 1875 census, and only 27 of them were listed in 1880. This extraordinary mobility rate was also found in other mining communities, such as Grass Valley and Nevada City, California.[18]

Men frequently traveled to the Comstock alone, and few women came to the Lode by themselves. The ratio of males to females in Storey County was never less than one and a half to one, and it was usually far greater. In late 1860 there were only 30 women and 2,206 men in Virginia City, and a decade later there were 2,323 women and 4,725 men.[19] The overall Storey County ratio was similar. The 1875 census listed 6,116 females and 13,415 males. However, only 3,572 women were eighteen years old or over or in the labor force. Assuming roughly equal numbers of male and female children, the ratio of adult men to women was closer to three to one than two to one. In 1880 the county population had decreased by about three thousand, as single men, the most mobile group, had begun to leave in droves. There were 9,294 males and 6,821 females listed.[20]

Marrying and bringing a wife to the Comstock took more money than many men possessed. For example, in 1875, fewer than one miner or carpenter in three was living with a woman. On the other hand, all mining superintendents resided with women. Table 1 indicates that

TABLE 1.   Selected Occupations and Living Situations of Men in Virginia City and Gold Hill, 1875

Occupation	Number of Men Living by Themselves	Number of Men Living with Women	Total
Mine superintendent or owner	0	10	10
Lawyer	16	22	38
Merchant	90	82	172
Boardinghouse, lodging house, or hotel owner or manager	9	49	58
Carpenter	266	144	410
Waiter or cook	311	18	329
Miner	2,908	1,052	3,960
Unemployed or no occupation listed	1,024	111	1,135

Source: Data compiled from the special Nevada State Census of 1875. All men eighteen years old and over or gainfully employed were counted.

upper- and middle-class men were more likely to be living with a woman (usually a wife) than working-class men. Some men saved for years in order to send for their wives, while a few lucky ones could afford large sums to bring brides from their old home villages in Europe.[21] The shortage of wives and marriageable women, along with formal prohibitions against adultery, created a demand for commercial sex. Most people believed that an infusion of respectable women would solve all of the Comstock's problems of prostitution and violence. An article about the men who hung about on street corners concluded, "Some eastern emigration society should send a cargo of marriageable young ladies. They would all do service here."[22]

Just such a scheme failed in San Francisco two decades earlier. Eliza Woodson Burhans Farnham, former women's matron at Sing Sing, was shocked at the number of marriageable men on the West Coast and the corresponding number of lone ladies in the East. With the endorsement of Horace Greeley, William Cullen Bryant, and Henry Ward Beecher, she constructed an elaborate plan to ship 100 respectable women to San Francisco. However, no women were desperate enough to enroll and her vision was forever labeled "Farnham's Fiasco."[23]

The Regular Economy

Since the first publicized ore strike, people rushed to the Lode seeking a piece of the not-quite-mythical pot of silver. Although very few individuals actually made their fortunes, Comstock lore emphasized the rags-to-riches characters such as Eilley Orrum Bowers, an illiterate boardinghouse keeper to whom miners gave a ten-foot claim in Gold Hill which netted one hundred thousand dollars a month before it pinched out at 190 feet.[24] Those streaks of luck were very rare, however, and most arrivals on the Comstock did well to find a job.

The Lode began in chaos with hundreds of miners staking indiscriminate claims, and between 1860 and 1865 twelve major mining companies were involved in 245 different lawsuits, generating an estimated ten million dollars in litigation fees alone.[25] When the dust from the suits cleared during the panic of 1865, it became obvious that a small number of capitalists controlled the Comstock. The legal process itself insured that people who already had money could influence corrupt judges, and gain access to promising ore veins. Corporate control was further strengthened by the referee's ruling of 1864, which supported a single-ledge definition of the Lode. The ruling that the Comstock was one ledge gave owners of claims on the main lode the right to follow their claims through all dips, spurs, and angles, and it virtually knocked out the claims of small, independent prospectors. Capital was essential for litigation and for the machinery and tunneling necessary to explore the full possibilities of each ore vein.[26]

A major depression first hit the Comstock in 1864, and that period marked the transition from independent capitalism to monopolization by the Bank of California. The bank, under the direction of its Virginia City manager, William Sharon, loaned money to mine and ore mill owners at 2 percent interest, undercutting other loan agencies charging 5 percent. As the depression dragged on, the "Bank Gang" foreclosed on mines, mills, and houses. The first great profits from this strategy came after the bank merged seven mills into the Union Mining and Milling Company which monopolized all ore milling and gradually expanded profits to more than a thousand dollars a day.[27] Other holdings supplemented the ore milling monopoly. The bank owned the Virginia and Truckee Railroad, which hauled ore and freight between the Comstock, the ore mills on the Carson River, and the recently built United States Mint in Carson City. It also owned part of the Virginia City and Gold Hill Water Company, and Tahoe basin lumber which was necessary to the timbered mines. The bank's holdings on the Comstock were so extensive that it would have collapsed from overinvestment if new ore strikes had not generated the 1871 boom. As one anonymous resident wrote, "All working men in Virginia City hate Sharon, but they tolerate him because he can cut off their bread and butter."[28]

In 1875 the bank's stranglehold was broken by a group which later came to be known as the Bonanza Four. John Mackay and James Fair were Irish immigrants who had become skilled, influential mining men, and James Flood and William O'Brien were San Francisco saloonkeepers who speculated in stocks with insiders' knowledge. The four began their rise to power by using stock manipulation to wrest control of the profitable Hale and Norcross Mine away from the bank group, which was then involved in a series of disastrous investments and stock speculations. The four later developed their claims adjacent to the Hale and Norcross into the Big Bonanza, the Comstock's greatest ore strike. The Bonanza Four acquired ore mills, lumber, and an interest in the water company, but unlike the Bank Gang, they always depended upon railroads owned by others. While the four partners in the Bonanza made great fortunes, they also lost huge sums by continuing to invest in development long after the Lode's last ore veins began to give out.[29]

Throughout the years from 1865 through 1880 one or another monopoly was omnipresent, symbolizing the Comstock's overall pattern of economic development. Most of the partners in the two monopolies did not even live on the Comstock, building their mansions in San Francisco while maintaining pro forma residences in Virginia City. They took enormous wealth from Nevada, but they reinvested few of their profits in anything other than the mines. This lack of economic diversification kept the Comstock in an almost constant state of social flux because most people worked in the mines or mining-related jobs. Daily life on the Lode was so unpredictable, so much a matter of apparent luck, that most people who could afford to plunged into the stock market to achieve economic security.

The San Francisco Stock Exchange was established in 1862 as a result of the first major Comstock ore strikes. The great silver boom was of interest to speculators throughout the world, and a special agent of the Rothschild firm visited the Crown Point and Belcher mines in 1873, as did a party of French capitalists.[30] Ordinary people literally went wild over the market, indulging in emotional buying and selling based on the belief that they had unique information.

The amount of "stock talk" heard in every saloon, public-house and shop on every street is at times enough to render an easy-going granger from one of the Eastern or Middle states, to whom it is all Greek, a raving maniac or a driveling idiot. The sidewalks on C-Street, the principal business street of Virginia City, are generally so thronged it is a difficult matter to pass along them except at the same slow pace at which the mass of pedestrians is moving; therefore at times when there is an excitement in regard to stocks, there are frequent blockades in front of the offices of the brokers, and persons wishing to pass are obliged to take to the streets—At times the police are obliged to clear passages through the throngs, as men become so interested in their stocks as to have neither eyes nor ears for anything else, and ladies and children find themselves unable to pass.[31]

Stock prices were so wild that small investors sometimes lost everything to behind-the-scenes manipulators in San Francisco. Other shareholders who clung to their stocks were wiped out by heavy assessments which far exceeded dividends. In 1867 there were approximately 400 organized mining companies and only 3 of them paid dividends. The Bullion Mine, a spectacular fraud, levied $3.8 million in assessments and produced absolutely nothing.[32] A small number of knowledgeable speculators with advance news about ore strikes forced most small investors out of truly lucrative mines, and speculators also inflated the price of worthless stocks by announcing false news of new ore discoveries. Major investors sometimes kept miners underground at the time of big discoveries, so that they could buy more stock before the information spread. It was equally common for owners and major investors to maintain total secrecy as ore veins gave out.[33]

There were speculative booms and ensuing panics in 1867, 1872, 1875, 1878, and 1886. Investment cycles grew more frequent and more extreme as the mines fell into permanent decline and stock trading came to be based on wishful thinking alone. In the early 1870s silver lost its sixteen to one parity with gold on European money markets and most European countries dropped silver from their monetary systems. Late in that decade the United States government stopped coining silver dollars, and the silver mining economy was further destroyed when the government dropped its obligation to purchase domestically mined ore.[34] Although the Comstock mines produced an alloy of gold and silver, rather than pure silver, the worldwide devaluation of silver combined with the exhaustion of accessible ore deposits to produce final depression on the Lode. In 1876, their peak year, Storey County mines produced more than twenty-seven million dollars, two years later production was down to slightly under twenty million dollars, and by 1880 it was a little more than three and one-half million dollars.[35] The Lode's long final decline was underway in 1880, and in 1883 a correspondent for the *Chicago Herald* wrote about the "wreck" of the community:

The 35,000 people [*sic*] have dwindled to 5,000. The banks have retired from business. The merchants have closed up and left. The hotel is abandoned; the gas company is bankrupt and scores of costly residence have either been moved away or given over to bats.[36]

During the brief twenty boom years, however, thousands of people came to the Lode, some looking for gold dust in the streets and others merely searching for jobs. They faced extraordinary prices in the early years when the Comstock was still a rough camp and eggs cost three dollars a dozen, flour was thirty to forty dollars a hundred pounds, and shovels sold for five dollars apiece. Prices leveled off with the establishment of regular freight lines and increased competition among businessmen, but for many years gold coins were in regular use and paper money was discounted as high as 40 percent.[37]

The Labor Force

Almost half of the men employed on the Comstock worked in the silver mines, and the largest of these employed from 500 to 700 miners. They each worked ten- and later eight-hour shifts under constant, obvious threat of death. Between 1863 and 1880 there were 300 mining fatalities, and when the mines were in full operation there was a serious accident every day.[38] In the late 1860s many mines were excavated at

1,000 feet below ground and by 1881 their deepest workings were far below that. As the level of the mines grew deeper temperatures grew higher, reaching 167°F at the 3,000-foot level of the Yellow Jacket Mine. Ordinary working temperatures often climbed above 100°, and the heat combined with noxious, stagnant air to force miners to spend more time recovering under fresh air vents than they spent actually mining. Men on the hot shifts chewed ice and carried it in their hands and in their boots. In the summer of 1878, every man working in the Consolidated Virginia and California mines consumed an average of three gallons of water and ninety-five pounds of ice each eight-hour day.[39]

At the mines' deepest levels men occasionally died from violent stomach cramps and heat prostration, but floods of scalding water and mine fires killed the most workers. Fires could break out at every level of depth, and in 1869, a disastrous one at the 800-foot level of the Yellow Jacket, Crown Point, and Kentuck mines killed forty-five men. Miners were also endangered by unprotected machinery and abandoned, unsealed mine shafts. Owners usually ignored all of these dangers, for safety legislation was ludicrously inadequate and employers had no legal responsibility for miners' health.

A Miners' Protective Association was organized in 1863 to care for the sick and disabled and to pay dead miners' burial expenses. The league, however, had a small membership which could do little when wages were lowered by fifty cents a day during the bust of 1864. In 1867, however, the protective association spawned the Virginia City Miners' Union and the Gold Hill Miners' Union. The two unions forced wages back up to four dollars a day, maintained first a ten- and later an eight-hour work day, kept Chinese out of the mines, and upheld a resolution for all miners to join the union after working a month.[40] These were tangible victories which the unions won because of owners' need for a stable work force and their desire to have the sick and disabled cared for at the unions' expense. Despite these gains, the unions could not alleviate terrible working conditions or give miners more control over their own labor.

Although the miners' four-dollar wage was exceptionally high for the times, the rampant inflation on the Comstock made wages less substantial than they appeared. Most single men paid from forty to sixty dollars a month for meals and a tiny room with stacked bunks and no outside windows.[41] In some cases, two sets of miners on different shifts shared the same room, with one group sleeping while the other worked. Board alone cost a dollar a day at a good restaurant and fifty cents at a simple

TABLE 2. Male Occupational Structure of Virginia City and Gold Hill, 1875

Category	Occupation	Number	Percent
Elites	Mine superintendent	10	0.1
	Ore mill superintendent	14	0.1
	Stock broker	15	0.1
	Other substantial persons (judge, corporate officer, etc.)	17	0.2
	Total	56	0.6
Professionals	Assayer	22	0.2
	Doctor or dentist	47	0.5
	Mining engineer	199	2.0
	Lawyer	38	0.4
	Minister	17	0.2
	Pharmacist	18	0.2
	School teacher	13	0.1
	Student	3	—
	Other professionals (surveyors, chemists, etc.)	95	0.9
	Total	452	4.5
Proprietors, craftsmen, and businessmen	Blacksmith, tinsmith, coppersmith (owns business)	187	1.9
	Boardinghouse owner	16	0.2
	Lodging house or hotel owner or manager	42	0.4
	Merchant	172	1.7

Restaurant owner	26	0.3
Saloon owner	113	1.1
White collar employees (clerks, salesmen, etc.)	390	3.9
Other business (barber, shoemaker, rancher, printer, etc.)	472	4.7
Total	1,418	14.2
Workers		
Carpenter	410	4.1
Laundryman (primarily Chinese)	217	2.2
Machinist	75	0.7
Miner	3,960	39.5
Ore mill worker	325	3.2
Criminal justice employee	30	0.3
Paid fireman	25	0.2
Teamster or stage driver	167	1.7
Theater or saloon employee	90	0.9
Waiter or cook	329	3.3
Other workers (mason, apprentice, plasterer, railroader, etc.)	1,221	12.2
Total	6,849	68.4
Dubious occupations		
Sport, gambler, gentleman of leisure	25	0.2
Speculator	81	0.8
Unemployed or no occupation listed	1,135	11.3
Total	1,241	12.4
Column total	10,016	100.0

Source: Data compiled from the special Nevada State Census of 1875. All men eighteen years old and over or gainfully employed were counted.

place serving plain, small meals; while individual meals cost fifty and twenty-five cents respectively.[42] Miners with kin shared cottages with other families or lived together in one or two rooms of a house belonging to someone else. Some miners owned small houses and others rented single family dwellings in Gold Hill's or Virginia City's working-class neighborhoods.

Other working men on the Comstock faced conditions of life and labor similar, but less intense than miners' situations. Almost all workers were employed in industries or service occupations dependent on the silver economy, as indicated in table 2. Many of them engaged in labor which was not quite so dangerous or uncomfortable as mining, but which held some physical risks. Carpenters who timbered mining tunnels and laborers who excavated them faced cave-ins, fires, and floods. Ore mill workers had to labor amid dangerous, noisy machinery. Teamsters drove wagons while maintaining control of thirty to forty spirited horses. Police and firemen were often in grave danger. Even the most pleasant working-class occupations, bartending or working in a boardinghouse or restaurant, promised encounters with unruly, if not violent, customers.

Working-class men were not the only ones to face special difficulties at their jobs which influenced the rest of their lives. Almost every employed man on the Lode had unique occupational difficulties because of the community's geographic isolation and complete economic dependence on the mines. The spectre of sudden financial ruin haunted everyone from the Bonanza Four to the boys who delivered groceries. Although economic organization in other parts of the country followed general cycles of economic booms and panics during the two decades following the Civil War, the Comstock's economy was extraordinarily volatile. Nevertheless, while prosperity was especially fragile on the Lode, it was also possible for men to make their fortunes as professionals, merchants, businessmen, or traders in stocks and real estate during bonanza periods. The Comstock's class structure was fluid compared with the social organization of established cities, and ethnicity or recent arrival to the Lode seldom hindered social mobility.

The possibility of mobility through the range of occupations open to men on the Lode was practically closed to women, and less than 10 percent of the Comstock's adult females were involved in a limited range of respectable occupations listed in table 3. The abundant supply of male labor, the desire to limit women's exposure to danger during their childbearing years, the harsh conditions of work in the mines, and the myths about women's fragility combined to limit their access to jobs.

On the Comstock and throughout the United States, women's labor was characterized by "constant changes or shiftings of work and workshop, accompanied by low wages, unsanitary conditions, and the want on the part of women of training, skill, and vital interest in her work."[43]

Most women workers on the Lode were domestics, employed by hotels, boardinghouses, or private families. More than half of them were Irish, although some employers hired only German or American women.[44] Servants in private homes earned from fifteen to forty dollars a month, depending on their experience, obligations, and whether or not they received room and board. Working at least ten hours a day for six days a week, servants' labor included cleaning, sewing, child care, and sometimes marketing and cooking as well. The women employed in public establishments could earn more money, from fifty to seventy dollars weekly, but they had to work about fifteen hours a day.[45]

In 1869, several articles on domestic labor in New York City and Boston described seven-day servants' work weeks of from twelve to fifteen hours a day. Work was done in dark, unventilated kitchens and servants' sleeping rooms were cold and cheerless.[46] Conditions on the Comstock were little better, and in 1874 one servant died and another came close to dying when an unsafe gas heater leaked in their room.[47]

Despite the low pay, there was considerable competition for domestic jobs with respectable families, and some women advertised for positions. They not only vied with one another, but also with Chinese men who were, according to Mark Twain, "good house servants, being quick, obedient, patient, quick to learn, and tirelessly industrious."[48] Most employers preferred to hire whites, however, although they vociferously complained about the "servant problem." According to "forgiving and forebearing" employers, many female servants couldn't cook, indulged in liquor, and had the audacity to entertain beaux.[49] Another much discussed tribulation involved servants' desires to marry and leave their situations. Louise M. Palmer, the Virginia City socialite, sarcastically remarked:

John is generally punctual at dinner; he knows that Bridget will scorn me and her forty or fifty dollar wage if he is not, and leave us in the lurch. Sometimes he annoys her by bringing a friend or two, and she threatens to leave, but, however, my humility generally conquers her ruffled dignity. I am very fortunate in this respect, for I have only had five different cooks within the last year.[50]

Some women worked solely as seamstresses and did not add sewing to a long list of other domestic tasks. The needle trades were a major

TABLE 3. Female Occupational Structure of Virginia City and Gold Hill, 1875

Category	Specific Occupation	Absolute Frequency	Relative Frequency (in percentage)
Dependent	Married women/living with husbands	2,446	68.5
	Adult daughters living at home	109	3.0
	Other female relatives of household head	41	1.1
	Widows with no other occupation listed	147	4.1
	Total	2,743	76.7
Working-class employment	Servant	208	5.9
	Laundress	3	0.1
	Seamstress	39	1.1
Petit-bourgeois employment	Lodging/boardinghouse owner or manager	44	1.2
	Saloon owner	3	0.1
	Merchant	2	0.1

	Milliner	5	0.1
	Other petit-bourgeois (e.g., hairdresser or telegraph operator)	5	0.1
Professional employment	School teacher	20	0.6
	Nun	13	0.4
	Total employment	342	9.7
Disreputable dependent/living with one man	No occupation, housekeeper, or euphemism for fallen woman	180	5.0
Disreputable	Madam	9	0.2
	Prostitutes	298	8.2
	Total	487	13.4
Column Total		3,572	99.8

Source: Data compiled from the special Nevada State Census of 1875. All women eighteen years old and over or gainfully employed were counted. The age of eighteen was selected because it was the legal age of marital consent for women. Many women, however, worked outside the home at an earlier age and the youngest woman worker in 1875 was a nine-year-old servant girl.

national source of employment for women, although only thirty-nine Comstock women were seamstresses in 1875. The Lode had no large clothing industry organized around the factory system, and seamstresses worked at home, at their employers' residences, or in small workshops with a handful of other women. Local newspapers regularly carried descriptions of the latest Paris fashions and affluent Comstock women bought patterns to be executed by seamstresses. Middle-class women also hired seamstresses to sew a few of their special clothes and to ready their childrens' wardrobes for school.

An accomplished seamstress earned three dollars for a full day of sewing, and her employment was seasonal and irregular. For a short time in 1866, Susan Caroll and Mary Conway tried to upgrade the sewing profession by establishing an employment office for respectable women, but seamstresses continued to be held in low esteem, and because they were sometimes employed by fast women, they were also tinged with disreputability.[51] When Mrs. Hungerford, a lady of moderate means, hired Mary McNair Mathews to sew her daughter's clothes, she paid a dollar a day and gave Mary and her son meals. Mary was dismayed at her overbearing employer, who treated her like a servant, demanding that she and her son eat leftovers in the kitchen.[52]

Mary McNair Mathews was a widow who came to the Comstock to trace her family and remained there long enough to write *Ten Years in Nevada*, published in 1880. She was an energetic middle-class woman who briefly took in sewing, laundry, and letter-writing commissions. With the aid of friends, she accumulated enough money to rent and furnish a house in which she tended respectable boarders. Mary always took in at least one lady, for she did not wish to attract gossip like housekeepers who only boarded men. She got up with her roomers who worked on the six o'clock shift, made her own breakfast, made her boarders' lunch and dinner, cleaned the house, and washed and ironed sheets on every day but Sunday.[53]

Mary belonged to the largest middle-class occupational group open to women. Some of the forty-four housekeepers ran lodging houses, merely offering rooms and supplying lodgers with relatively clean linen; but the majority of these women ran boardinghouses in which people received both rooms and meals. In 1875 there were almost as many female housekeepers as males, and the large number of women in the occupation was legitimated by the widespread belief that their work was a logical extension of women's traditional domestic roles. Women were such an important part of the Lode's lodging business that they were eagerly welcomed into the Protective Organization of Hotel, Boarding House, and Restaurant Keepers of Virginia City and Gold Hill at a time when ladies were not permitted to join any other professional association or union. Of course, it was very much in the male owners' interest to invite women to join, since they had organized to compile a list of people who did not pay their bills, whom association members agreed to exclude from their establishments. While the association was not particularly influential, it was unique because it was the only such group to invite women to join.[54]

All of the major women's occupations noted so far were tinged with disreputability. "Servant" and "chambermaid" were fairly common Victorian euphemisms for prostitute, in part because a number of fast women were recruited from those ranks. Women who took in lodgers and boarders were sometimes sexually involved with those men. The only women's occupation generally considered to be both ladylike and comparatively lucrative was teaching. School teachers could make from $60 to $125 a month, and it was not surprising when 120 unmarried women applied for less than twenty public school posts in 1877.[55] The clamor for teaching jobs was so loud that it prompted Professor J. N. Flint, the male Superintendent of Public Instruction for Storey County to write:

It is greatly to be regretted that school teaching is, in the estimation of the female sex, the only respectable occupation which a young lady can follow.

Some women who would be good clerks or waitresses are not good teachers. They must realize any occupation giving them an honest living is respectable.[56]

In 1877 there was also growing opposition to married school teachers whose husbands could support them. They were admonished to give up their jobs to some young lady who was "reduced to the hard necessity of fighting for her daily bread all alone."[57] Actually, as of 1875 there were only two married women employed by the school district, and that number probably changed little in two years. Very few married women listed occupations outside the home, and in 1875 only eighteen did so. This figure is somewhat misleading, however, because many wives were not listed as gainfully employed in the census, although they helped their husbands manage restaurants, lodging houses, or shops, or else they raised hogs or chickens for market. Nevertheless, most married women's primary commitment was to family life.

The law reflected the widespread ambivalence toward financially independent wives. In 1867 the state legislature recognized all women's rights to own businesses by passing the "Act to Authorize Married

Women to Transact Business in Their Own Names as Sole Traders."
This stipulated that a woman could use her own name for business
purposes, if it was not with the intent to defraud her husband's creditors.
There was a catch in the law, however, for once a woman availed herself
of those provisions, she assumed complete responsibility for her children, regardless of her husband's assets.[58] In effect, the legislature forced
married businesswomen to be "superwomen," by offering them business
responsibility only if they accepted full family responsibility. The act
also implicitly denigrated a man's ability as a breadwinner and family
provider, if he were so silly as to permit his wife to own a business.
While the legal provisions concerning sole trading probably deterred a
handful of women at most, this statute illustrated women's marginality
to the labor force. Few women could attain economic independence by
means of respectable jobs; but while the regular occupational structure
was nearly closed to them, the irregular marketplace welcomed women
as part of its own raucous working class.

The Irregular Marketplace

The irregular marketplace was not a building or geographical area,
although it was easy to associate it with the fleshpots, dives, and faro
parlors lining C and D Streets. Instead, the marketplace was a set of
economic relationships involving the creation and exchange of goods and
services which were either formally or informally condemned. While
prostitutes, faro dealers, and dubious stock speculators were not au-
tomatically defined as criminals on the Comstock, they lived outside of
the respectable community's moral boundaries, participating in routine
economic relationships with opium peddlers, stage robbers, and other
obvious criminals. Despite its unsavory denizens, however, the irregular
sector operated under the same economic laws as its regular counterpart,
and it was a most competitive and fruitful economic arena, offering
individual entrepreneurs and investors high rates of return as compensa-
tion for risks of disorder or legal penalties.

On the Comstock, the line separating sharp practices from downright
immoral ones was usually a matter of opinion, and it was inevitable that
some highly successful irregular entrepreneurs would be drawn into the
respectable marketplace and the social life surrounding it. Silver was
mined, milled, transported, and sold through established channels. No
matter how questionable the original claim on a mine or how shady its
owners' stock manipulations, the people who controlled bonanza profits

were soon embraced by the community elites and they in turn had to pay lip service to respectable customs and morality.

Throughout the boom years, the Lode's regular and irregular marketplaces merged in a symbiotic relationship. Irregular institutions stabilized the mainstream labor force by providing lone and lonely men with diversions in return for a portion of their wages. Thus men who might have organized militant unions or simply fled from the Comstock probably stayed at their jobs in order to partake of immediate gratification in the vice districts. The vice districts also offered respectable elites avenues for investment with a very high rate of return, and capital secretly flowed between the two sectors.

For at least a century, much of the property in United States brothel districts has been owned by respectable elites who often masked their investments behind corporate and individual fronts.[59] In 1877, John Piper, owner of Piper's Opera House, state senator, chairman of the Senate Committee on Public Morals, alderman, and former mayor of Virginia City, was publicly chastised for his concurrent ownership of brothel land and efforts to block legislation limiting the location of houses of ill fame.[60] Piper rationalized his opposition on the grounds that legislation would harm individual property owners and the community's overall tax base. However, the editor of the *Virginia City Evening Chronicle* asserted that Piper was motivated solely by his own avarice.

For the increase of his income our citizens should be compelled to walk their wives and daughters to church or along the promenade past rows of Senator Piper's demoralizing and disgusting tenements, with their open doors and windows.[61]

Piper's Row, as it was commonly known, was not listed under his name in the assessment rolls of 1875. In fact, those rolls yielded some vague, puzzling information about land ownership in the heart of the main bawdy district, on D Street from Taylor to Sutton Streets. Of the nine male owners who could be clearly identified, three were reputable merchants, one was an assayer, and another worked as a gunsmith and rented out his upstairs to three prostitutes. There were also two saloonkeepers and one speculator. Seven women also owned brothel district land. Four were madams, two were prostitutes, and one owned and operated a disreputable lodging house.[62] Sarrah Pottle's lodgings at 5 South D Street housed a cross section of the disreputable community. By 1880, Sarrah and her husband were divorced and she claimed the land and building registered to him on the 1875 assessment rolls. In 1880, she lived there along with seven male gamblers, a carpenter, a blacksmith, a stage company agent, and three prostitutes.

The irregular occupational structure resembled its larger legal counterpart, although there was somewhat more room for individual entrepreneurs within the irregular marketplace. While respectable investors secretly owned a good deal of real estate, most irregular businesses were owned and run by a set of disreputable elites, including major saloon owners and madams of large brothels. Below the disreputable elites, there was a small stratum of middle-level professionals and managers: doctors and attorneys who catered to the disreputable community, small-scale madams, high-status prostitutes who worked on their own, and skilled professional criminals. Most people living in the disreputable community, however, were workers. Men served in saloons, dealt cards in gambling halls, and labored at menial jobs ranging from running errands to cleaning livery stables to watching for vulnerable travelers on the Divide. While a few women owned or managed disreputable businesses, most of them were prostitutes. Just as women were denied access to high-status respectable occupations because of pervasive discrimination and sex role stereotyping, they were also confined to the lower echelons of the irregular labor force.

Some irregular activities, like fraud, burglary, robbery, and mayhem, are almost universally outside the law, and no community could survive without prohibiting them. Other lucrative businesses, like prostitution, gambling, and purveying liquor are somewhat destructive, but they contributed to the Comstock's overall economic stability. The irregular marketplace functioned because it indirectly benefited most respectable people by providing attractive goods, services, and investment opportunities. The disreputable subculture was a community within a community, and its very existence also stabilized the wider community by permitting the respectable upper and middle classes to define immorality and criminality and clarify their own identities by providing an example of what they were *not*.

When the first boom began in 1860 no established pattern of market relations governed the Lode's economic and social life and there was a free-for-all for community control. However, the contours of traditional civic life swiftly developed, and in 1863 the respectable community fought a final symbolic battle with the city's sporting men. A fire in a carpenter's shop provoked a brawl between Engine Company No. 1 and its adjunct hook and ladder company (the sports) on one side and Young America Engine Company No. 2 (the respectables) on the other. The two companies fought to determine which should put out the fire, and before they finished one man had died and a portion of Virginia City had burned. The melee was the first and only large, overt conflict between the two groups and the legal decisions in its aftermath sealed the respectable community's dominance.[63]

Commercial sex on the Comstock could scarcely be separated from the violence permeating the community. Economic instability and concurrent demographic flux created a situation in which "social disorganization" was a literal description rather than a neat academic phrase, and the Comstock burst its seams during major booms and disintegrated during busts. For the community to survive, thousands of rapacious individuals had to be bound into some consensual moral arrangement. A unified collective conscience or even a set of widely shared moral sentiments could not develop in a community divided by class, status, ethnicity, and race. However, compromises forged through necessity and upheld by violence brought a semblance of civic order to the Lode.

Law and Disorder on the Lode

During the first wild boom years when street brawls and shootings went unpunished, mining litigation glutted Comstock courts. Civil and property law developed at much faster rates than criminal law in terms of numbers of statutes and ordinances and pressures for enforcement. Of course, there were immediate prohibitions against capital crimes, but many crimes against persons were still treated as private disputes. The first ordinances which legislated morality, regulating prostitution and saloon keeping, were passed in 1863; but they were seldom enforced. Neither civic consensus nor due process fully developed, and there was a constant tension between the respectable and disreputable communities.

For three months during the massive economic slump of 1871, about seventy men organized a vigilante movement which hanged two well-known outlaws, brought other men to confess to crimes, and forced a number of others off the Lode.[64] The spectre of the vigilantes was evoked periodically over the next nine years, but they never organized again. Instead, people on the Comstock depended upon notoriously lax police.

The Virginia City police force was too small and too corrupt to preserve order. It ranged from five to fourteen men who were required to enforce local ordinances, serve as truant officers, and keep the peace at the sites of elections, hangings, and other large gatherings. Police were accused of brutality, corruption, and graft, as well as dubious relations with prostitutes.[65] Judges were considered to be equally venal and they were accused of corruption in everything from complicated mining litigation to straightforward murder trials.[66] Local justice was such a joke that in the city's formative years the Storey County sheriff used to amuse himself by composing juries of Virginia City's fattest men, thinnest men, ugliest men, and tallest men. Finally a local judge ordered him to stop because the crowds coming to see the juries were a threat to order in themselves.[67] Jurors in every sort of trial took bribes, as did witnesses.

In 1876 the city attorney of Virginia City halted jury trials for offenders against city ordinances, such as drunks, prostitutes, and vagrants, justifying his actions on the grounds that it saved citizen jurors time and trouble.[68] The curtailment, however, indirectly struck at the common corruption of jurors and witnesses, while at the same time depriving the accused of rights of due process.

The organization of criminal justice on the Comstock mirrored the deep fissures in the fabric of civic life. There was no moral agreement and representatives of the criminal justice system were just as corrupt as the disreputables whom they were supposed to control. Simple order was barely maintained and many crimes were ignored. The combined inadequacy and corruption of the criminal justice system allowed prostitution to flourish.

Prostitution was always legal during the twenty year boom. Various attempts were made to regulate the location and organization of sexual commerce, but there were no crusades to eliminate it. Any attempt to eradicate the vice districts would have been foolhardy, for prostitution was very important to the Lode's overall economic life. Moreover, the criminal justice system was stretched to its limits protecting personal and property rights, and the enforcement of morality was far beyond the capacities of the police and the courts. However, prostitutes became the targets of bitter condemnation because they symbolized the threat of the disreputable subculture to the rest of the community and because their presence challenged the social prerogatives reserved for ladies.

Theoretical Implications

The Comstock provided prostitutes with the rocky social soil in which they could thrive, and some material features of the Lode were unusually conducive to sexual commerce. No single aspect of material life on the Comstock generated prostitution or made it an integral part of community life, but a number of material forces combined with family organization and the system of ideas defining masculinity and femininity to produce a social situation extraordinarily supportive of prostitution. The theoretical implications of this chapter are answers to the question,

"What outstanding features of life on the Lode sustained prostitution?"
If the case study approach is useful, those features will be found to support sexual commerce elsewhere, and future historical and comparative
research on prostitution can focus on some of those features and refine
the implications presented here.

The single most important variable making prostitution central to
social organization on the Comstock was the overwhelming ratio of men
to women. At no time was there more than approximately one adult
woman for every two men. The imbalanced sex ratio, of course, only
generated demand for prostitutes because of its social context. The lone
men who came to the Lode had sometimes left behind their wives and
had often set aside some of the sexual constraints characteristic of the
established communities where they had previously lived. On the Comstock there was a shortage of marriageable women and there were also
widespread formal prohibitions against adultery. Prostitutes were the
only available sexual partners for many men whose desire was fueled by a
widespread popular "volcano theory" of sexuality which held that unless
men had regular sexual contact, they would explode in orgies of adultery, rape, physical violence, or even homosexual embraces.

The rootless men who came to the Comstock participated in an urban
situation fostering both the demand and supply for prostitution. Large-
scale prostitution in America has always been associated with urban
settings, and a number of early sociologists asserted that individual
isolation in large cities and the fast pace of metropolitan life gave rise to
prostitution.[69] The Comstock's size, heterogeneity, and social geography permitted the development of specialized brothel districts in
which prostitutes could visibly ply their trade and customers could keep
their visits somewhat secret.

The Comstock rapidly grew into a city which attracted men and
women from all over the world because of the fabulous wealth in the
mines and the availability of many jobs. The organization of the mines
combined with the Lode's urban characteristics to create an atmosphere
in which human life was generally devalued. The many deaths and daily
injuries in the mines and the routine violence in the streets were symp-
tomatic of the makeshift mining economy. That economy epitomized
laissez-faire capitalism in which there was unregulated competition for
resources, markets, and jobs without the cushion often provided by
community roots or lasting affective ties. In order to compete successfully in the economic arena, Comstock residents had to separate their
private and public selves and attempt to isolate their work from the rest
of their lives.[70] Segmentation of various roles supported prostitution,

because organized sexual commerce depends on participants' ability to keep various parts of their lives separate and treat one another as means to different personal ends. In the most basic transactions women are merely instruments for sexual satisfaction and men are agencies of economic remuneration. There are obviously different demands for role segmentation in different occupations, but overall role segmentation is likely to be greatest in situations like the Comstock, where there is unregulated economic competition along with consistently dangerous working conditions.

The danger and difficulty of work in the mines and the lesser perils of most other workingmen's occupations fueled the market for prostitution. Danger and the absence of family life have traditionally combined to increase the demand for commercial sex. Although men who work at dangerous occupations may find means to deny or routinize the possibility of harm, once they are no longer in imminent danger they may use sexual contact as a release for accumulated tensions. The immense brothel districts in nineteenth-century English garrison towns and the legions of camp followers traveling with the Union army during the Civil War bore witness to the connection of danger, isolation, and demand for prostitution.[71] Discomfort and occasional terror in the mines probably produced immediate emotional strains which set many men in motion toward the bawdy districts after their shifts were over.

The physical conditions of lone workingmen's leisure also supported prostitution because saloons, gambling halls, melodeons, and brothels were practically the only places on the Comstock where they could relax. Their cramped rooms were barely large enough to sleep in, let alone unwind, and men were almost driven out on the streets and into the bawdy quarters. On weekend evenings the streets were filled with men seeking amusements, while the air carried the mixed sounds of hoisting machinery and hurdy house pianos.

Because of inflation workingmen's comparatively high wages actually bought little, and they had few opportunities to spend or invest money wisely. However, they had every chance to gamble at cards or stocks or chase prostitutes. Workingmen patronized prostitutes more than men in any other social class because they made up the bulk of the Lode's male population, but the throngs in the bawdy districts included men from all walks of life. (Patronage will be discussed in chapters 3 and 5.)

Respectable working-class women were more likely to face grinding tedium than sudden danger, but their jobs payed far less than men's, and they could sometimes find no work because many occupations were closed to them. Inadequate pay, indecent working conditions, and lack of access to good jobs contributed to women's decisions to enter prostitution in order to earn a living. Some women saw prostitution as an attractive alternative to respectable jobs, while others saw it as the only available occupation. Women's marginality to the labor force and segregation in a few ill-paid occupations were the most important structural forces sustaining the supply side of prostitution on the Lode and supporting it in the rest of the country. In 1875 only 10 percent of all Comstock women were respectably employed, as were only 14 percent of the women over sixteen years old in the United States.[72] Women could neither depend upon kinship networks for support as they had in traditional agrarian societies nor be assured of earning an adequate living on their own. The partial opening of the respectable labor force to women guaranteed that some of them would slip into the crevices of the irregular marketplace.

The existence of an irregular marketplace in symbiosis with the larger economy sustained both the supply and demand for prostitution on the Comstock. Irregular institutions underlaid stratification patterns within prostitution, and the large disreputable subculture fostered the development of prostitutes' support networks, a specialized occupational argot and ideology, and a set of professional customs. Prostitution, gambling, and drinking all complemented one another, and a man beginning the evening in a saloon could easily wake up the next morning in a prostitute's arms. Prostitutes benefited from the proximity of many irregular institutions and from the fact that those institutions had their own agents of social control who could protect patrons' safety and property far better than official law enforcement officers.

If the majority of Comstock residents had supported laws against prostitution and the community had maintained honest and effective police, prostitution would have been diminished and controlled, although probably not eliminated. Minimal legislation and law enforcement against prostitution merely reflected the overwhelming structural forces supporting the growth and spread of sexual commerce on the Lode. The Comstock would have been a very different place without prostitution, and it is possible that community life on the Lode could not have survived without it. Hubert Howe Bancroft briefly described the centrality of the irregular marketplace to social and economic life on the Lode.

In Virginia [City] might be found, not withstanding statutes to the contrary, every form of vice, and all kinds of degrading amusements. On Saturday nights the underground population came to the surface; and while business houses were closed on Sunday, barrooms, gambling dens, fourth rate theatres, and bagnios were liberally patronized.[73]

2

Women's Work and Ladies' Leisure:
Marriage on the Comstock

There's too much of worriment goes to a bonnet,
There's too much of ironing goes to a shirt,
There's nothing that pays for the time you waste on it,
There's nothing that lasts but trouble and dirt.
                                    Traditional Folksong

ALTHOUGH WOMEN were marginal to the labor force, they were crucial to the home, and most Comstock women identified themselves as housekeepers to census enumerators. The high ratio of males to females on the Lode placed women in a paradoxical position in courtship and marriage. The shortage of adult females raised respectable women's exchange value on the marriage market and wives' importance to their husbands, but the exigencies of life on the mining frontier made women extraordinarily dependent on men for their physical comfort and safety. Most respectable women who were alone on the Comstock couldn't support themselves, and they had to marry or establish a long-term liaison with a man willing to care for them and defend their reputations. Marriage was essential to most women's social and economic survival, while it was merely desirable and important to men.

Respectable matrons of all classes led lives which were very different from the disreputable women's, but prostitution supported the social organization of courtship and marriage. Wives' major obligations were maternal, as they nurtured their children and spouses, while prostitutes' primary services were sexual. To be sure, there was sex in marriage and intimacy in prostitution, but the central functions of each institution were opposite and complementary.

Courtship

In the mid-nineteenth century respectable women learned courtship behavior from etiquette books, ladies' magazines, and bound gift treasuries which poured forth advice on appropriate courting for the first time in American history. Most of the advice was directed toward new members of the middle class, whose mobility generated the demand for written etiquette codes. Chaperonage was also introduced to middle- and upper-class Americans in the 1850s, as were rigorous stipulations about when suitors might call and what gifts they might bring to a lady. Regulated courtship was designed to limit the types of young men with whom young ladies could become acquainted, while also providing structured protection for their chastity.[1]

Chastity was among a woman's most valuable assets in the system of social exchange leading to marriage, and it was also the only truly effective form of birth control available at that time. Recently published studies about late-nineteenth-century women's sexuality, however, suggest that close to 10 percent of American women in all classes engaged in premarital intercourse.[2] Other women probably exceeded appropriate limits of sexual contact during courting but did not engage in actual intercourse, and much evidence indicates that the rigid ideology denying Victorian women's sexuality was never fully accepted in the United States.[3] While some of the Victorian emphasis on chastity was probably prescriptive rather than descriptive, chastity was normative and violations of the norm ideally occurred behind a screen of privacy.

Chaste young women were supposed to restrain all of their impulses in order to preserve their worth as future wives. Manuals advised women to wait cautiously for men's declarations of matrimonial intentions before they displayed any interest in their suitors at all, unless they wished to risk being trifled with.[4] Feminine purity was celebrated everywhere and even the "Language of Flowers" offered a dried white rose to symbolize "death preferable to loss of innocence."[5] Chastity was a serious matter for both bride and bridegroom, and some men searched for proof in the form of a bloody mark on a bride's nightgown. One late Victorian marriage guide suggested that new husbands abandon the custom of searching for a stain, for women's physiology varied and some may have accidentally broken their hymens. Instead, the author advised his male readers to search for purity in their wives' words and deeds.[6]

There were comparatively few respectable women available for courtship on the Comstock. Most married men brought their wives with them or sent for them after they had settled on the Lode, and there were only 1,456 marriages in Storey County from 1867 to 1880.[7] Women who were attractive and marriageable usually had a number of suitors.[8]

Various churches sponsored strawberry festivals, socials, tableaux, benefit performances, bazaars, and dances at which maidens of every class could meet appropriate beaux. Women flirted as they presided over bazaar tables and charmed men with entertaining letters which they sold for fifty cent donations to church funds. Once they were introduced, eligible men could call on young women at their homes or escort them to social functions. Virginia City ladies often set aside Monday afternoons for gentlemen callers, and when they became better acquainted, men might also call on ladies in the early evenings to chat or to play music on the piano or banjo. Most of these courtship situations offered couples no privacy, but evening parties did provide opportunities for discreet sexual play, as Alf Doten noted in his diary:

About a dozen couples in all assembled—Surprise party—Jolly girls—Jolly time—One of the pleasantist parties I ever attended—music & singing—Played "log cabin" and "consequences"—Ever so much kissing—most I ever saw— Had lunch [antiquated usage] of cake, fruit, nuts, candies, champagne, etc.— left 11 ½ [P.M.]—Saw the girls home.[9]

Courtship on the Comstock usually lasted less than a year, and the shortage of women probably made men extraordinarily eager to find wives. Parents were quite concerned with the brevity of courtships, fearing that their daughters might elope with unsuitable mates, and the age for young women's marriage without their parents' consent was legally set at eighteen.[10] Men similarly worried that they might make misalliances with women whose past histories were unknown to them. Thus, a local man was congratulated for setting a good example and breaking his engagement after discovering that his fiancee left an illegitimate child in Indiana.[11] Couples who married on the Lode were often little more than briefly acquainted and the vagueness of Comstock residents' past histories contributed to the probability of broken engagements or mismatches.

Family Organization and Wives' Roles

Marriage and family organization on the Comstock differed little from the dominant forms found throughout the United States. Even though basic nuclear family units were always the major family form in the United States, the American family of the era after the Civil War differed markedly from the typical family of earlier times. By the mid-1860s the growing concentration of labor in urban centers had all but destroyed the close-knit, multigenerational rural family oriented toward production.[12] Most Comstock families were nuclear units composed of parents and children, and few of them produced goods or services.

Although children were generally considered to be the major goal of nineteenth-century marriage, almost one-third of the Comstock families recorded in the 1875 state census had no children living at home. Out of 2,466 family units, 769 had no visible offspring, 531 had 1 child, and 455 had 2. Mean family size was 1.8 children per unit. Such small families were typical of late-nineteenth-century America, as parents directed their energies toward helping individual children ascend in the world, rather than encouraging the family to achieve mobility as a collective entity.[13] The maximization of expectations meant that people had to be willing to leave the families into which they were born, and the decline of conscious commitment to multigenerational families was linked to the general economic trends permitting thousands of people to rush to the Comstock in the first place.

The privatization of family life isolated almost all Comstock wives from the public arenas of work and political power and from the private support networks provided by their own kin. While the nature of women's isolation and of the work they did within their families varied according to their husbands' social class, all wives were responsible for doing or supervising housework, consumption, emotional work, and child care. They were also supposed to create an idyllic refuge from the world of work and take a major role in their children's socialization.

Wives were obligated to maintain the family dwelling, and inadequate housing, frequent windstorms, and occasional mudslides affected every Comstock woman but those few elites who maintained their residence in the Bay area. While more stone and brick houses were built after the Great Fire of 1875, most housing was still made of wood. Many families lived in rented rooms or in rickety two-room cottages consisting of a kitchen and a sitting room.[14] A few homes had impressive paneling, but the majority of inexpensive wood buildings had cloth walls and ceilings.[15]

These physical settings shaped housework, since poorly built, small dwellings often required extra cleaning and organization. Dust, mud, and pollution from the mines and ore mills forced most wives into an endless battle with dirt. Upper- and middle-class women cluttered their homes with carved furniture and ornate bric-a-brac requiring constant attention, and working-class women sometimes emulated middle-class styles by buying a few pieces of fashionable furniture or mass-produced prints to brighten their homes.

Cooking and cleaning, the basics of housework, were further complicated by the absence of labor-saving devices.[16] Preparing meals took a great deal of time in ill-equipped kitchens with few if any canned goods. Many Comstock cottages lacked rudimentary cooking facilities, and women either prepared food on the hearth or borrowed their neighbors' kitchens. Housecleaning also involved hard physical labor, and some popular cleaning solutions were dangerous because they contained caustic substances like sulfuric acid.

Water shortages and the poor quality of water in Storey County also hindered housework, cooking, and routine personal hygiene. Most people depended on the Virginia City and Gold Hill Water Company which provided a polluted product at high rates of one dollar a week per small family and higher rates for larger families and businesses.[17] One-family dwellings ordinarily had a single faucet in the kitchen at which individuals filled their pails and pitchers. Broken pipes were common during freezing winters, and housewives left their faucets on all night to prevent the problem. The water company's executives, dismayed at the overuse of their product, turned off residential water supplies at five in the evening and did not turn them on again until six the next morning.[18] Women hoping to cook or clean or wash in the evening had to plan ahead and store a supply of water before they could even begin their other work.

Upper- and middle-class women usually hired servants to do their cleaning and all ten of the mine owners' or superintendents' wives living on the Lode in 1875 had at least two servants residing in their homes. Other wives hired only one servant or employed a daily domestic who maintained her own residence. If she could not afford regular help, the least a respectable middle-class woman did was send her laundry out to the Chinese quarter and have someone come in to help with heavy cleaning.[19] Employing servants indicated that a woman was a lady dedicated to higher tasks than routine drudgery. Most wives, however, did their own housework and received little recognition for the hard labor.

Some women also worked at home to raise their families' living standards. Close to 100 Comstock wives helped keep boarding or lodging houses and other women sometimes took in one or two boarders to earn money.[20] Few wives worked at home to produce goods for profit, and home production on the Lode was usually limited to sewing family garments, raising hogs and chickens for meat and eggs, and growing vegetables for the table. The productive plots of beans and cabbages tended by working-class women provided a marked contrast to the profuse decorative flower gardens which ladies cultivated, and working-women's simple calico dresses which cost about eleven dollars for materials and labor presented a far different image than ladies' elaborate silk confections for which the labor alone cost forty dollars.[21]

Women who could afford it patronized dressmakers or purchased the growing supply of mass-produced dry goods. Clothing was not only a necessity, it was also a badge of respectability, and the process of buying or sewing new clothes and keeping old ones in good repair was part of the creation and maintenance of a family's social position within the respectable community. By the end of the Civil War consumption of clothes, foodstuffs, and other goods for family use was beginning to supplant production as a major part of women's work within the nuclear family. Shopping for goods and services was often difficult, crucial work which included tiresome bargain hunting in inconvenient shops.[22] The Lode's wild inflation and capricious investment possibilities also made consumption important as a form of investment for families of limited means, and the purchase of a piece of furniture or a valuable, durable item of clothing like a cashmere shawl was sometimes the best possible investment.[23] Wives' work as consumers functioned to secure necessities, maintain family status, and at times even make small investments. It was also a diversion, however, and shopping was among the few free, public pastimes open to respectable women. Reputable women did not go downtown to drink or gamble, but they could indulge in the main street's carnival atmosphere while they were shopping.

While working-class women struggled to buy essentials, affluent wives' consumption far exceeded the broadest possible definitions of necessity. Leisured upper- and middle-class ladies turned shopping into art and enhanced their husbands' reputations by devising fashionable rituals and entertainments.[24] Louise Palmer critically described a typical Comstock luncheon:

It is curious that we all protest against lunch parties, yet continue to give and attend them. It is stupid to dress in one's newest silk, and handsomest corals to partake of chicken, creams, ices and Champagne, with a dozen of one's own sex. Who can help being painfully conscious that each and every one of them have priced the silk at Rosener's and the corals at Nye's, before they came to one's wearing. It is a trying thing for one's dress to be subjected to the test of its value, not of its adaptability, or becomingness.[25]

Wives were also obliged to provide for their husband's sense of well-being by creating shelters from the brutal marketplace. *Reveries of a Bachelor,* a bestseller during the 1850s, described the attractions of domesticity, noting that man's greatest pleasure at home came from

the ecstasy of conviction that *there* at least you are beloved; that there you are understood; that there your errors will meet with gentlest forgiveness . . . ; and there you may be entirely and joyfully——yourself.[26]

Women were expected to be sources of patience, kindness, and inspiration for their husbands and children. A number of late-nineteenth-century social reformers even argued that if wives could only inspire their husbands and children to moral purity, all society would be cleansed and fundamentally improved.[27] On the Comstock, wives were idealized as a civilizing group who "shed the comforts of life o'er the barren hearth, causing the desert to blossom as the rose."[28] Women could sometimes gain power through attending to husbands' happiness, and one late Victorian ladies' publication discussed the power of persuasion, commenting that "the empire of woman is softness . . . her commands are caresses, her manacles are tears."[29]

There was a common division of labor in the nineteenth-century family in which men took care of their children's material well-being by financially supporting them and women took care of the bulk of their emotional, intellectual, and spiritual development. Fertility in the United States declined throughout the last half of the nineteenth century, but children were still very important to family life.[30] Child care or the supervision of a child care worker was usually a wife's central role. According to the dominant nineteenth-century ideology, motherhood provided women with "a higher place on the scale of being."[31] Child-rearing literature told women that children were molded within their families and that it was up to mothers to shape "the infant mind as yet untainted with evil."[32]

Comstock children were exposed to public and private schools, church groups, professional dance instructors, and a range of other private tutors, but the major responsibility for their welfare still rested with their mothers. Families were held accountable for their children's moral training and supervision.[33] During the community's formative years the small number of children on the Lode were regarded as a naturally civilizing element, discouraging profanity and inspiring rough men and unruly women to better behavior.[34] Children were defined as naturally good and innocent, and when they grew old enough to become troublesome to the community their mothers were held accountable. Child care, like all of wives' other functions, was often taken for granted as naturally following from women's character.

All of wives' activities occurred within a social institution characterized by male dominance. A large part of that dominance rested on husbands' roles as breadwinners, but men also had power because of ideology, custom, and law. Nevada law permitted wives to formally register property which they had inherited or acquired alone, but for the duration of marriage a husband had the legal right and duty to control and manage his wife's property, and a married woman could only dispose of her property in her husband's presence.[35] The law acknowledged the possibility of women's independent financial contributions, but it affirmed men's control of their wives' economic lives.

Wife beating was the most evident symptom of the power differential within marriage. Comstock newspapers reported thirty-six cases of brutality, fourteen of them occurring in 1877 when public attention focused on the problem because of the passage of a state law against the practice. Divorce figures provide some additional evidence that wife beating was a widespread problem. Cruelty, which referred to physical abuse, was cited as the sole cause of divorce in 230 decrees granted to Nevada women from 1867 through 1886, and an additional 149 wives listed it as one of several causes.[36]

Few husbands were arrested or punished for the offense, for the issue of wife beating involved thorny legal puzzles about the relationship of the criminal justice system to the privacy of marriage and other problems about how to punish offenders without penalizing their families. Fines and jail sentences usually imposed financial hardships on wives and children who depended on the family head, but the legislature managed to devise a law penalizing only husbands. Any man convicted for the first time of beating his wife or another woman would be tied to a permanent post erected in the county seat for two to ten hours. During that period of public humiliation he would wear a sign stating "wife or woman beater." Convictions for second offenses would result in jail sentences. The legislators realized that police might react against embarrassing another man whose only criminal activity occurred within his family, so they also provided for fines against lawmen who did not enforce the new penalty.[37]

Public comments on the new wife beating penalty were made by men who predictably believed that it constituted cruel and unusual punishment, and through 1880 no wife beater on the Lode was ever tied to the post.[38] No one publicly defended the practice of wife beating, but several newspaper articles discussed the ways in which wives provoked beatings. These beatings were defined as "mutual affairs, demonstrating how easy it is for a woman to get false sympathy."[39] "As we have this post for men, we should have our ducking stool for women."[40]

Wife beating went virtually unpunished because of the privacy surrounding the nuclear family and also because of widely shared support of men's patriarchal roles. Family violence was regarded as an individual problem, rather than as a course of action reflecting wider social relationships.

Volunteer Work

Because of their many household obligations and also because of formal and informal restrictions, most respectable wives were virtually cut off from community life. Volunteer work was one of the few areas in which women could work for goals beyond their immediate family circles and for which they could receive public recognition. Volunteer work allowed women, especially affluent ones, to engage in valued public activity that was complementary to their duties as wives. As volunteers they extended their time-honored maternal and inspirational functions outward from the family circle to embrace the wider community, and they could receive public recognition and gratitude which reflected on their husbands. Moreover, most volunteer work offered respectable women a rare chance to gather in groups and engage in worthy sociability.

Comstock women were involved in four interrelated types of volunteer work, all of which had some formal or informal connection to religious organizations. They were church groups, disaster relief organizations, reform groups, and spontaneous charity. Almost all charity on the Lode was based on a consistent differentiation between the deserving poor who lived within the law and conformed to the ethics of hard work and sacrifice and the undeserving or disreputable poor who did not. This differentiation made it possible for people on the Comstock to deny prostitutes access to charity or moral reform. Respectable women in eastern and midwestern cities had created groups to aid and rehabilitate prostitutes since the 1830s, but Comstock volunteers simply avoided the whole issue of commercial sex.

Volunteer work was the prerogative of the "wives and daughters of our best citizens."[41] As volunteers they could gather together to make plans, gossip, work, and sometimes behave in a manner bordering on disreputability. For the sake of charity ladies sang and danced on the stage, sold tickets to balls and festivals, and used charm to sell goods at charity bazaars. They could briefly enter public life and even defy conventional mores for the sake of a higher cause, so long as they avoided contact with the disreputable subculture. Quite simply, good women were expected to do good deeds for good people in good company.

After 1865 prostitutes were excluded entirely from volunteer activities and from public notice of their individual good works, but in the first years of the Comstock's settlement a few prostitutes had assumed integral roles in community life—nursing the sick, visiting the poor, sponsoring volunteer fire companies, and organizing innocent picnics and parades.[42] Mary McNair Mathews commented:

This class of women is always very kind-hearted and gives liberally to any charitable purpose, and is always ready to assist the poor and suffering. It seems as if they wish to atone for their many sins by doing charity, for "charity covereth a multitude of sins."[43]

Volunteer activities and the gratitude and recognition they commanded were the traditional prerogatives of respectable women. The highmindedness and personal goodness associated with volunteer work could have been easily questioned if disreputable women joined volunteer organizations, so respectable women on the Lode somehow crowded prostitutes out of volunteer work in order to preserve their own reputations, power, and status.

Adultery, Divorce, and Consensual Liaisons

Sex in marriage was a private topic seldom openly discussed by people on the Comstock, but the many marital and medical advice books published in the second half of the nineteenth century offer some clues on that delicate subject. While some writers conceded that women's sexual urges were as strong as men's, the majority believed that "good" women had less need for sexual satisfaction than did their husbands.[44] Partners in marriage were urged to create an ideal family circle, and issues of their interpersonal compatibility were usually defined as secondary. Sexual satisfaction was never considered to be a major marital goal, although some writers gave it more importance than others.

The minimization of respectable women's sexuality denied them some conjugal satisfaction and formed the foundation of an ideology affirming men's right to seek out prostitutes as alternative sexual partners. On the positive side, however, their alleged lack of sexuality enhanced wives' positions in the family by defining them as morally superior to their spouses. The widespread belief in feminine asexuality also allowed women to control their husbands' sexual demands and reject advances which might have led to unwanted children in an era of imperfect birth control.[45] Contrary to popular belief, however, a number of Comstock wives desired sexual satisfaction and some of them had extramarital affairs.

Adultery was one of seven grounds for divorce in Nevada and from 1867 through 1886 simple adultery was listed as the sole cause for 100 Nevada divorces. Sixty-seven of them were granted to irate husbands, and it is possible that more women strayed than men.[46] All other evidence suggests, however, that women's transgressions were taken far more seriously than men's because of the double standard of sexual behavior.

The pattern of blaming women and absolving men was played out in the famous Beecher-Tilton affair which rocked America in the 1870s. Victoria Woodhull, the explosive feminist-adventuress, exposed the renowned Henry Ward Beecher's affair with Elizabeth Tilton, a member of his congregation and the wife of one of his good friends.[47] On the Comstock as elsewhere the public generally excused the minister and condemned both his morally frail partner and the reckless woman who betrayed their secret.[48] Senator John P. Jones of Nevada declared that he would stand opposed to women's suffrage in Congress because "he has been interviewed by Woodhull and Claflin [her sister] and has concluded that, since they demand the ballot, it is scarcely possible that the better classes of American wives and mothers do."[49]

One husband on the Lode shot his wife because he suspected her of intimacy with a lodger and another shot a friend whom he discovered embracing his wife in the outhouse. Local juries acquitted both men.[50]

Since the burden of blame for adultery fell most heavily on wives, so did the burden of concealment. In a farce bordering on tragedy, Alf Doten was nearly caught in bed with his mistress when her husband, a close friend of his, came home unexpectedly. She slipped out the back door and knocked her elbow out of joint, later telling her husband that she had accidentally fallen on her way back from the privy. In his diary for that day, Alf congratulated himself for sitting up late with his mistress while she endured the pain of her injury.[51] More affluent wives often avoided discovery because they had time to spare, resources for concealment, and husbands whose devotion to work kept them away from home, and stylized adultery rituals emerged on the Comstock as they had in aristocratic New York City and London. It was common for bachelors on the Lode to escort married ladies to club functions, private card and supper parties, and church entertainments. So long as husbands acknowledged the apparent innocence of these arrangements there was no scandal, and the assumptions about women's minimal sexuality allowed everyone to deny possibilities of adultery. Louise Palmer noted:

This proves an excellent arrangement where one's husband is old or disagreeable, or even when there are no such drawbacks, and greatly lessens the chances of domestic feuds, by rendering impossible the familiarity which is said to breed contempt.[52]

Sometimes familiarity led to divorce and from 1867 to 1886 there was approximately 1 divorce for every 4 marriages in Storey County, or 353 divorces and 1,412 marriages.[53] Although rates in the United States had been rising dramatically since the Civil War, divorce was still considered deviant.[54] Comstock newspapers published articles lamenting rising divorce rates and urging couples to stay together.[55] Separation was only permissible under extreme circumstances, and one writer exhorted:

Our courts are beginning to get as notorious for divorce cases as the California tribunals. Ladies and gentlemen, keep your tempers and remain with your better halves, and thus save our climate from a bad name.[56]

There were seven grounds for divorce which could be cited alone or in combination in Nevada. They were adultery, cruelty, desertion for more than one year, habitual drunkenness, a husband's willful neglect to provide for his family, conviction of a felony, and impotence. From 1867 through 1886, 879 Nevada divorces were granted to women and only 249 were granted to men. The four most common single causes were cruelty (254), husband's neglect to provide (171), desertion (169), and adultery (100). More husbands than wives were granted decrees because of their wives' adultery (67) or desertion (113).[57]

In 1880 there were twenty divorced men and twenty-six divorced women living alone on the Lode, and twelve of the divorced women were prostitutes. Divorce represented an enormous step for women because it threw them out of their previous social positions. Some women could return to their families of orientation, others quickly remarried, and still others were thrust into an unwelcoming labor force. No matter who sued for divorce, however, women lost status when the intimate details of their lives were subjected to public scrutiny. The double standard permitted many male transgressions, but women's sexual misbehavior was seldom excused by ideology or practice.

Desertion was a functional substitute for divorce in the late nineteenth century.[58] In Nevada, 169 divorces were granted to men and women whose spouses had deserted them for more than one year and an additional 143 decrees were obtained by wives whose husbands had both deserted them and failed to provide for them for over one year.[59] Many more men and women in similar circumstances probably did not file for divorce because of the expense and the social stigma involved, and the whole transient aura surrounding the silver booms must have facilitated the casual dissolution of marriage.

Desertion was one part of a dynamic giving rise to consensual unions in which men and women lived together as if they were married but had no formal legal ties.[60] Members of those couples usually lived in working-class districts and conformed to the norms of respectable behavior, sometimes pretending they were married, although many of these disclosed their real names to census enumerators. There were 180 consensual unions in 1875 and only 20 in 1880, indicating that most of those involved in them either married or were among the first to leave the Lode as the final depression began. Fourteen of the men involved in liaisons in 1880 were single, four were married, one was divorced, and one was widowed. In contrast, nine of the women were widows, four with children; two were divorced, one with a child; five were married; and only four were single.

These figures suggest that many of the women in liaisons, especially widows with children, desperately needed men to support them. They were willing to be bound to men who could not or would not marry them in order to follow traditional patterns of daily life. Very little was written about them and they wrote nothing about themselves, but census data provide some bare bones of description. Mary Ronan, an Irish widow with two children, and Thomas Welsh, an Irish miner, set up housekeeping in a small house on South E Street. Clara Kane, another widow, who was born in Kentucky, lived with Amidee Dupas, a New Orleans locksmith, at 152 South C Street. Mary Howe, a thirty-five-year-old widow, resided with A. Fairbush, a Prussian glazier, at 133 Main Street in Gold Hill. Most of the other couples were similar.[61] The men were workers and they lived in working-class neighborhoods, unlike the sporting men who took up residence with their mistresses in the bawdy districts.

Some people in consensual unions probably refused to marry because they had spouses elsewhere. Anna Mittlman deserted her first husband and married another man who brought her to the Lode. Eventually her first husband discovered them and Anna went to trial for bigamy, but her attorney successfully defended her by arguing that she told no bigger lies than the many Comstock women who pretended to be married when they were not.[62]

Adultery and consensual unions involved extramarital sexuality which went against the grain of Victorian morality. That morality was ideal rather than real, and it is doubtful whether most Comstock wives denied their sexuality. Nevertheless, sexual satisfaction was not considered to be an essential part of marriage, and men and women alike entered erotic extramarital relationships. Alf Doten was one of the many who strayed. He has been introduced earlier in the book, but now he will be more formally presented in order to provide readers with a view of the social organization of sexuality in one Comstock man's life.

Alf Doten's Private Life

Alf was local editor of the *Virginia Daily Union* and the *Territorial Enterprise,* and editor and proprietor of the *Gold Hill News* during the 1870s. Born in Plymouth, Massachusetts, in 1829, he was directly descended from two Mayflower families, but he left his roots to sail around Cape Horn and find his fortune in the California gold fields in 1849. The afternoon of his first day at sea Alf conquered his queasiness and began to keep the methodical journal in which he wrote entries almost every day until his death in 1903. There were seventy-nine small leather-bound diaries, and twenty-five of them, volume numbers 30 through 54, cover the Lode's boom years and the early period of its final depression. [63] The pages of Alf's diaries reveal his attitudes and priorities concerning sexual arrangements and there is no way to measure whether his ideas or activities were typical or representative. Certainly Alf himself was no ordinary fellow, although he described his adventures as commonplace and his descriptions correspond with many of the patterns described earlier in this chapter.

Alf was a moderately attractive man about five feet eight inches tall, who was something of a dandy and sported a black mustache and beard. When he arrived on the Comstock at age thirty-three he was slender, but two decades later he began to grow stout as he changed from being a sociable drinker to a drunkard. He enjoyed a short period of affluence at the beginning of his marriage in 1873, when he rode the crest of the Big Bonanza along with other investors. As the Comstock slipped into final depression, however, Alf became bitter and despondent, filling his diaries with rationalizations and blame. He moved to Austin in 1882, later commuted between Reno, Carson City, and Virginia City, and finally died in Carson City at age seventy-four.

When he arrived on the Comstock Alf was a highly eligible bachelor—a literate man with a trade who had traveled to San Francisco, Calaveras County, Spanish Gulch, the Palmyra District, and other towns on the Mother Lode that promised romance and high adventure. He was not an archetypal ladies' man who could magnetize women, but Alf could be charming and witty, and during his nine years as a bachelor on the Comstock he threw himself into assignations in the bawdy districts, polite courtship, a clandestine affair, and a whirlwind engagement.

Alf quickly adjusted to life on the Lode and joined comrades in cruising bars, burlesque shows, and brothels. He regularly visited Jenny

Tyler's Box Windows Brothel; he was a special customer of Ida Vernon, a former music hall performer who went to work for Jenny, and of Belle Neal, a dancer who "showed plenty of shape."[64] Although Alf often visited prostitutes during his first years on the Lode, he seldom noted whether he went to them for sexual contact or for simple companionship. Many of his brief comments about sex had been erased by a family censor (probably his wife), and those entries that survived briefly summarized his adventures as a "jolly time" or "Ho Joe."[65] Alf treated his interest in prostitutes casually and matter-of-factly, and he frequently abated his pursuit of immediate satisfaction in the bawdy districts in order to court young ladies.

Alf was seriously interested in Miss Frankie Cross, Miss Mira Morrill, Miss Cora Kelsey, and Miss Lizzie Lansdell, all of whom he had known previously in California. They were all young, marriageable maidens with whom he corresponded, exchanged valentines, and passed brief, enjoyable visits. Lizzie was forward enough to send Alf a lock of her hair and a bouquet and Frankie went farther and allowed Alf to kiss her several times. There was no other sexual contact in their courtship rituals and Alf's interest gradually waned as he became enmeshed in a torrid affair with his landlady, the wife of Ellis H. Morton, an old schoolmate from Plymouth who drank too hard and scrambled to earn a living as a marginal entrepreneur. In reacquainting himself with the Mortons, Alf dined with them, and when Morton was away or tied up with business Alf properly escorted his spouse to the theater, parties, and church functions, while she gradually became the grand passion of the journalist's life.

Alf and Mrs. M., as Alf always called her, began their physical affair in March of 1867, after they had been living under the same roof for some time. Alf compulsively tallied their sexual encounters in his diary, cryptically entering numbers like "OK 30," and they completed more than 526 successful rounds.[66] In the rapturous beginning of their relationship Alf also recorded physical details, using a simple letter substitution code to maintain secrecy. The romantic affair was over well before Mrs. M. informally separated from her husband and moved to San Francisco to become a dressmaker in April of 1871, but on her subsequent visits to the Comstock Mrs. M. managed to crawl into Alf's bed once or twice.

Their romance peaked in 1867, and after 1868 Alf and his paramour became more friends than lovers. Alf kept on sleeping with Mrs. M., but he began to cruise the bawdy districts once more and he also resumed his search for a wife. For almost two years, however, his mistress was at the center of Alf's life.

On September 10, 1867, the lovers celebrated an anniversary of sorts.

—Evening at home—11 PM OK—100—Me & my love had thus far just one hundred good square fucks together—the best fucking on the face of the earth—Heavenly . . .[67]

In other entries Alf was far more explicit about the nature of their intercourse. Sometimes there was "no skin" and at others they "went at it naked."[68] Alf usually satisfied himself, although he occasionally went away disappointed.

—Evening we were in bed together one hour, fucking & having a jolly time & all sorts of styles—I fooled so that I could not get my gun off.[69]

He joyously acknowledged his partner's sexuality, and he was willing to follow her lead in experimenting.

I came home at 9 this evening and me and my love went to bed and had one of our best fucking matches—we felt each others cocks all we pleased and then she got on and fucked me bully & I lying on my back—got my gun off in that position for the second time in my life—[70]

Alf and his mistress were constant companions in private and public life, and Ellis Morton could scarcely have ignored the reality of their affair. All three members of the triangle, however, kept up the fiction that Ellis was blissfully unaware. The clumsy Morton interrupted the lovers on several occasions, and Alf and Mrs. M. did not spend a full night together until June of 1868, when her husband was away.

Alf may have intended to marry Mrs. Morton early in their affair. He happily noted Ada Hoyt Foye's spiritualist prophecy that he would someday marry a Virginia City lady who "loves you better than she does her husband."[71] But even during the same passionate romantic period of their affair, Alf refused to deal with an early miscarriage of Mrs. M's. After describing her great pain he remarked, "I get no fucking now."[72] When his mistress finally departed for the Bay Area, Alf simply shrugged, "at 4 PM Mrs. M. left for San F—took her bird and all her things—leaves me for good, I think—."[73]

Three nights later he was sparking with Mira Morrill and commencing his final quest for a wife. Mira married someone else, but by the time Alf heard the news he was already courting his future spouse, Mary Elizabeth Calista Stoddard, a young widow. Their romance began in

November of 1872 when Mrs. Stoddard returned from Lake Tahoe with some friends of Alf's and presented him with a trout. In the next five months they saw each other occasionally, as Alf paid her formal calls. Then in June of 1873 he accelerated courtship, escorting her to the theater and the circus and taking her on buggy rides. Next month Alf and Mrs. Stoddard joined two respectable married couples on an expedition to Lake Tahoe. The men sailed and fished and the women read. In the evening the couples sat by the fire and played whist until 9:30 when everyone retired, with Alf sleeping in discrete solitude. Finally, less than a week before his forty-fourth birthday, Alf proposed: "We had an *interesting talk—I proposed and was accepted.*" [original emphasis].[74]

Nearly one hundred people showed up for the unusual ceremony on a yacht in the middle of Lake Tahoe. Mrs. Stoddard became Mrs. Doten and the newlyweds set out for Glenbrook and a round of visiting and parties once they returned to the Comstock. Given his previous writing, Alf was extraordinarily reticent about the sexual aspects of his marriage. For a few weeks he entered numbers such as "-22-" in his diary, but after awhile he merely used check marks to indicate intercourse.[75] Surprisingly, he wrote "-3-" on his wedding night, for during the preceding week he and his fiancee sampled the delights of marriage. Sex became less important to Alf as he assumed the duties of a household head and anticipated raising a family. The Dotens eventually reared four of their own children and Mrs. Doten's daughter by her previous marriage, and some of Alf's diminished interest in sex may have reflected his young wife's practical desire to limit their family's size. Throughout his first seven years of marriage Alf was fairly faithful to his Mary. He stayed away from married women and only strayed down to the bawdy districts on rare occasions to see a melodeon show or attend a prostitutes' ball. Alf did not forsake prostitutes, but he severely limited his encounters with them, just as he had limited his courting during the first years of his great affair.

Alf's attitudes toward the women in his life conformed remarkably to the customs of the times. He enjoyed prostitutes but did not become emotionally involved with them, as he did with his mistress, a respectable married woman. Emotional involvement, however, did not mean formal ties, and Alf failed to marry his mistress after she had separated from her husband. The high sexuality of his affair contrasted with the minimal place he accorded sex in his marriage. He and his fiancee bent courting customs once or twice, but sex never appeared to be a central part of their lives and Alf was far more concerned with his finances and his offspring.

Theoretical Implications

Alf Doten's diaries suggest that wives and prostitutes had very different but complementary functions, as does other information about marriage, family life, and sexual commerce on the Comstock. The idea that marriage and prostitution are opposite social forms contradicts a traditional feminist argument about similarities between the two institutions. Emma Goldman persuasively discussed the parallels between righteous marriage and sexual barter in her famous pamphlet, "The Traffic in Women":

Nowhere is woman treated according to the merit of her work, but rather as a sex. It is therefore almost inevitable that she should pay for her right to exist, to keep her position in whatever line with sex favors. Thus it is merely a question of degree whether she sells herself to one man, in or out of marriage, or to many men.[76]

Although married women and prostitutes on the Lode shared a common economic dependence on men, little else bound them together. Wives implicitly exchanged housework for financial support, and a portion of husbands' wages paid for women's work in the home.[77] Housework and the creation of a supportive environment separate from the public sphere were crucial parts of women's marital obligations which did not involve many sexual obligations. Their central maternal roles of bearing and raising children were also distinct from, if not in opposition to, their expression of sexuality. Sexual satisfaction had minimal importance in marriage because husbands and wives had so many other duties to one another and also because abstinence was the only completely effective means of limiting procreation.

The sustained interaction characteristic of marriage provided more fruitful opportunities for the development of genuine intimacy than the sporadic encounters characteristic of most prostitution. Prostitutes offered their patrons sex without the emotional or ethical obligations characteristic of marriage, and once men paid a fee they had fulfilled their part of the transaction. These critical differences in the material and emotional obligations of wives and prostitutes point to the possibility of functional complementarity between marriage and sexual commerce. It appears that marriage and family organization on the Comstock were strengthened by prostitution, and that prostitution was particularly functional for marriage during courtship and after wives had ceased to desire more children.

The importance attached to feminine chastity before marriage and the equivalent emphasis on masculine virility made it necessary that single men find nonmarriageable women to initiate them sexually and continue to satisfy their needs. The purity of respectable maidens and their value in the marriage market partially rested on the sacrifice of another group of women, prostitutes. The minimization of feminine sexuality during marriage also supported and was in turn supported by prostitution. It is probable that married men were most likely to seek out prostitutes if their wives refused to bear any more children. The connections among prostitution, courtship, and marriage are extraordinarily complex, and the relationship of sexual commerce to the family life cycle is an empirical question requiring further investigation of the past and present.

Prostitution on the Comstock also functioned as a means of symbolic social control to keep women married. Visible, organized sexual commerce clarified the social norms surrounding wives' sexual behavior, indicating the potential consequences of promiscuity. Being a housewife was often romantically frustrating, emotionally unsatisfactory, and physically demanding, but it provided women with far more social and emotional resources than prostitution. The physical hazards and psychic consequences of sexual commerce were so great that the possibility of becoming a prostitute probably served as a powerful deterrent to wives' sexual or social nonconformity.

Respectable wives were intent upon protecting the scarce public recognition and status resources which they gained from volunteer work, and they emphasized the differences between themselves and prostitutes. In condemning prostitutes, however, they inadvertently limited their own alternatives by refusing to forge links with a whole caste of other women. Wives' proper parlors were as constricting in many ways as the bawdy quarters' alleyways, for each place offered women a limited set of roles and rewards.

3
First Impressions:
An Overview of the Bawdy Districts

I wish I were a fascinating bitch:
I'd never be poor—I'd always be rich.
I'd live in a house with a little red light.
I'd sleep all day and work all night.
Traditional college sorority song

NO MATTER HOW sheltered or oblivious they were, no one on the Comstock could be entirely ignorant of prostitution. Its traces were everywhere, just like the chronic pollution from the mines and ore mills or the fine dust from the surrounding countryside. Language, residential patterns, and customs all reflected the substantial presence of prostitution on the Lode. This chapter will offer a general overview of Comstock prostitution, focusing on social geography and on prostitute's age, race, ethnicity, and marital status. It will be a basis for exploring some of the qualitative dimensions of prostitutes' lives in the three following chapters.

The rich vocabulary applied to Comstock prostitution suggests its size and importance in the community, and thirteen different words for prostitution were used regularly in newspaper stories and contemporary commentaries. While some of those words reflected a Victorian penchant for euphemisms and reporters' attempts to pepper their writing with arresting terms, the large number of synonyms for prostitute also indicates the centrality of commercial sex to people on the Lode. Just as Eskimos and Laplanders use a number of words for snow, Comstock residents routinely used thirteen different words or phrases to refer to prostitutes. The sheer number of terms and phrases, which often conveyed nuances of meaning, indicated the importance of prostitution to social life.[1]

Some phrases which were synonymous with the word "prostitute" implied general conceptions about commercial sex. Thus, "soiled dove" and "fair but frail" communicated the idea that prostitutes were fragile creatures who had fallen into sin. On the other hand, "woman of the town," "woman of easy virtue," and "woman of ill repute" indicated the promiscuous, public nature of prostitutes' sexuality.

Other words were more straightforward. "Courtesan," "prostitute," "harlot," and "whore" were used interchangeably in reference to prostitutes. However, "madam," "mistress," "waiter girl," and "prostitute of the lowest order" indicated different occupational groups within the profession. Other terms and phrases were used infrequently, but serve as superior illustrations of inventive language about prostitution. They included "cyprian," which originally denoted those who worshiped Aphrodite, "nymph du pave," and "keeper of a hotel de refreshment."

The language which was explicitly connected with prostitution was supplemented by four plain euphemisms: "actress," "servant," "dressmaker," and "housekeeper." The meaning of these words could only be clarified by their context. A servant who kept house for a mine owner's wife had a very different occupation than a "servant" who worked in a chebang on the Barbary Coast. Also, six "housekeepers" who resided in the same house in the heart of the main bawdy district could only have been prostitutes.

The rich vocabulary people applied to prostitution reflected some key features of commercial vice on the Comstock where women of many ages and many countries plied their trade in many situations. It is hard to image anyone on the Lode having enough time, money or energy to experience the full range of prostitutes who lived there and it is even harder to imagine such a person acquiring a sociological perspective on the subject. People's images of the fast life were undoubtedly shaped by their experiences with it, and occasional patrons of Cad Thompson's high-status Brick House would view prostitution somewhat differently than sporting men who regularly smoked opium at China Mary's.

At best someone may have been able to develop impressionistic accounts much like those found several decades later in the *Denver Red Book* or the New Orleans *Green, Red,* and *Blue Books.*[2] The latter, first published in 1895, was the most complete of such volumes. It was a veritable *Guide Michelin* to the Storeyville district, containing an initial listing of prostitutes, a section of advertisements for cigars, liquor, and other diverting goods, and a large final section of elaborately illustrated inducements to visit various brothels.[3] These guides were for pleasure rather than for understanding, yet they offered excellent representations of the fast life's shiny surface. No such publications ever described Comstock prostitutes, but the 1880 manuscript census lists women's addresses and also provides dry but accurate details about some of their other attributes.

Social Geography of the Fast Life

Final depression had settled on the Comstock in 1880 and total ore production was less than in any year since 1860. The market value of all local mineral production was approximately $3.5 million, compared with more than $38 million in the peak production year of 1876.[4] More than sixteen thousand residents remained on the Comstock, although many of them were making plans to leave. Some people believed that deep mining would eventually pay off, so they reluctantly turned over large sums of assessment to keep their stocks and their hopes alive.[5] Others simply had no place to go.

While the Comstock's overall population size had declined by about 15 percent since 1875, its prostitutes had diminished in number from 307 to 146 in 1880. Virginia City's large population of prostitutes always appeared to be in constant motion through western cities and mining camps, and only 7 prostitutes and two madams were listed in both censuses. The rate of turnover may not have been quite so high as census figures indicate, however. Some Comstock prostitutes went uncounted in one or another census because they commuted between the Lode and San Francisco, the California gold towns, or Carson City.[6] Also, some prostitutes changed their names frequently or used two or more names simultaneously. For example, one woman known as Hattie Willis was born Belle Bateman, while another changed her name from Hattie Knapp to Laura Steele. Madam Caroline Thompson was also known as Cad or Cad the Brick or simply the Brick. The 1880 roster of prostitutes revealed that Mary, Alice, Kitty, and Fannie were among the most popular prostitutes' first names, and it is probable that some women were not born with them. Nevertheless, several features of frontier prostitution encouraged geographic mobility. Dependence on large numbers of customers forced women to follow men moving to new boomtowns and new ore discoveries and the many hazards of commercial sex contributed to prostitutes' early deaths. So long as the Comstock boom lasted, however, new women came to take others' places. The contours of prostitution on the Lode were much the same in 1880 as they had been at the peak bonanza, and while the actual size of the disreputable subculture had grown smaller, it maintained its variety and vitality. Prostitutes lived everywhere on the Lode, but they congregated in

Virginia City's main bawdy district and in Chinatown. (See appendix 2 for a roster of prostitutes living on the Lode in 1880, the first census year in which addresses were specified.)

At the peak of the big bonanza in the early seventies, the Barbary Coast on South C Street near Silver was famed for its small but very wicked bawdy saloons. Those dives included Mr. and Mrs. Corcoran's Union Saloons at 158 South C, Nellie Sayers' place at 146 ½ South C, and Peter Larkin's at 146 South C. All of them could be described as

gin-shops of the lowest class. . . . The buildings are low one story doggeries, with an appearance such as to warn most people of the nature of their occupants. The front part of both are bar-rooms [about 12' by 14'], the back part are bed-rooms . . .[7]

A massive cleanup campaign in 1877 forced the temporary closing of the Coast saloons, but by 1880 commercial vice once again flourished on that block. A lodging and boardinghouse at 194 South C housed four prostitutes and a disreputable female owner, as well as seven miners and a male Chinese cook. Five other prostitutes lived alone or in pairs on C between Potosoi and Taylor streets.

The block along C Street from Taylor to the center of town at Union and C Streets included dry goods stores, furniture emporiums, saloons, and melodeons in which women sang and sometimes danced with customers. On the west side of the street, five prostitutes lived in a brothel at 17 South C, close by the Delta Saloon and the Sawdust Corner Saloon at 1 South C.[8] The Fredricksburg and Milwaukee saloons stood directly across C Street on the east corner, and they were sometimes lauded as "the two most famous beer houses on the Comstock."[9] They were famous, however, for more than beer, as both saloons had rooms over them and employed women to entertain during and after hours.[10]

The fast action on the corner of C and Union streets was a target of citizen complaints for many years. At all hours, but especially after the day shift left the mines, loungers harassed pedestrians on the west side of C between Taylor and Sutton.[11] Street corner society was in full flower between four and eight in the evening, and ladies hesitated to appear on C Street at that time.[12] Despite protests by members of the respectable community, the saloons, melodeons, and gambling halls near the corner of C and Union remained open throughout the boom.

The northeast corner, 1 North C, was dominated by the International Hotel, a six-story edifice boasting one of the first elevators west of the Mississippi.[13] It was the Comstock's "Grand Hotel" and in 1880 it contained 160 rooms filled with mahogany furniture, ceiling-high mirrors, and chandeliers.[14] According to observers, "It would compare favorably with the Sherman House at Chicago, or any of the first class hotels in the East."[15] From its beginnings in 1859, the International had been the Comstock's most elegant hotel, occupying the same site it did ten years later.[16] Dignitaries such as President Rutherford B. Hayes and General William Tecumseh Sherman stopped there, as did more dubious celebrities such as Victoria Woodhull and Tennessee Claflin. Although no prostitutes resided there in either 1875 or 1880, the International most certainly was not isolated from vice. Not only did it face two of the Comstock's most famous saloons, but it also stood opposite the city's largest, noisiest bawdy theater. Dick Bermann's Alhambra Theater in the basement of Frederick House was renowned for its loose and pretty entertainers. Several Comstock campaigners sought to limit the theater's attraction for youths, and one editorial caught the flavor of the whole bawdy quarter in commenting:

There is a theater called the Alhambra here in Virginia which is known for neither the chasteness of its performance nor the moral tone which it seeks to exert on its frequenters. Good people go there sometimes and very bad people offtimes. This is a free country and the grown men and women who go there might find a worse place if it were closed.

However, a dozen to three dozen boys are there each night. Parents must stop this. Authorities must forbid minors on penalty of license loss. Boys attending regularly will surely become hoodlums.[17]

C Street became increasingly proper as one moved north past Sutton and on toward the Geiger Grade. Respectable lodging and boarding-houses and small homes lined the street, and in 1880 only five prostitutes lived north of Union Street on C. Nine prostitutes lived west of C Street by themselves, in pairs, or in one small brothel near the county jail on B Street; but most women of ill repute lived below the main street, down the hill nearer the mines.

When Comstock ore was first discovered, some of the city's major institutions such as the railroad depot and the city hall were built on D Street alongside major brothels and prostitutes' cottages. By 1880 city hall, the county courthouse, and the Miners' Union Hall all occupied imposing buildings on B Street and the prostitutes stayed on D Street. Neither local ordinances nor citizens' complaints nor the fires which swept the Comstock could destroy the sprawling D Street district.

In 1880, fifty prostitutes lived on D Street between Washington Street and Sutton Avenue in the four-block heart of the bawdy district, and in the mid-seventies, far more women had lived there. The D Street district included saloons and bawdy theaters on C Street between Taylor and Sutton, as well as prostitutes living on cross streets and alleyways in the crude, imaginary rectangle from the northeast corner of C and Washington, through the northeast corner of E and Taylor, through the northwest corner of C and Sutton. It was *the* red-light district for the Comstock, although none of the bawdy institutions or prostitutes needed such beacons to identify themselves. During the early sixties, a few prostitutes hung blue lights outside their establishments as discrete reminders of their occupation, but later on word of mouth and location were advertising enough.[18]

Housing within the D Street district changed greatly over twenty years, because of the many fires and hasty rebuilding efforts. The bawdy district was unusually vulnerable to fire because of its flimsy dwellings and the incendiaries who made prostitutes their targets.[19] Small fires damaged a number of houses, and major fires in 1871 and 1875 leveled the whole quarter, although it was always speedily rebuilt. After one major fire an *Enterprise* reporter marveled:

D Street has immense vitality and in rising from its ashes it beats that fabled fowl the Phoenix, while its inhabitants are no suckling salamanders when it comes to living in the midst of flames.[20]

The 1880 census suggests that four women lived in single dwellings, probably cottages, near the southeast corner of D and Union and three more lived one block north, while there had been dozens of prostitutes living in cottages in the early years. By the mid-seventies brothels had replaced most cottages, and twenty-two women in the D Street quarter lived in small brothels with three or four residents in 1880. An article on a Mexican prostitute's suicide provided a glimpse into one of those establishments run by an old woman with dyed hair who employed only two or three prostitutes. The waiting room contained a badly worn horsehair sofa, three chairs, and a stained Brussels carpet. According to the article, it was as comfortable as three quarters of the brothels in Virginia City.[21]

The top houses included Cad Thompson's Brick House, the longest established brothel on the Lode, which was in constant operation under the same owner from 1863 through 1880. Cad started her brothel on D Street near Sutton, but she moved south to 15 South D Street after Rose Benjamin vacated those premises and quit the Lode in 1877.[22] Cad's old place and her new were two-story buildings with individual rooms for each prostitute. The downstairs parlors were large and comfortable and the South D Street house had a kitchen where prostitutes' dinners were cooked before the brisk evening business began.[23]

D Street was synonymous with vice. No respectable women dared to live in the quarter and when Belle West, a prostitute, was asked her occupation in court, she simply replied, "I live on D Street."[24] Prostitution, however, by no means stopped at D Street, and prostitutes occupied dwellings below I Street, although their status usually declined along with the altitude of their abodes. A small alleyway on E Street held four low-status prostitutes who lived in individual one-room cribs resembling the San Francisco and New Orleans cubicles containing little more than a bed, a chair, and a basin. The occupants stood in doorways and sat in the windows to attract passersby.[25] A few other Caucasian prostitutes lived on F and G Streets, but the bulk of sexual commerce outside of the main bawdy quarter could be found in Chinatown.

There were twenty Chinese prostitutes on the Comstock in 1880, while there had been seventy-five in 1875. In 1880, all but one of them lived on I Street or below it. Most lived in small two- and three-women brothels located from just south of Union Street through the north edge of Chinatown. Many of their dwellings were not listed by street because much of the Chinese enclave consisted of alleyways and tiny, muddy paths. Both whites and Chinese trod those paths, seeking out women, opium, or games of chance. The Asian section was at the north edge of Virginia City and its end marks the end of this brief guided tour.

Prostitutes' Ages

The legend of the frontier prostitute describes her as uncommonly lovely, and a few individual Comstock prostitutes may have fit that ideal. However, all evidence suggests that most of them were rather ordinary. Three surviving photographs of high-status prostitutes depict women who were attractive, but who were by no means great beauties by either modern or Victorian standards (see illustrations). The picture of Julia Bulette is particularly interesting because it lays to rest the rumor that she was a devastatingly beautiful mulatto.

Newspaper stories provide other clues about prostitutes' appearances, and none was ever lauded as a great beauty, although there were occasional references to women's "shapes." Other information suggesting that Comstock women were other things before they were beautiful is in their nicknames. Some women were distinguished by their country of origin, and the Irish Blond, Spanish Lize, English Gussie, Dutch

Mary and Jew Annie all lived on the Lode. Other women had more graphic titles. They included the German Muscle Woman, Suicide Frenchy, Bigmouthed Annie, Buffalo Jo, the Spring Chicken, the Big Bonanza, and the Carson Banger. While most of them probably were not beautiful, Comstock prostitutes were indeed young and in both 1875 and 1880, most of them were less than thirty years old.

In 1875, thirty-five prostitutes were eighteen or younger and in 1880, nine were (table 4). It is possible that other fancy women were also underage, but lied to the census taker to protect themselves from being "saved." That is unlikely, however, because national or state legislation stipulating the age at which girls could consent to "carnal relations with the other sex" was either absurdly lax or nonexistent.[26] Until 1889, Nevada had no age of consent laws and in 1893, age fourteen was finally specified.[27] Thus, youthful prostitutes had little legal reason to disguise their ages.

The legal laxity surrounding age of consent was commensurate with public disinterest in that issue. There were no protests when Susie Brown, a Barbary Coast prostitute who witnessed a murder, publicly announced that she would be sixteen in two weeks.[28] People on the Comstock simply ignored prostitutes' youth as they denied other problematic aspects of the fast life, and they only protested the abuse of young prostitutes when local girls were enmeshed in blatantly bizarre situations.

One case involved thirteen-year-old Maggie Gorhey, who had been drugged by her mother and placed in a squalid bawdy saloon.[29] Another case was that of a fifteen-year-old who joined a brothel of her own volition because her mother alternated between permissive fits of encouraging her daughter to drink and punitive moods of forcing her to wear a sixteen-pound weight around her neck.[30] The thirteen-year-old was rescued, but the fifteen-year-old remained in Rose Benjamin's brothel where she was more comfortable than at home. These were the only two incidents evoking mild public protests about prostitutes' youth. The possible downfall of "sons and daughters of fine citizens" was noted in a handful of articles about the dangers of opium dens, but people usually admitted that confirmed pimps and prostitutes were found there rather than fine sons or daughters.[31]

Much of the folklore and social theory about prostitution emphasizes the negative relationship between a prostitute's age and her status within the profession. The younger the prostitute, the higher her status, and the downfall and progressive impoverishment of prostitutes is a key theme in early reports on sexual commerce.

Anyone conversant with the subject knows that there is a well understood gradation in this life, and as soon as a woman ceases to be attractive in the higher walks, as soon as her youth and beauty fade, she must either descend the scale or *starve* [original emphasis]. Nor will any deny that of those who commence a life of shame in their youth under the most specious and flattering of delusions, the majority are found, in a short time, plunged into the deepest misery and degradation.

Here is seen, in a glance, a reason for the large number of juvenile prostitutes. Youth is a marketable commodity, and when its charms are lost, they must be replaced. [32]

Sanger's 1897 commentary on nearly inevitable downward mobility in prostitution combined moralists' warnings against the fruits of evil and social scientists' analysis of youth as a desirable exchange commodity. Like the opposite vision of glorious gain through frontier prostitution, the widespread belief in prostitutes' sudden, almost certain downward mobility is not supported by evidence from the Comstock. Most older prostitutes *did* live in near poverty, but so did most younger prostitutes, and material degradation was simply a condition of commercial sex on the Comstock. Whether a woman was one of the few elegant prostitutes or one of the many impoverished ones probably depended upon what type of prostitution she first entered. Certainly there was some upward and downward mobility within Comstock prostitution, but that mobility was associated with far more than simple age or longevity within prostitution.

TABLE 4. Age Structure of Prostitutes, 1875 and 1880

Age	Prostitutes in 1875	Prostitutes in 1880
1–18	35	9
19–24	101	39
25–29	75	39
30–34	42	22
35–39	29	18
40–44	19	9
45–49	5	6
50–59	0	4
60 and over	1	0
Total	307	146

Source: Data compiled from 1875 Nevada State Census and the 1880 United States Census.

In the 1860s some of the Comstock's high-status prostitutes, such as Julia Bulette, Martha Camp, and the actress Adah Issacs Menken, were in their mid-thirties and almost "middle-aged." Age alone did not affect prostitutes' careers until they were visibly unappealing. Of course, the longer a prostitute remained in the profession, the greater her exposure to drug addiction, alcoholism, venereal diseases, and brutal customers. Those hazards often left their marks but some women escaped them to remain high-status prostitutes for many years, and their age may have operated in their favor. While youth served to attract customers, it was not the sole attribute defining a prostitute's appeal. Sexual experience and diversity, fashionableness, and ease at conversation also enhanced a prostitute's value and those abilities could increase with age, thus mitigating the direct effect of age on a prostitute's specific status within the profession.

Evidence that age in itself was unimportant to status until a prostitute became visibly "old" is fragmentary. In 1875 and 1880, the census takers were capricious in their categorization of prostitutes. "Courtesans," "prostitutes," and "prostitutes of the lowest order" lived beside "housekeepers" and "harlots." Only three distinct occupational categories could be distinguished in the census: madams, who managed houses of ill fame; saloon or hurdy girls, who entertained and/or waited on tables; and all other prostitutes. No terms systematically differentiated the third group, and its members could have been anything from mine owners' mistresses to outcast slatterns. Thus, according to census data, the only clear association of age with occupational status occurred in the case of madams, and in both 1875 and 1880 only one madam was under thirty years of age. Madams' maturity reflected the fact that both capital and experience were necessary to run a successful bawdy house or saloon.

The lack of a clear relationship between prostitutes' age and professional status is further confirmed by looking at the women who inhabited the best-known, most comfortable brothels. At the peak of the boom, brothels housed anywhere from three to a dozen women. By the census of 1880, when street addresses were accurately transcribed, the brothels had grown smaller, but it is best to look at the internal organization of brothels in that year because location and residents could be identified clearly. Houses could be ranked according to their size and location, and better brothels were larger than others, located in the main bawdy district on C or D streets between Sutton and Union. In 1880, the city's two best brothels each housed one madam and four prostitutes whose ages ranged from eighteen to thirty-two years. Most were twenty-five or older, while all Comstock prostitutes' average age was twenty-five.

Prostitutes' Ethnicity and Race

Because the Comstock rose and fell in a brief twenty years, most prostitutes necessarily came from other places, and the majority of them probably were already established in the *demimonde*. Many American-born women drifted to Nevada from cities where they were unable to support themselves in other occupations. Others were immigrants who became prostitutes after they reached the United States, while some explicitly journeyed to America to earn money through sexual commerce. In 1875, approximately two-thirds of the prostitutes were foreign-born, while in 1880 54 percent were. Some women gained status because of their race or ethnicity, but most lost it.

French and American-born prostitutes were regarded as desirable *because* of their ethnicity and they were residents of the community's best houses, as indicated in table 5. The French made up about 4 or 5 percent of Comstock prostitutes in 1875 and 1880. American-born women, however, comprised about 29 percent of the prostitutes in 1875, and by 1880 they represented 46 percent of all women in the fast life, so mere scarcity could not explain the allure of the women belonging to those two ethnic groups.

On the Comstock, ethnocentric notions about human nature added to the status of American-born and French prostitutes. Like the ladies who employed servants, the men who hired women often wanted "wholesome, clean American girls." Thus, when a native-born hurdy girl committed suicide, the report of her death noted her comparative advantages, stressing the fact that she was "an American girl and good looking."[33]

On the West Coast, French prostitutes had a special reputation for mysterious fast living that added to their allure. An observer of booming San Francisco in the early 1850s commented:

Men would look hopefully at them [American women] in the streets, at least men who had just come to California, but they much preferred the French women, who had the charm of novelty. Americans were irresistibly attracted by their graceful walk, their supple and easy bearing and charming freedom of manner, qualities, after all, only to be found in France; and they trooped after a

TABLE 5. Rosters of Virginia City's Best Brothels in 1880

Name	Occupation	Age	Marital Status	Birthplace
1 North D Street				
Mollie Wiston	madam	36	single	Southern or border U.S.
Blanche Lebo	prostitute	22	married	Canada
Alice May	prostitute	26	single	Eastern U.S.
Donette Pomerory	prostitute	24	divorced	Midwestern U.S.
Jessie Winter	prostitute	27	divorced	Southern or border U.S.
15 South D Street				
Cad Thompson	madam	53	widowed	Ireland
Annie Burnett	prostitute	28	single	Eastern U.S.
Kitty Caymont	prostitute	29	single	Southern or border U.S.
Emma Hall	prostitute	27	single	Southern or border U.S.
Annie Miller	prostitute	32	married	France
34 South D Street				
Jane Robinson	madam	40	divorced	France
Mary Browly	prostitute	25	single	Great Britain
Tessa Goodwin	prostitute	25	married	Canada
Hattie C. Robinson	prostitute	18	single	France
39 South D Street				
Mary Allen	madam	40	divorced	France
Eliza Duffield	prostitute	20	single	Midwestern U.S.
Mamie Duffield	prostitute	18	single	Great Britain
Rose Duval	prostitute	31	single	France

Source: Data compiled from the United States census manuscripts of 1880. Brothels' quality were determined by size, location, and references to them in other sources.

French woman whenever she put her nose out of doors, as if they could never see enough of her.[34]

Some Frenchwomen were present in California from the earliest gold strikes, but in 1852 and 1853 hundreds of French prostitutes traveled to the Pacific Coast. Their passage was paid through giant national lotteries conducted by Louis Napoleon, who sought to rid France of its criminal and potentially revolutionary elements.[35] Some of those skilled women rose to the top level of San Francisco's disreputable community, and their exotic reputations and the general glamour associated with Second Empire France contributed to the high value placed on French prostitutes on the Comstock. Women who were or claimed to be French found that their ethnic origin enhanced their professional status, but many other women were hindered by their ethnic and racial origins. With one exception, Asian women were always segregated in Chinatown and none of them lived in brothels also housing whites.[36] This segregation reflected anti-Chinese prejudice supporting an explicit local ordinance allowing any citizens living west of H Street the right to petition for the removal of neighboring Chinese.[37] In the summer of 1868 Asian prostitutes were further confined to the area below H Street and the chief of police removed a number of them from H.[38]

In the system of stratification within prostitution Chinese prostitutes had lower status than any other group of women. A few Chinese immigrated to the Comstock as free-agent prostitutes or the concubines of rich Chinese, but the majority were either indentured for about five years or were the lifetime slaves of brothel keepers with ties to the secret societies headquartered in San Francisco.[39] Prostitutes who had signed body contracts for a period of years were turned over to exporters in China who received a fee from brothel owners once the women reached San Francisco. The Hip Yee Tong netted an estimated two hundred thousand dollars from importing women from China between 1852 and 1873.[40] After 1870, the majority of prostitutes were outright slaves who had been kidnapped or sold by their parents, and they usually passed through the hands of several owners before reaching the Comstock.[41]

The full or partial enslavement of Chinese women was common knowledge on the Lode, but whites simply accepted it, and a newspaper article reporting the kidnapping of a prostitute urged readers to treat it lightly, noting that among the Chinese women stealing was comparable to horse stealing among Americans. It was a serious crime against someone's property, but not a grave offense to someone's person.[42] Whites on the Comstock ignored the brutal semifeudal organization of Asian brothels because of their sense of racial superiority to the Chinese. Contemporary commentators and newspaper reporters usually defined "John Chinaman" and "Susie Chinawoman" as vastly inferior to whites, if not of a subhuman species.[43]

In both 1875 and 1880 there were only three black prostitutes on the Comstock. Black prostitutes did not work in white brothels, but they did live in some of the same boardinghouses as whites in the main bawdy district. For a brief time during the early sixties, black fast life centered around the Hotel d'Afrique.[44] However, for most of the Comstock's boom years, a small number of black prostitutes, gamblers, and sports lived among their white counterparts.

"Spanish" prostitutes were far more common than blacks. The term "Spanish" did not refer to women from Europe, but instead denoted those from Central and South America. In 1875, forty-five prostitutes from that area lived on the Comstock, but by 1880 that number had dwindled to six. The largest "Spanish house," Madam Reyes' at 15 North D Street, and the six Mexican women who worked there in late summer of 1875 had all disappeared by 1880.

In Virginia City there were noisy celebrations of Mexican Independence Day, a ball in honor of Juarez, and other private but equally rowdy festivities. One such event was:

—Spanish fandango out to the summer pavilion this PM and evening—lots of people went—Evening all the D Street whores were there—lanterns from the district looked beautiful—Jolly time I expect—[45]

The next evening that wistful diarist was drawn to the fandango and stayed until 3:30 A.M.[46] In spite of some of their exotic attractions, Spanish prostitutes were devalued as a group because of their color. Most of them were Mexicans who worked alone or in lesser brothels. Castellana Morales' brief life history illuminates the careers of similar women. She came from Sinaloa, Mexico, to Stockton, California, to live with relatives when she was a child. By 1878 she was twice divorced and living at Mme. Reyes' brothel on D Street.[47]

Central and South American prostitutes were among the first to reach the California gold fields in the early 1850s.[48] Famines in Mexico, Nicaragua, Brazil, Peru, and Chile forced many of them to immigrate. Some of the women indentured themselves to ships' captains to pay their passage and they usually plied their trade in shanty towns and crude mining camps. Early prejudice against Spanish-speaking women partially reflected anti-Mexican sentiment fanned by clashes over titles to mining claims in California, but later on the Comstock it reflected racist stereotypes about feminine attractiveness. William S. McCallum observed Panamanian prostitutes on his voyage to California and wrote:

The senoritas are not fascinating because they are not pretty—they are very willing to be gazed at, however, and are inclined to coquetry. I must confess I prefer something lighter—and less greasy—more graceful and less indolent, and above all, something which can speak English.[49]

Most Comstock prostitutes spoke English, although many could neither read nor write the language.[50] Their ethnic and racial diversity contributed to the rich texture of the irregular marketplace on the Lode. Prostitutes came to Nevada from five continents, from the city and the countryside, from farms and from factories. They also came with different histories of relationships with men.

Prostitutes' Marital Status

In 1880, almost half of all Comstock prostitutes had been married at one time (table 6). Seventy-five prostitutes were single, 31 married, 27 widowed, and 12 divorced. Most of those who were married no longer lived with their husbands, and they had simply ignored complicated divorce procedures. This marital pattern also occurred in New York City, where Sanger found that 784 of 2,000 prostitutes had once been married.[51]

Many of the married women whom Sanger interviewed told stories of desertion, infidelity, and abuse by their husbands, and many Comstock prostitutes probably had similar experiences. The hardships slowly driving married women to prostitution seldom made news, but their sudden

TABLE 6. Prostitutes' Age and Marital Status, 1880

Age	Single	Married	Divorced	Widowed	"Mistress"	Total
1–18	7	2	0	0	0	9
19–24	28	8	3	0	0	39
25–29	21	8	4	5	1	39
30–34	12	3	2	5	0	22
35–39	4	7	1	6	0	18
40–44	1	2	1	5	0	9
45–49	2	0	0	4	0	6
50–54	1	1	1	1	0	4
Total	76	31	12	26	1	146

Source: Data compiled from 1880 United States Census. The 1875 Census listed neither marital status nor relationship to household head.

flights into the fast life did. Three women were reported to have left
their husbands and immediately assumed work in brothels on the Lode.

The most colorful incident involved a young wife who took the household furniture and moved into a house of ill fame while her husband was
away. He returned and went to the brothel to reclaim his furniture,
while solemnly assuring his audience that he would never reclaim his
wife.[52] In another case, Katie Thompson quarreled with her husband
and left him to reside in Rose Benjamin's house.[53] Rose was also involved in strife between a Salt Lake City husband and wife, Mr. and Mrs.
Gamble. Mrs. Gamble was pregnant when she left her husband to enter
a nearby brothel owned by a friend of Rose's. After her baby was born,
she deeded him to Rose and the infant lived in Rose's D Street brothel
until Mr. Gamble secured custody through the Nevada Supreme
Court.[54]

These anecdotes deal with some women's sudden, extreme entrance
into prostitution, but other women were drawn to the bawdy districts
more quietly. Those individual paths to prostitution were probably as
varied as the prostitutes themselves, although certain routes were more
common than others, and poverty and racial or ethnic stigma were more
likely to spawn prostitutes than affluence and high status. Comstock
prostitutes were a heterogeneous group and their diverse backgrounds
interacted with varied forms of prostitution to create an intricate stratification system within the bawdy quarters.

4

Stratification in the Fast Life

Girls in this way fall every day,
And have been falling for ages;
Who is to blame? You know his name,
It's the boss that pays starvation wages.
    Joe Hill, "The White Slave"

PROSTITUTES' STATUS within the disreputable community reflected the type of work they did, and the less blatantly they bartered sex, the more money and esteem they commanded. In other words, the most successful prostitutes were usually the most "ladylike." San Francisco madam Bertha Cahn stated the issue squarely when she preserved the tone of her brothel by demanding polite conduct from her thirty employees and their patrons and posted a sign stating "NO VULGARITY ALLOWED IN THIS ESTABLISHMENT."[1]

According to the most widely accepted sociological definition, prostitution involves sex for extrinsic purposes, and it is characterized by hire, promiscuity, and impersonality.[2] However, the higher the status of the prostitute, the less obvious her connection with any of these four characteristics. High-status prostitutes try to convince customers (and occasionally themselves) that their activities involve intrinsic rather than extrinsic rewards.[3] They often camouflage the element of hire, and they are seldom promiscuous, relying instead upon a handful of generous customers. Their relationships are ostensibly personal, involving more than sexual exchange.[4]

These criteria for status were defined in terms of modern prostitutes, but they also apply to the women who worked on the Comstock. Prostitution on the Lode could be ranked from high- to low-status, depending upon whether a woman was: (1) clandestine or flagrant in soliciting customers, (2) subtle or open about obtaining payment, (3) selling talents or attributes other than straight, impersonal sex, (4) involved with few or many men, (5) expensive or cheap, and finally (6) patronized by rich or poor men. All of these interrelated criteria determined how much a woman earned, shaping her class and status within prostitution.

Although the six criteria for stratification were deeply intertwined, it was theoretically possible for a clandestine prostitute to be involved with many men, for a promiscuous prostitute to sell companionship as well as sex, or for the other women to combine both lower- and higher-status attributes. Despite these possibilities, however, most specific forms of prostitution were congruent in terms of all six criteria. Thus, there was a fairly clear hierarchy of specific occupations within the fast life, although there were better and worse living situations and employers within each rank. For example, waiter girls in saloons belonged to the middle rank, but they might have slightly different status depending upon the size and comfort of the saloon in which they worked. Even within the same brothel, saloon, or boardinghouse, different women were more or less well regarded by their peers and patrons.

In general terms, there were elite, middle-, working-, and lower-class prostitutes, as well as madams and saloonkeepers who remained essentially outside of active prostitution. All of the women in the irregular marketplace lived beyond the respectable community's moral boundaries, but the difference between the lives of elite and lower-class prostitutes was almost as great as the difference between leisured ladies and working women. There is no surviving scale of Comstock prostitutes' earnings, but material from San Francisco and information about lifestyles permit fairly accurate generalizations.

An Outline of Stratification

Land and building owners, many of whom were men, made the big profits from prostitution; but madams operating brothels and saloons made a fair share of money themselves. Owners of course made more money than mere managers, but regardless of their holdings, madams fared better than prostitutes. While an extraordinary prostitute, Julia Bulette, owned little more than her personal possessions, a small-time madam, Mit Raymond, the fifty-six-year-old owner of a one-woman bawdy saloon on the Barbary Coast, could leave a substantial estate, including another saloon in San Francisco and $40,000 worth of real estate in Oakland, Sacramento, and Marysville, California.[5]

The madams seldom competed with their employees for customers, although many of them took lovers. Certainly promiscuous by respectable Victorian standards, madams were practically celibate compared to other women in prostitution. The madams' comparative lack of promiscuity enhanced their status within the disreputable community and the structure of the fast life, but it also made them targets of some respectable people's hatred and detracted from their status in the larger community. The madam's role was even more foreign to the Victorian ideal of womanhood than the prostitute's, because she had to be active and shrewd in order to profit from other women's sexual exchange, while prostitutes could be viewed as soiled doves passively fallen from grace because of men or because of their own wayward sexuality. Critics of prostitution sometimes blamed madams for luring girls into the fast life and for founding the whole structure of sexual commerce.[6]

Madams gained esteem within the disreputable community for the very management skills which some respectable people condemned. Running a brothel was an exacting job, and the better the house, the more obligations a madam had. High-status madams, such as Cad Thompson, both lodged and fed their prostitutes, while low-status madams merely lodged them. The women who ran the best houses had to organize meals, send out laundry, supervise servants, discipline prostitutes, and also humor customers and police. For these services they received either a percentage of their prostitutes' earnings or a flat fee.

Sometimes their jobs were easier because of storekeepers who catered to fancy women and who were willing to charge supplies and deliver them. In at least one case, however, the arrangement backfired when a white sporting man hired a Chinese to pose as a brothel servant and use a well-known madam's credit to obtain illuminating oil from Fredrick's store and cigars and snuff at Mr. Friedman's.[7]

The women who ran brothels provided both prostitutes and customers with tangible services which pimps did not. Top brothel madams were among the disreputable community's elites and most others belonged to its middle stratum. Their lack of sexual promiscuity and visible skills at management contributed to madams' high status in the fast life, but their obvious venality and public stance detracted from it. Madams' entrepreneurial role forced them to be direct in demanding payment. They were also flagrant, since running a house involved their mediation between the public and the women working for them. Maintenance of a successful establishment involved prolonged residence on the Comstock, and this also made it difficult for madams to conceal their occupation. Economically successful, calculating, and sensible, madams were both respected and scorned.

Very few Comstock prostitutes led lives so lucrative and so clandestine that they could be considered elite. The important element of secrecy in elite prostitutes' activities protected them from publicity, and their ranks were only penetrated by major scandals. They were a small, non-cohesive group of adventuresses who were other things besides prostitutes. All of them engaged in prostitution, for they bartered sexual contact for economic considerations, but many adventuresses earned some or even most of their livings from stage appearances, confidence games, or their own investments.

Elite prostitutes were secretive, selective of clients, subtle in receiving payment, and expensive. Although individual women might play several roles at once or in succession, most elite prostitutes fit into only one of three general categories at a given time. They were celebrated entertainers, rich men's mistresses, or confidence artists.

Celebrities accepted a few patrons, as they toured the United States and sometimes other countries as well. Some of those patrons, such as aristocrats or industrial royalty, added to their attraction for other men, because celebrity-prostitutes reflected their clients' wealth and power. Rich men's mistresses, supported by one or two regular patrons, also gained prestige from their clientele. The final group in the elite category, confidence artists, were true adventuresses who lived by their wits, traveled, and sometimes adopted the role of mistress or entertainer to find additional means of economic support or to hide from irate victims.

Unlike elite prostitutes who often attempted to conceal their liaisons, middle-rank prostitutes relied upon discreet publicity. The middle rank included prostitutes living in cottages and employed in better brothels, saloons, and melodeons. Their prostitution was open within their workplaces, but it was confined indoors. Customers came to them, and they did not solicit passersby from their windows and doorways or approach pedestrians or street corner loungers. Waiter girls, entertainers, and cottage prostitutes made arrangements themselves, while brothel employees worked through a madam. Comparatively unpromiscuous, these women saw only one customer a night, and they could support themselves comfortably. They sold companionship, conviviality, and sometimes dancing and singing ability as well as sex.

Sex was *the* commodity sold in smaller brothels and saloons, cribs, and single rooms where most prostitutes made a bare living as part of the disreputable community's vast working class. Small brothels and saloons employed from one to three prostitutes who were available to several customers a night. If customers paid enough, these women could be more selective of both their partners and the time they spent with them; but working-class prostitutes usually had to accommodate as many customers as possible. When customers did not search for them, working-class prostitutes hustled flagrantly—hanging out of windows and doorways, walking the streets, and shouting enticements to men and insults to ladies.[8] These women's income, blatant solicitation, promiscuity, and impersonal sexuality combined to offer them little comfort or public esteem within the disreputable community.

The final rank in the fast life included Asian prostitute-slaves and Caucasian prostitute-vagrants. These women were indeed "prostitutes of the lowest order," a quixotic phrase used by census takers in 1875. Members of the lowest order resembled working-class prostitutes on most status criteria, but their prostitution was overshadowed by a more salient spoiled identity. As slaves or servants indentured to brothel keepers, Chinese prostitutes kept nothing of what they earned and lived according to their owners' whim. They were more chattels than prostitutes. The other group within the lowest order, outcast slatterns, were more vagrants than prostitutes. They occasionally took money from men willing to pay them for sex, but they subsisted primarily on gleanings of rubbish and sporadic charity. Unlike working-class prostitutes who were much involved in the irregular marketplace, women in the lowest order belonged to a caste set apart by race or utter demoralization.

The remainder of this chapter will describe specific women in each of the five general groups of Comstock prostitutes. All of them were unique, while at the same time all of them represented particular strata. These prostitutes were selected for the reason that some information existed about them as active individuals, rather than as mere categories on census takers' sheets.

The Madams

The madams owning or managing brothels or saloons had to be shrewd in order to be successful, but aside from their business acumen and the fact that most of them were over thirty years old, Comstock madams differed tremendously. Newspapers sketched the careers of four very different Comstock madams: Nellie Sayers, Rose Benjamin, Cad Thompson, and Jessie Lester.

Ellen (Nellie) Sayers lived in the back of her small Barbary Coast saloon, located next door to one lover's establishment and down the street from another's. Nellie rented her saloon in a one-story building at 146 1/2 South C Street. It had a kitchen, a barroom, and two bedrooms housing Nellie and three prostitutes.[9] The *Enterprise* described Nellie as the worst specimen of femininity ever to crawl down C Street. She was a liar, a cheat, a robber, a drunk, and of course, a whore. Nellie preferred to employ very young girls, such as fifteen-year-old Susie Brown and thirteen-year-old Maggie Gorhey, and she was also linked to a ring of Barbary Coast saloonkeepers engaged in robbery and fencing stolen goods.[10] When she was finally brought to trial for keeping a disorderly house, Nellie was accused of trying to bribe the jury.[11] All of these charges, however, were little compared to Nellie's role in the murder of Daniel Corcoran.

Some people accused Nellie of murdering her lover during a rendezvous in her saloon, but Peter Larkin, an estranged lover, was convicted of the deed and hanged on the basis of Susie Brown's and Nellie's testimony. Larkin's jealousy of Nellie was cited as a major motive, although he was also accused of malice toward her because she had spirited away Susie, his star employee. Nellie, on her own part, had reason to be annoyed with Larkin, for he had tried to influence the aldermen to revoke her liquor license.[12]

Although there was some reason to believe that Nellie framed Larkin, the coroner's jury, trial jury, and Nevada Supreme Court all chose to believe her in spite of her bad reputation and misbehavior in the courtroom. Larkin's appeal to the Nevada Supreme Court rested on Nellie's lack of chastity and her misconduct during the coroner's hearing. No one could deny the former accusation, but the Court ruled "though a female may lack this great moral quality [chastity], still it does not follow that because of such deficiency she is not to be believed on oath."[13] Still, Nellie's oath was rather hard to take seriously, since she changed her testimony between the hearing and the murder trial. She first stated that she had not seen Larkin fire at Corcoran, but she later claimed that she had seen him shoot her lover. Nellie excused her contradictory testimony on the grounds that she was very frightened and very drunk during the coroner's hearing. "She claimed to be perfectly oblivious of everything that transpired before the coroner's jury."[14]

There was a great deal of community feeling against Nellie and she was successfully pressured to leave town after Larkin's hanging. During the final Barbary Coast cleanup of 1877 the board of aldermen revoked her license to sell liquor, stating, "This . . . closes another den of iniquity on our great public thoroughfare."[15]

While Nellie was a very bad madam, Rose Benjamin was an average brothel keeper who sometimes elicited devotion from her prostitutes, sometime disobedience. Rose ran a tight house, regulating prostitutes' leisure activities as well as their working hours.[16] She also employed young women, taking in fifteen-year-old Miss Duffy and inviting sixteen-year-old Hattie Willis to leave the Amelia Dean Melodeon Troup and join her establishment.[17]

Three of Rose's prostitutes committed suicide while working for her, and at least two other made attempts. Rose's brothel was relatively large and suicides among prostitutes were common, but the fact that five women tried suicide indicates that Rose's place was not all that pleasant. One of the successful suicides, Laura Steele, killed herself early in the morning, after Rose's birthday celebration of "revelry and high carnival."[18]

Tragedies in Rose's house included fires as well as suicides. One young customer played with matches and started a small fire that did little more than scare the women; but in another case, a prostitute turned over an oil lamp which caused fire to gut one room, while firemen's hoses created water damage in the rest of the brothel.[19] Both of these fires were accidental, but another small fire was started by one of Rose's former lovers. At age thirty-six, Rose married another lover, George E. Perkins, with whom she resided in a respectable part of town far away from her house.[20]

She loved the law with an irrational conviction which drew her into court when she would have been better off at home. In one case, she lost her claim to a child whom a prostitute had placed in her custody.[21] In another, Rose defended a special police officer, asserting that he only shot a man named Ash because of great provocation.[22] Rose also attempted to use the law for her own ends, when she brought in all seven of the women in her brothel and charged them with larceny for assisting another prostitute who stole back a trunk which had been left with the madam to guarantee a debt. The case was dismissed after much laughter on the part of the judge and courtroom loungers who felt that the petty madam had no right to complain of petty larceny.[23]

Practically everyone on the Comstock knew how Rose earned her money, but she chose to live outside the bawdy district and hold her brothel and the land on which it stood in her niece Carmen Julio's name. Rose managed the business during the evening, but Phil Escobar, her old houseman, took over during slack times.[24] Rose appears to have left the Comstock shortly after her marriage in 1878, leaving some friends and some enemies.

While Nellie Sayers and Rose did much that was bad, two other Comstock madams, Cad Thompson and Jessie Lester, came as close to resembling the legendary golden-hearted prostitute as any human being could. Cad Thompson's life on the Comstock stretched from 1866 through at least 1880. Cad's brothel was one of the Lode's most convivial, best-run houses. She was called "the Brick" or "Good Sport" and her establishment was known as Brick House. There were no suicides among Cad's prostitutes, although several customers were shot. Officer Hawkins, a corrupt policeman, killed John Dalton at Cad's place and Hugh Kerrin of Engine Company No. 1 "accidentally" wounded Zink Barnes in the leg.[25]

Cad was christened *Caroline* in Ireland in 1827 or 1828. She was widowed when she came to the Comstock and her son Henry lived with her some of the time until he committed suicide. Cad owned the land and building housing herself, four or five prostitutes, and a Chinese houseman. Little else is known about her life, although Cad was mentioned with affection in Alf Doten's diaries and Comstock newspapers. She kept up a loving correspondence with one of her former prostitutes named Jenny, and if those letters are ever disclosed to the public they could reveal much about a madam's private world.[26]

Jessie Lester, another beloved madam, was fatally shot by an unknown assailant on Christmas of 1864. She lingered for almost a month, until January 24, 1865, but she refused to name the man who shot her.[27] Throughout that time Jessie was in great pain:

—had to have her right arm amputated at the shoulder joint this afternoon— poor creature, she was just recovering from the taking of chloroform during the operation, and was shrieking with pain—and in her delerium calling on her mother.[28]

Jessie's funeral was formal and proper. She was buried in a mahogany coffin wearing a silk shroud, silk gloves, and silk stockings.[29] Father Manogue, who had performed last rites, officiated at services held in the church and saw that Jessie was buried in consecrated ground. The Church's largesse came from an exchange, for Jessie left the bulk of her estate to the Sisters of Charity. Her money went toward the care of orphans, where it had previously gone toward keeping up her D Street brothel.

Jessie purchased her ramshackle two-story parlor house on D Street from J. A. Batchelor for $2,000 and a 5 percent interest in the proceeds of her house. The place was built to be a brothel or lodging house, for there were no cooking or dining facilities or indoor plumbing and the frontage of her lot was only thirty-two feet. Like most Virginia City dwellings built during the first five years of the silver boom, it was designed for simple utility rather than comfort.

One entered from D Street into a hall lit with coal oil lamps placed on a sideboard. Off the hall were the main parlor and another smaller one. Both parlors were hung with chandeliers and lace curtains and decorated with Brussels carpets and antimacassars. There were two sofas and ten chairs in the two rooms, but with the exception of two ornate carved armchairs, nothing matched. This haphazard assembly of furniture carried over to the bedrooms, which contained a few fine pieces and many makeshift furnishings.

Jessie's own lace-hung room contained a magnificent matched mahogany bedroom set consisting of a marble-topped washstand, lamp tables, bureau, and bedstead.[30] Her bed had a spring mattress topped by one stuffed with horsehair and wool and a bolster rather than a pillow. She also stored the extra house linen in her room, and there were eleven blankets and four extra bedspreads. Like all of her prostitutes' rooms, Jessie's contained a spittoon and a basin and pitcher.

The five upstairs bedrooms had linen window shades rather than curtains, thin carpets, and bedsteads with spring mattresses topped by ones stuffed with wool or wool and horsehair. Odd souvenirs and pieces of furniture which Jessie had collected supplemented these basics of a prostitute's workplace. One bedroom was personalized by a collection of dishes and water pitchers and another was enlivened by four plaster busts. The best of the prostitutes' bedrooms contained a huge carved mahogany bedstead, a clock, and assorted fancy bottles and vases.

None of Jessie's clothing or jewels were itemized in her probate. In the weeks prior to her death she prepared by making her will, planning her funeral, settling her debts, and she probably sold or gave away her intimate belongings. The final value of Jessie's estate was $5,294. It was not a great amount, but Jessie had only been in business a few years, and as a madam she owned far more than all but the most successful prostitutes.

The Adventuresses

The handful of elite Comstock prostitutes avoided the brothel district, and, except for celebrities, avoided the spotlight of publicity. These clandestine elites were among the few frontier prostitutes who could realistically aspire to die wealthy and respectable, but the women leaving traces of information because of scandals did not achieve those goals.

Confidence artists were skilled professionals whose earnings and technical knowledge separated them from the ranks of ordinary prostitute-criminals. Their success often depended upon their having enough money to impress clients with their standard of living, and wardrobes, furnishings, and education or its semblance were important assets for adventuresses. Like all elite prostitutes, they were differentiated from other fast women because of their highly developed specialization, expertise, and professional norms.[31]

Fighting Annie who clumsily shoplifted jewelry from Bloch's was not an adventuress nor was another prostitute who passed stolen checks at various gambling houses.[32] They were simply working women trying to earn a bit extra. The real confidence artists used sexuality to supplement their game, as in the case of an Englishwoman who posed as an aristocrat in distress. A number of gentlemen thrust financial aid on the lady, who assured them that she was expecting a stipend from her family fortune momentarily. After insisting that her benefactors accept a portion of her diamonds as collateral, she precipitously left town and they discovered that the jewels were fakes.[33]

Two other attractive women independently used men's avarice to their own advantage, claiming to be clairvoyant about mining stocks. Patrons showed good faith by placing money and mining stock certificates in the women's hands—where they promptly vanished.[34] More explicit kinds of gambling involved adventuresses who lured men to the tables where they earned their livings by sleights of hand. Mme. Eleanor Dumont, also known as Mme. Moustache because of the fuzz above her lip, was one of the most famous female gamblers in the West. She brought tables and cards with her when she dealt losing blackjack hands, served champagne, and charmed patrons. She worked various confidence games from 1854 to 1879 when she killed herself. Mme. Dumont conducted games of chance in San Francisco, Boise City, Cheyenne, Bannock, and briefly in 1860 in Virginia City.[35]

Confidence artists came to public attention when their schemes were discovered, and rich men's mistresses gained notoriety when their relationships failed. Surely many of the Comstock's men of property kept mistresses at some time in their lives, for in some high circles a mistress was not only a lover and companion, she was also a status symbol. Bonanza king James G. Fair kept several women in San Francisco and was also rumored to court his Comstock employees' attractive wives.[36] Theresa Fair divorced him on grounds of adultery with Fannie Smith, Inez Leonard, and other loose women. Fair denied nothing, pleading only that he was no worse than this peers. Moreover, he asserted that he had always been discreet and would never embarrass his wife by open adultery. These arguments were persuasive enough to make a Storey County court award him custody of his two sons and the bulk of the family fortune. No one knows what became of Fair's fancy women, but his young son, Charles, carried on the dubious family tradition when he married a San Francisco parlor house madam in 1892 and lived happily with her until they died in an automobile accident ten years later.[37]

Other rich men's mistresses were also brought to public attention by scandals. Nellie Davis overdosed on morphine in her room in Mrs. Gray's B Street lodgings. She had separated from her husband several years earlier, after she became involved with a married man. When that affair ended, Nellie was kept by a wealthy mine owner who urged her to go east after he tired of the affair. She did so, but came back to the Comstock to die in destitution.[38] Like other mistresses, Nellie was not very promiscuous, and she shared her favors with comparatively few men.

Another hapless mistress suffered temporary injury and embarrassment when her lover's wife discovered them together upstairs in the International Hotel. The affronted spouse did nothing to her husband, but shattered a bottle of champagne over his companion's head.[39] Sometimes, however, men were victims. Judge Livingstone of the third and fourth wards intentionally overdosed on morphine. According to Alf Doten, it was because of

defalcation, induced by too much running with a little Spanish whore named Louise—She bled the old fellow literally to death—the County Commissioners were investigating his books & accounts & he couldn't face the music.[40]

Although the Judge's case was unusual, some men pursued glamorous entertainers with similar heedlessness. It was quite common for Comstock audiences to toss coins at their stage favorites, and at one typical burlesque featuring disreputable entertainers

Audience [was] enthusiastic—a shower of money almost continually going on stage to one or another of the actresses or actors—Miss Lizzie Fillmore had over $100 thrown at her—three "twenties" among it—her sister Minnie had some $50, all in half dollars—Maria got some $20—must have been over $200 thrown on stage.[41]

These burlesque actresses were a status rank below the true elites who quietly earned large sums offstage. "Actress" was a common Victorian euphemism, but there was an obvious distinction between genuine actresses and "the many loose women parading on the stage."[42] The first, very small group included touring nationally famed legitimate actresses or singers, such as Adelina Patti or Modjeska. These great ladies of the stage were as ostensibly virtuous as any other Victorian grandes dames. The second group of actresses and entertainers appeared in light dramas and musical evenings, and their ranks included a number of elite prostitutes who traveled from city to city accepting carefully chosen patrons. The final, largest group of entertainers sang and danced in melodeons and bawdy theaters and they belonged to prostitution's middle rank.

In the 1850s, Lola Montez, the former mistress of the King of Belgium, made a disastrous tour of the California gold towns. If she had been as successful onstage as off, Mme. Montez would have been a celebrity courtesan. Sue Robinson or Sue Robinson Getzler was a famous entertainer in Virginia City and San Francisco and she was practically a "native daughter" of the Comstock. She played Piper's in confections such as *Theresa's Vow, The Countess for an Hour, The Robber's Wife*, and *The Stage Struck Chambermaid*. But she also distinguished herself in *Julius Caesar* and *Hamlet*. She was divorced and died suddenly at age twenty-six, stricken by a mysterious complaint labeled "cancer of the bowels."

Kind hearted and generous even to a fault, Sue Robinson was endeared to all who knew her, and . . . upon the stage she was always a prime favorite, and especially so at Piper's Opera House . . . Her path through life was not all sunshine and devoid of domestic trouble, by any means, for she was at times a hard-working woman, toiling at menial labor to support her little family, as well as professionally an actress upon the stage, but at last she finds peace and rest.[43]

Another actress, Adah Issacs Menken, was by far the most famous courtesan-actress to ever play before Comstock audiences. She did so briefly in winter 1864, bringing her notorious play, *Mazeppa,* to Virginia City and to Macguire's Theater in San Francisco. Although Mark Twain briefly lauded and courted her, Menken sustained no known liaisons on the Lode.[44] She was four times married, however, and otherwise entangled with famous men, including Algernon Swinburne and Alexandre Dumas. Her low character, high literary tastes, great ambition, and rounded "shape" attracted enthusiastic Virginia City audiences; and, according to legend, one mining venture was named the Menken Shaft and Tunnel Company. It issued stock certificates illustrated with a naked lady bound to a galloping stallion.

That sexually charged image was Menken's trademark. Her triumph, *Mazeppa,* featured a famous scene in which the actress appeared on stage in the third act in a "nude" flesh-colored bodysuit, bound to the back of a live horse. Wherever she played, that scene created a sensation, and on the Comstock it was subsequently replayed by other actresses. *Mazeppa* also spawned a host of local burlesques in dance halls and bawdy theaters. At the same time that Miss Grace Daley was recreating Menken's original role before a slim house at Piper's the disreputable Black Crook Melodeon was filled with a boisterous, appreciative audience taking in

"Life Among the Circassians"—Mazeppa Piece—6 Mazeppas, including Mrs. Sherwood (The Diamond Widow)—She showed the best shape of all—[45]

Adah Issacs Menken's very notoriety made her marginal to the elite prostitutes; but her dramatic talent, international fame, and fleeting fortune clearly differentiated her from ordinary melodeon girls. Menken left little more than a burlesque tradition to the Lode, but another elite prostitute, Laura Fair, left an enduring scar. Laura (no relation to the bonanza king) rocked the Comstock and much of the nation when she murdered her protector, Alexander P. Crittenden. She is an appropriate character to close this section, for she was a confidence artist, a mistress, and a celebrity at different times in her life. Also, a great deal of information is available from the transcripts of her 1870 trial in San Francisco.[46]

Laura was a beautiful blue-eyed blond, who had deserted one husband and lost two others before she arrived in Virginia City. She was born in Holly Springs, Mississippi, in 1837, and her family wandered throughout the South. Laura's first husband, whom she married when just sixteen years old, was an alcoholic liquor dealer from New Orleans. After he died a year later, she entered the Convent of the Visitation to prepare to teach school; but she left to marry in less than a year. She abandoned her second husband, another alcoholic, and joined her mother in San Francisco where the two operated a boardinghouse. They moved to Shasta, California, where she met an attractive attorney, William D. Fair, and she married him, believing that her second husband had divorced her. In less than three years they were separated, and Fair shot himself in San Francisco, leaving Laura to support herself, her sixteen-month-old daughter, and her mother.

So far Laura Fair's history resembled those of many other women of dubious virtue who needed to earn a living but had few real skills or job prospects. She had been raised in shabby gentility to please an affluent husband; unfortunately she never married that sort of man. At the time of Fair's suicide Laura had no assets other than her looks and charm, so she went on stage and appeared opposite Junius Brutus Booth in a benefit performance of Sheridan's *School for Scandal*. The San Francisco benefit netted her enough money to pay her debts and rent a lodging house in Virginia City.

Laura opened Tahoe House on South C Street to more than thirty lodgers in September of 1862. Her mother, brother, and several chambermaids aided Laura in its management, and she also rented out the store on the bottom floor of the building. In 1863 she netted about one thousand dollars a month and also secured the attentions of one of her star lodgers, Alexander P. Crittenden. He was a successful San Francisco attorney who included major politicians and financial elites among his friends. In fact some of those influential friends tried to "save" Crittenden once he became deeply entangled with Laura.

During the next seven years Laura and Crittenden lived together and apart, alternately torturing, teasing, and tickling one another. For a brief, bizarre period, Laura was landlady to her lover, his wife, and children. Crittenden engaged in staggering vacillations, promising Clara, his wife, that he would forsake his mistress, and pledging eternal devotion to Laura, swearing that he would obtain a divorce as soon as possible. High comedy and melodrama occurred daily in the triangle until Laura transformed it into tragedy, when she shot her lover on the crowded San Francisco–bound ferryboat, *El Capitan.*

Laura's trial involved conflicting claims about the nature of chastity, feminine hysteria, culpability in adultery, and feminists' rights to attend murder trials. While Laura was in jail awaiting trial Susan B. Anthony and Elizabeth Cady Stanton visited her, and Miss Anthony set aside a portion of a suffrage speech to comment:

If all men had protected all women as they would have their own wives and daughters protected, you would have no Laura Fair in your jail tonight. . . . I declare to you that woman must not depend upon the protection of man, but must be taught to protect herself, and there I take my stand.[47]

The noted suffragist did not state whether self-protection extended to murder. After a lengthy trial, Laura was judged guilty of murder, but her execution was stayed and an appeal on grounds of prejudice led to a new trial in which her conviction was overturned. However, Laura, an unbalanced woman, did not change her ways. She irrationally estranged her mother, cheated her attorney of his fees, and embarked on an ill-fated lecture tour. After the tour she retired in San Francisco, lived modestly, and died more than fifty years later.

Laura was not a kept women who relied solely on her protector. If her lodging house was full she made a good living; but when she was strapped for cash or simply wanted luxuries, she turned to her patron. He advised her on mining stocks and arranged loans for her with William Sharon of the Bank of California. When Laura was in strained circumstances in San Francisco she wired Crittenden and he sent $500 from the Comstock in the next mail. Crittenden also paid for a number of "gifts" which Laura picked out for herself, wheedling in the time-honored fashion of rich men's mistresses. She spent $600 on a Steinway grand piano to celebrate their "engagement," and also replenished her wardrobe at the City of Paris Department Store. During the brief, euphoric time when Laura believed herself to be on the road to marriage, she also charged three portraits to Crittenden. However, it soon became clear that her patron had no intention of leaving his wife, and she answered a letter Crittenden wrote with these classic words of a kept woman:

Poverty I am willing to bear without complaint if I have only you; but when you sleep with another—live with another—protect, cherish her—and she to call you husband, *then I want money* [emphasis added].[48]

Laura Fair's twisted, intense liaison with Crittenden far exceeded the emotional boundaries defining prostitution. However, she did barter sex for money, and the prosecutors in her murder trial and the popular media called her a whore. The very exclusivity of a mistress-protector relationship encouraged emotional complications for both parties. Touring celebrities and confidence artists had an easier time avoiding emotionally draining involvements with patrons, because they traveled so much. Women in the next rank of prostitution also avoided those complications, because they entertained large numbers of customers.

The Middle Rank

The middle group of Comstock prostitutes included women living alone in cottages, working in melodeons and saloons, or residing in the city's best four or five brothels. All of them earned enough to live comfortably, but they seldom accumulated capital enough to enable them to leave prostitution. Middle-rank prostitutes usually saw only one customer a night, and they did not have to solicit publicly because men sought them out. Moreover, they had enough steady customers to allow them to reject men who were obviously diseased or violent.

Julia Bulette, the Comstock's most celebrated courtesan, belonged to the middle-status group. Because the publicity surrounding her murder provided a trail of information unlike that available about any of her contemporaries, she has become a central figure in this book, and this section on the middle rank provides the best framework for describing her life and death in more detail.

Julia lived near the corner of D and Union streets in a small white frame cottage with two rooms stuffed with ornate, recently purchased furniture. The small parlor could accommodate almost a dozen visitors on a carved black walnut set of a sofa, a rocker, and four matched chairs, with additional unmatched cane-seated chairs and another rocker. All of these were arranged around a large stove and set off by lace curtains, a Brussels carpet, hanging gas lamps, and a spittoon.

Julia's huge mahogany bed dominated the other room, which was darkened by damask curtains and extra window shades. The bed was covered by a fancy worked wool spread in winter and a plain white bedspread in summer, and there were few other decorations in the room. Practicality determined the rest of the furnishings of a small box stove, two spittoons, and two washbasins. Julia's cottage lacked plumbing or a kitchen, yet it was far more comfortable than most other prostitutes' dwellings.[49]

On January 19, 1867, she left her small cottage and went to see *The Robbers* and a farce of *Willful Murder* at Piper's Opera House. Julia was denied admission "by the front door," and refusing to sit in the section reserved for women of ill repute, she returned home to wait for a midnight customer who had already made arrangements with her.[50] That was the last time she appeared in public, for later that night Julia was strangled, shot in the forehead, and left to be discovered the next morning by the Chinese manservant who did her menial work.

Newspapers described the crime as "the most cruel, outrageous, and revolting murder ever committed in this city." Julia was characterized as

belonging to that class denominated "fair but frail," yet being of a very kind hearted, liberal, benevolent, and charitable disposition. Few of her class had more true friends.[51]

People honored the request that "her faults be buried with her and her virtues live," and she was revered for her golden heart.[52] Her charity included nursing sick and injured miners during the community's formative years and donating money to needy individuals. She also contributed money and spiritual support to Virginia Engine Company No. 1, which had a number of disreputable entrepreneurs on its roster.[53] The fire company marched in her funeral procession, and its band played while "16 carriages loaded with friends and sisterhood of the deceased went out with her."[54] Julia's murder was not forgotten, and more than a year later, John Milleain was hanged for the crime while about four thousand people watched the spectacle from the hills above the Geiger Grade.[55]

Milleain was brought to justice (and perhaps framed) because a number of Julia's valuables were found in his trunk, which was searched after he tried to sell her diamond pin to a jeweler who knew her. There was a $400 sable muff and cape set, coral earrings, chains, rings, a Masonic emblem, a silver brick stamped with Julia's name, and a jet cross. Five of Julia's silk dresses also turned up in Milleain's trunk. Those stolen items barely represented the surface of her wardrobe and she must have spent the bulk of her earnings on clothes and jewels.[56]

Julia had twenty shirtwaists, fifteen jackets, twelve dresses, five cloaks, and two riding habits. Just before her death she had purchased seven fine linen chemises to supplement the large amount of fancy lingerie she already owned. Her most expensive dress, a wide-skirted brown silk creation, sold used at auction for $37.50. Most of her clothing was fashionably conservative, made from dark silks, fine wools, and calicoes. Julia wore a few splendid, eye-catching garments, however, such as a magnificent black velvet riding coat, a circular red wool cloak, and a huge cashmere shawl. Some of the jewelry left behind in her cottage included a small diamond ring, a matched pair of gold bracelets, and a locket and chain.[57]

Her estate inventory and the prices her possessions fetched at auction indicate that Julia owned some very good clothing and jewelry. She did not, however, wear the ornaments and apparel of an elite prostitute or an upper-class lady of fashion. Julia dressed exceptionally well for her time and place, spending far more money on apparel than was necessary to her trade; but she did so in the manner of a successful businessman's wife. Her jewels also could have belonged to a middle-class lady. They were *bijoux bourgeois*— solid, well-made articles of massive appearance which lacked the imaginative design or precious stones found in pieces of great value. Compare Julia's trinkets with some of those belonging to La Barucci, a *grande horizontale* (great courtesan) of Second Empire Paris. Her jewel casket

was as high as the mantlepiece, and divided into twenty drawers. Each one, upholstered in silk, contained a special kind of stone; there was a compartment for diamonds and others for emeralds, pearls, rubies, sapphires, ancient and modern jewels, and gems of all descriptions.[58]

Julia did not live lavishly and her extravagance on clothes and trinkets was and is a common pattern among prostitutes.[59] One psychodynamic explanation is that they want to rid themselves of money obtained through prostitution and the guilt associated with it. Perhaps this explains Julia's behavior, or perhaps she was simply a generous woman who was also generous to herself. At any rate, Julia died leaving more debts than assets in her estate. While she never earned a fortune, she might have slowly saved enough money to buy her own cottage, invest in real estate or mining stocks, or even open a small brothel.

Julia gave parties for patrons and friends, and her last liquor bill of $141.50 indicated that she was a generous hostess whose largesse exceeded the demands of her trade. Over a three-and-a-half-month period in which she was ill and did not work for much of the time she purchased bourbon, whiskey, Sazerac, cognac, port, Jamaica rum, Old Sazerac brandy, thirty pints of ale, and several champagne baskets.

Julia was born in Liverpool and immigrated to Louisiana where she married, left her husband, and entered prostitution. She came to the Comstock at the beginning of the boom in 1861 or 1862, and she befriended other prostitutes, men associated with the sporting community, and patrons.[60] Many of those who knew her recognized that Julia was an extraordinarily kind woman, but despite her unique qualities, she was also a fairly typical cottage prostitute who lived comfortably but amassed little capital. Like other middle-status prostitutes, Julia belonged to a well-regarded ethnic group and offered customers companionship as well as sex. Most other women in the middle rank did not have Julia's personal magnetism, but like her, they provided men with more than impersonal intercourse. The women employed in gambling houses, dance halls, large saloons, and melodeons also entertained men. Only melodeon performers actually sang and danced on stage, but all of the prostitutes in this group had to amuse patrons, relying upon flirtation and conversation to entice customers.

A few large places, such as the Alhambra Theater and the Villa de Belvelier, had private dressing rooms used for sexual dalliance, but most bawdy establishments merely employed women to attract drinkers, and they arranged for customers to meet them at their own rooms after work.[61] Prostitutes had different tasks in each type of business, but all of them drew patrons to their workplaces and urged men to consume liquor or lager. Melodeon prostitutes entertained on stage and during breaks they either sat with customers or served drinks; saloon girls or "pretty waiter girls" served and sometimes drank with customers; gamblers presided over games of chance, dealing cards or turning fortune wheels; and hurdy girls charged customers to dance with them.

During the first two years of the California gold rush, when women were far scarcer than on the Comstock, San Francisco waiter girls earned an ounce of gold for merely sitting and drinking with a customer or standing by a man while he gambled. Scarcity and novelty also allowed these prostitutes to charge from $200 to $400 for a single night of sexual contact.[62] On the Comstock few women of middle rank earned a tenth as much as comparable San Francisco prostitutes of the early gold rush era.

The Alhambra Melodeon was the largest and "best" bawdy establishment. It featured licentious burlesque musicals in which performers revealed their "shapes" in brief clothing. During hard times the Alhambra operated as a dance hall, but for most of the boom years it was the Lode's central bawdy theater. Sometimes the major theaters, Macguire's and Piper's, staged light musicals such as *The Black Crook* and *Lady Godiva,* and the actresses in those were usually prostitutes. A troup from Lancashire, the Swiss Bellringers went en masse from the stage at Piper's to prostitution.[63] Sixteen-year-old Belle Bateman from Utica, New York, left the Amelia Dean Melodeon Troup at Piper's and joined Rose Benjamin's "troup" on D Street, and Ida Vernon moved from Max Walter's Music Hall to Jenny Tyler's Bow Windows.[64]

All of the Alhambra's "actresses" were prostitutes, but only some of those at legitimate theaters also bartered sexuality. Sometimes prostitutes avoided the footlights and gave private exhibitions for customers. One group of middle-rank prostitutes staged a private exhibition of *tableaux vivants* for which they charged twelve wealthy men $100 each.[65]

Prostitutes moved easily from the bawdy stage to their own cottages or to brothels, and they probably drifted among other middle-rank situations as well. Women worked at Sissa's B Street gambling hall, the Crystal Peak, the Grecian Bend, the Bon Ton, and other nameless establishments. All of them were available for a price, but they supplemented their income from prostitution by entertaining men with charm and conversation. Unlike brothel prostitutes in even the best houses, the entertainers, lady-gamblers, waiters, and hurdy girls could choose among their prospective customers, picking the richest or most attractive man "to see Nellie Home."[66]

In 1880, prostitutes in four brothels belonged to the middle rank. The institutions in which they lived and worked fronted on D Street in the block from Union to Taylor, a choice location. The brothels were the largest in the city, and two had five women living in them while the others had four. All but one brothel were managed by a madam living on the premises. The two largest also had Chinese manservants living in, and the others probably had daily help. All of these were parlor houses where customers and prostitutes congregated in the downstairs rooms for conversation or music and group singing.

There is no available information about the brothels' price structures; but during the 1870s, the best San Francisco brothels charged a ten- or twenty-dollar gold piece for an all-night stay. These prices did not include gratuities to prostitutes and servants or the mandatory five-dollar bottle of champagne included in the package.[67]

Some brothels set a single price and in these establishments all prostitutes charged flat fees varying only by the length of contact, but in others women charged variable rates depending upon their youth and willingness to accommodate special sexual requests. In "boarding-houses" prostitutes simply paid "rent" for a place in the establishment, commonly five dollars a day; but in most better houses madams took from 25 to 50 percent of a prostitute's earnings.[68] Brothel prostitutes probably earned less than some other women in the middle rank, giving up raw cash and autonomy for the comforts of brothel life. Women working in better brothels did not have to worry about meals, laundry, and other routine tasks. The proximity of other prostitutes and especially of a madam also mitigated violence and police harrassment.

The women working in the best brothels in 1880 were a remarkably homogeneous group. All but one prostitute were from North America, Great Britain, or France. Their ages ranged from eighteen to thirty-two, and most of them were in their twenties. They usually traveled the parlor house circuit, and their independence and mobility hid their individual stories from public scrutiny. Newspapers carried many brief items about prostitutes living in brothels, but none of those women left her mark on the Comstock like Cad Thompson or Julia Bulette.

Scotch Laura, who killed herself after attending Rose Benjamin's birthday party, might be a representative middle-rank brothel prostitute. She was described as a twenty-two-year-old beauty with regular features, very fair skin, and jet black hair. Laura was born in Aberdeen, Scotland, and immigrated to Santa Clara, California, with her mother and sister. She accompanied her saloonkeeper husband to Gold Hill about six months prior to her death. Shortly after arriving on the Comstock, Laura left him, changed her name, and moved into Rose's.[69]

All of the women of the middle rank had some personal attributes most respectable ladies would have been delighted to possess. These prostitutes exchanged their looks, talent, or charm as part of the sexual bargain and received relatively high remuneration in return. They did not have to disgrace themselves by flagrant solicitation or accept customers who were diseased, violent, or overly demanding. The women in the fast life's working class had no such options, however.

Working Women

Most working-class prostitutes labored alone, in small brothels, or in one- or two-woman bawdy saloons belonging to the disreputable working class. No exact figures can be presented because of ambiguous classifications of a few living situations, but all census and qualitative data suggest that more than half of all prostitutes were working women. Some of these women lived in lodging houses along with higher-status entertainers and waiter girls, but most of them occupied small brothels, small houses, cottages, or cribs. In 1880, there were two small brothels housing three women each, nine houses shared by two women, and twelve cribs.

Working women were of every age and non-Chinese nationality, ranging in age from forty-year-old Margaret Cluny from Ireland to fifteen-year-old Fannie Palmer from the Midwest. All but one of six Latin American prostitutes in 1880 were working-class, as were most other foreign-born women apart from the Chinese. Working women were more anonymous and interchangeable than middle-rank brothel prostitutes. An occasional crime or suicide received brief public notice. Castellana Morales, for example, divorced her second husband, a miner, because he beat her, and went to work in a room on A Street.[70] None of the many other descriptions of working-class prostitutes is more detailed or meaningful than Castellana's story. When women sold pure sexual contact, unembellished by inessential interaction, their individuality and humanity was often overlooked. Like other basic working-class purchases, sexual exchange had few frills.

No working-class prostitutes left enough property behind to warrant probate and there are few other available records. In San Francisco at the turn of the century women charged customers a dollar for a short visit, and fees were probably comparable on the Comstock.[71]

All surviving information suggests that Comstock working women earned subsistence wages, allowing them to survive physically and remain at their jobs. They were involved in routine sprees, brawls, and suicides, but they caused no real trouble for the police or the respectable community. These prostitutes took care of themselves, getting by, albeit barely, and their survival skills contributed to their anonymity. Some women in the final group, the lowest order, were constant public nuisances, forcing the respectable community to notice them. Others, Chinese slave girls, suffered and sometimes died in silence, but their extreme exploitation could not be ignored entirely.

Prostitutes of the Lowest Order

Both outcast slatterns and Asian slaves stood at the edge of the irregular marketplace, far more socially stigmatized than ordinary prostitutes. Neither subgroup had any social or economic options. Prostitute-vagrants occasionally found customers or men who briefly lived with them, but they usually lapsed into dependence on charity. The Chinese women's earnings, possessions, and very selves usually belonged to the Chinese men who bought them or their contracts in San Francisco. Vagrants were dissipated and unattractive, while some Chinese women were quite lovely, but women in both groups had spoiled identities which irrevocably separated them from the mainstream of the irregular marketplace.

Five female vagrants could be identified from living situations listed in the 1880 census, and probably one or two of the women housed in the B Street jail also fit that description. All five lived in shanties and were either Irish- or American-born. None had any children, except for Mary Dillard, who had three.

One or another vagrant woman could always be found begging around Comstock saloons, but some of them were too debilitated even to beg. For example, Catherine Curran, a widow from St. Louis, left four children when she died from alcohol abuse.[72] Another prostitute-vagrant abused her children so flagrantly that respectable ladies begged the authorities to place them in custody of the Sisters of Charity.[73] Ellen Farey, also known as Irish Mary, served three months in jail for public drunkenness and child abuse, and died two years after she was released.[74]

So long as prostitute-vagrants hid from public view and did not visibly hurt their children, respectable people ignored them. Thus, a woman would have died alone in a squalid C Street basement if two local hurdy girls had not offered her aid.

Two women of the neighborhood . . . were informed of the condition of the woman, brought her food, wine and did all else that seemed to be required.[75]

Mary Ramshart was the most persistent and problematic prostitute-vagrant on the Comstock because of her vulgar public behavior and her many illegitimate children. According to newspaper reports, when she came to the Lode in the early sixties, Mary was an industrious, hardworking mother, but two years later she was ravaged by "local, domestic, and physiological causes."[76] Two respectable seamstresses who lived near the Gould and Curry Mine tried to take her in after she was found wandering about in a stupor, visibly pregnant by some unknown man, but Mary finally had to be committed to the California State Asylum at Stockton, along with two other Comstock residents.[77] At that time, Nevada had no state mental institution and poor people who were visibly deranged were sent to the neighboring state. She died one month later and Alf Doten wrote a private epitaph:

Mrs. Ramshart died at Stockton Insane Asylum in the 11th inst—30 yrs
old—The crazy, weary wanderer at length finds rest, and a friend—God—[78]

Vagrants were isolated and friendless and most of them were al-
coholics as well. Their lives were tragic, but they enjoyed a freedom
denied the other women of the lowest order, Asian slaves or indentured
prostitutes. In some ways Chinese prostitutes had more comforts than
vagrants, for their masters usually fed and clothed them adequately.
They were well-kept because of their owners' desires to protect an investment, rather than because of any humanitarian impulses, and slavery
was the single, overwhelming condition of these prostitutes' lives.

In 1875 there were 1,254 Chinese men on the Lode and eighty-four
Chinese women, only nine of whom were not prostitutes. By 1880, more
than half of the Chinese on the Comstock had left for Bodie and other
new bonanza camps and only 613 men remained along with twenty
women, all of whom were prostitutes.[79] The high ratio of men to women
was common, for most Chinese men came to the West Coast to labor,
send money back to their families, and eventually return home. Following traditional customs, almost all of their wives remained in their
husbands' parents' homes, and village heads frequently insured men's
loyalty by demanding that they marry prior to departing for the United
States.[80]

During the period of unrestricted Asian immigration from 1850 to
1882, more than 100,000 men but only 8,848 Chinese women entered
the United States.[81] The Act of Exclusion of 1882 officially barred all
but the wives of the wealthiest Chinese, although an underground traffic
in prostitutes kept up past the turn of the century. As Mary McNair
Mathews observed, "respectable [Chinese] women do not come to this
country."[82]

The incredible sex ratio and the isolation of Chinese men from white
communities generated nearly ideal demand conditions for prostitution,
but white prostitutes rarely accepted Chinese customers. The same merchants and members of protective associations who had arranged passages
and jobs for male sojourners leaped into the breach, supplying Chinese
prostitutes to their own immense profit.[83]

Chinese secret societies based in San Francisco or their individual
tributaries controlled Asian prostitution on the Comstock. Virginia
City's Chinese quarter was organized by tongs who frequently fought to
establish exclusive control over legitimate and illegitimate trading, and
one tong war ended with two deaths and fifteen arrests.[84]

Most Asian prostitutes in the United States were "big-footed" peasant girls from southern China, and in 1880, all of the Comstock's Chinese prostitutes had Cantonese surnames.[85] After the 1851 Taiping Rebellion famines and fighting swept South China, and conditions were so bad that some families were willing to sell their daughters to slavers. Other women were kidnapped from their villages, and a few others were lured to the Pacific Coast by promises of proxy marriages.[86] Profits were immense, and a woman who sold for a little over $400 in Hong Kong brought $1,800 in gold when she landed in San Francisco in the 1880s.[87] Prostitutes cost from $300 to $3,000 once they reached the Pacific Coast, and domestic slaves unsuitable for brothel work sold in the $100 to $500 range.[88]

A few wealthy Comstock Chinese owned concubines, but the majority of prostitutes worked in public establishments. In 1875, the largest single Asian brothel in Virginia City housed six prostitutes, while in 1880, the two largest brothels had two women each, and eight Chinese prostitutes worked in rooms adjoining gambling dens or opium shops.

Whites seldom observed status gradations among Chinese prostitutes, yet there were marked differences determined by the quality of the establishments in which they worked. Brothels were distinguished by both class and race, and the best Chinese brothels in San Francisco, and probably on the Comstock as well, catered only to Chinese, because Chinese men believed that the most degrading thing a Chinese woman could do was to have sexual intercourse with a white. High-status Asian women often dressed in silks and jewels, as did other Chinese prostitutes who catered to whites with a taste for the exotic. By and large, however, Chinese prostitutes dressed in plain cotton and worked for fees ranging from twenty-five to fifty cents a customer.[89]

Faro, fan-tan, and other games of long chance flourished in Chinatown, where lonely, indebted laborers had few other opportunities to become solvent. The same conditions encouraging prostitution and gambling also encouraged opium dens, which continued to operate openly after the Nevada legislature prohibited them in 1877. Mark Twain described his excursion to some of those dens in the Chinese quarter:

In every little cooped-up, dingy cavern of a hut, faint with the odor of burning Josh lights and with nothing to see the gloom by save the sickly, guttering tallow candle, were two or three yellow, long-tailed vagabonds curled upon on a sort of short truckle-bed, smoking opium, motionless and with their lusterless eyes turned inward from excess satisfaction—or rather the recent smoker looks thus, immediately after having passed the pipe to his neighbor—for opium smoking is a comfortless operation, and requires constant attention.[90]

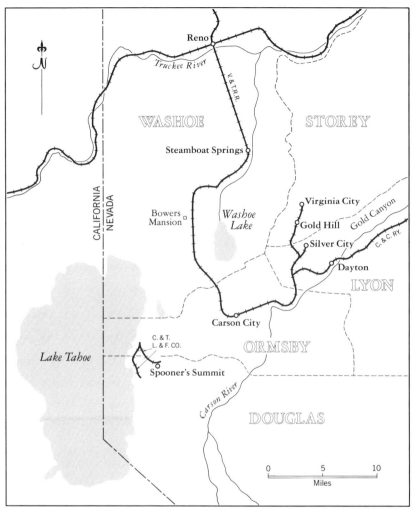

This map indicates the proximity of Virginia City and Gold Hill and shows
how the Virginia City and Truckee Railroad linked the Comstock
to Carson City, Reno, and the Central Pacific line bound for San Francisco.
(*Redrawn from the endsheet of the 1958 edition of* Reproduction of Thompson and
West's History of Nevada, 1881, *edited by Myron Angel. Courtesy of Howell-
North Books. All rights reserved.*)

Panorama of Virginia City, 1861, highlighting major buildings and institutions. (*Courtesy of I. N. Phelps Stokes Collection; Art, Prints, and Photographs Division; The New York Public Library; Astor, Lenox, and Tilden Foundations.*)

THO'S TAYLOR

OFFICE OF THE TERRITORIAL ENTERPRISE

S. BLOOMFIELD & Co.

LOUIS FEUSIER

A. DRAKE'S CARPENTER SHOP

J. ROSTAND & CO.

RESIDENCE OF W.H. BRYAN

SIERRA TEMPLE BAKERY

J. H. GARDINER

TUNNEL IN THE MT. DAVIDSON G. & S. MINING CO.

BLACKSMITH'S & WAGON SHOP

WILLARD & ZELLE, PR.

PAVILION

JOHN L. MOORE PR.

RESIDENCE OF JAS. A. COLLINS

BLACKSMITH & X BUILDING

PIONEER DRUG STORE

LANGTON'S EXPRESS

INTERNATIONAL HOTEL

BLACK & HOWELL

PROVISIONS HARDWARE GROCERIES & LIQUORS

PAUL & BATEMAN, PROPRIETORS

A. FLEISHHACKER & CO.

L. HERMANN

S. HALDENBACH

DR. E. SMITH.

NELSON W. WINTON, AGENT

BRITTON & Co. PRINT.

C.C. KUCHEL LITH. 176 CLAY ST. S. FRANCISCO, C.

GINIA CITY.

NEVADA TERRITORY.

Writing on the back of the original photograph identified these women as "visiting French actresses." They were probably embarking on a brief tour of one of the mines. (*Courtesy of Nevada Historical Society.*)

This picture was taken at the upper level of a Comstock mine. The men had no effective safety equipment or protection against heat and water at the mines' lower levels. (*Courtesy of Nevada Historical Society.*)

Alf Doten and some of the women in his life. *Above left to right:* Mary Stoddard Doten, his wife; Mrs. M., Alf's mistress; *below left to right:* Alf Doten; Lizzie Lansdell, a respectable young lady; Cora Kelsey, another young lady Alf courted; and Adah Issacs Menken, the adventuress. (*Courtesy of the Special Collections of the Library of the University of Nevada at Reno.*)

Alf Doten identified this hurdy girl of the mid-sixties as "Julia ——, hurdy
and beer jerker . . . afterwards wife of Ernest Zimmer leader of the orchestra at
the Music Hall." (*Courtesy of the Special Collections of the Library of the University
of Nevada at Reno.*)

Except for her honorary fireman's hat, Julia Bulette resembles a stolid Comstock matron captured in front of a standard photographer's backdrop. (*Courtesy of Nevada Historical Society.*)

This frame house was the residence of an affluent Virginia City family around 1870. Note the child's elaborate rocking horse and the nursemaid with the baby in the upstairs window. (*Courtesy of Nevada Historical Society.*)

Two different Virginia City parlors in the late 1870s. (*Courtesy of Nevada Historical Society.*)

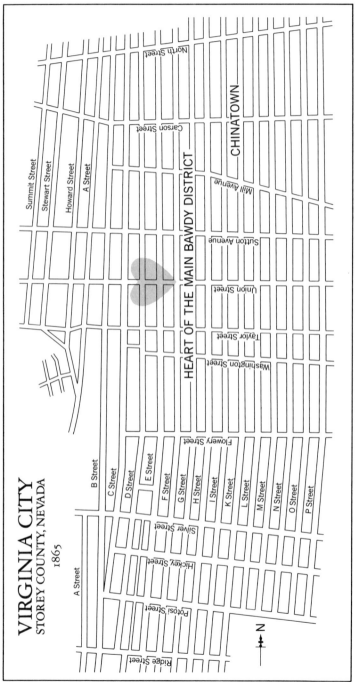

VIRGINIA CITY
STOREY COUNTY, NEVADA
1865

A Street
B Street
C Street
D Street
E Street
F Street
G Street
H Street
I Street
K Street
L Street
M Street
N Street
O Street
P Street

Ridge Street
Potosi Street
Hickey Street
Silver Street
Flowery Street

Summit Street
Stewart Street
Howard Street
A Street

North Street

Carson Street

CHINATOWN

Mill Avenue

Sutton Avenue

Union Street

Taylor Street

Washington Street

HEART OF THE MAIN BAWDY DISTRICT

N

By 1865 the street plan for Virginia City was fixed. Although a flurry of building after the Great Fire of 1875 led to some changes, the city's fundamental contours were set five years after settlement began. The main bawdy quarter and the Barbary Coast were well within the city limits and were geographically and socially central to the community. (*Redrawn from the Official Map of Virginia, Storey County, Nevada, 1865. Courtesy of the Special Collections of the Library of the University of Nevada at Reno.*)

This is a very rare photograph of three Chinese prostitutes in 1866, who were identified only as Marie, Susie, and Nellie. (*Courtesy of the Special Collections of the Library of the University of Nevada at Reno.*)

While legend held that respectable Mrs. O'Leary was responsible for the great
Chicago blaze, drunken Crazy Kate and her friends became symbols of Virginia
City's Great Fire of 1875. (*Courtesy of Nevada Historical Society.*)

Prostitutes also required constant attention from their owners, for like other property, they were vulnerable to thieves. Four Comstock women were kidnapped by rival tongs. One of the victims was discovered alive on the railroad, nailed into a crate being shipped from San Francisco to Reno.

This event was accepted by the wider community, and white observers looked on with much amusement when a few Chinese made complicated arrangements to marry domestic slaves and then held American-style weddings.[91] Marriage, however, was no protection for a woman. The Sam Sing Company arranged to kidnap Ah Quong's bride by swearing out a complaint for both husband and wife's arrest. When the woman alone was released from jail, she was kidnapped and taken to San Francisco.[92] In another case, a tong representative swore out a petty larceny complaint against a woman whose husband was leaving for Belleville, in the hope that he would go without her. The case was dismissed, however, and she was able to accompany her mate.[93]

Owners had absolute control over their women, for on the Comstock there were no public protests or institutionalized rescue work. The white community permitted the owners to retain feudal power and owners bolstered that power with a fierce capacity for violence. Six Asian women who killed themselves were the only ones known to have escaped from slavery, and it is probable that other kinds of escape attempts were punished privately and fiercely. Si Yowh, a twenty-year-old woman from Hong Kong, was found dead under her owner's house at Union and I Streets. Ah Pan, the owner, swore that she was his "cook" and that she had stolen a ring and six dollars from him. He stated that after discovering the theft, he went away to his friend Tom Poo's. The two returned together to find Si Yowh gone, and her badly beaten body was found much later. On the basis of that testimony, the coroner's jury brought in a verdict of death by unknown causes.[94]

Tom Poo asserted that his friend, Ah Pan, would not hurt anyone, and Poo's testimony helped the case, for he was a liaison between the white and Chinese communities in Virginia City. Poo controlled various enterprises, including a saloon where he sometimes stood drinks for newspaper reporters like Dan De Quille and Alf Doten. The many white men who visited Chinatown simply denied the forced aspects of prostitution, preferring to see friendliness and quaint customs. Alf wrote of Chinese New Year in 1866:

—Then I ran with Dan—went to Chinatown—China New Year commences this night—women in their best rig—rudders in their hair behind—houses set out with nice little lunches of sweetmeats, preserves, etc.—they invited us to eat & we did taste a little—pretty nice—lots of fancy colored candles burning also rushes burning—firecrackers exploding by the million in the streets.[95]

Whites referred to Chinese prostitutes as "celestials" or "moon-eyed damsels" when they wished to make a point of politeness, but the women were no more than slaves. They ranked at the bottom of the internal stratification pyramid in the most oppressive situation within prostitution.

Theoretical Implications

Laura Fair, the headstrong adventuress, and Si Yowh, the concubine, had little in common. Even though each of them was kept by one man, they occupied nearly polar positions in the stratification system within prostitution. Sharing a common isolation from the respectable community, the two women were separated by differences in class, race, and living situations. The complexity of stratification among Comstock prostitutes indicates how difficult it is to generalize from one form of sexual barter to others and demonstrates the hollowness of a legend based on a small number of elite prostitutes. The vast differences among prostitutes also makes it difficult to use a single theoretical framework to explain sexual commerce.

The dimensions of stratification, however, reveal how closely prostitution was tied to the wider community and to definitions of femininity within that community. Elite prostitutes derived their status from many of the same personal attributes and interactional skills with which respectable women achieved advantageous marriages, and specific sexual abilities or willingness to accommodate perversions were seldom important to a woman's position within the profession. The highest-status prostitutes sustained relationships resembling marriage in their privacy, lack of promiscuity, intimacy, and subtle economic exchange.

With some surface changes, the organization of prostitution on the Comstock resembled urban prostitution in the United States from the beginning of the nineteenth century through the present, and the ubiquity of internal stratification suggests its importance to the maintenance of prostitution. Stratification functioned to regulate prostitutes' work roles, mitigate competition among prostitutes and also entrepreneurs, and accommodate customers. The division of prostitutes into various strata allowed them to learn specific customs and norms surrounding their work roles and their relationships to one another. Once a prostitute was familiar with a narrow role she could fully utilize the parlor house circuit or other migratory routes and have the resources to arrive in a strange city with contacts or at least the working knowledge to seek out an appropriate niche within a community's disreputable subculture. Prostitutes in the same working situation could also maintain bonds of solidarity by befriending one another and competing with women in other status groups.

Stratification within prostitution encouraged employee loyalty to individual melodeons, saloons, or brothels. Stratification also facilitated the development of differentiated labor pools, so entrepreneurs like Rose Benjamin, Nellie Sayers, and Tom Poo did not compete with one another to attract women to their establishments. The greatest benefits of stratification, however, accrued to customers.

The organization of Comstock prostitution made it possible for any man to have sexual contact if he could pay something. Affluent men could enjoy elite prostitutes or sample a range of women, and men with less money could choose among working-class prostitutes or perhaps save for women "above their station." There was a vision of infinite variety that added to the allure of the bawdy quarters. The class lines within prostitution also allowed customers to maintain class lines among themselves. Men patronizing prostitutes usually associated with their male equals directly or indirectly. The men who kept mistresses rarely had to enter the red-light districts and the middle-class patrons of Cad Thompson's brothel seldom saw ordinary miners. Obviously patrons could choose women above or below their own class, but the organizations of prostitution supported stratification within the wider community and was in turn supported by it.

Friends and Enemies

Hangtown Gals are plump and rosy.
Hair in ringlets mighty cosy.
Painted cheeks and gassy bonnets;
Touch them and they'll sting like hornets.
Old Mining Camp Ballad

THERE IS LITTLE specific information about the men who wandered through the Lode's vice districts. The large, differentiated irregular marketplace allowed most of them to remain anonymous, and, with the exception of pimps, men faced few legal or moral sanctions because of their interaction with prostitutes. Social definitions and individual emotional responses made it likely that women who bartered their sexuality would organize their daily lives and self-concepts around prostitution. Customers and most other men involved with prostitutes, however, could escape the taint of association with sexual commerce because they had a number of social roles outside of the context of sexual barter and those roles were salient to them and to their community.

The majority of Comstock prostitutes probably came into contact with hundreds of men during their working lives. There were five important male roles associated with prostitution, and they were not mutually exclusive. Commonly, however, a man occupied only one major social role in relation to a specific prostitute at a given time. Men's usual relationships with prostitutes were brief and impersonal. As customers men exchanged money for sex, as lawmen they offered protection for bribes, and as property owners and landlords they provided institutional services for a percentage of prostitutes' profits. Lovers and pimps had longer, more intense relationships with prostitutes that were rooted in emotional attachments rather than material concerns.

Long-Term Lovers

Relationships based primarily on mutual affection between a prostitute and a man were difficult to define because a lover might also take money from her, earn money through her, or have the power to imprison her. There is some information suggesting that a very few Comstock prostitutes sustained long-term liaisons because the relationship was intrinsically rewarding to both partners. Those relationships may have been based on one partner's illusions or perhaps on shared delusions masking avarice; but in illusion or in reality romantic lovers were important to prostitutes and thus they must be mentioned here.

A man could be considered a prostitute's long-term lover if he were involved with her for several months and that involvement was based primarily on affective considerations of both parties. A few prostitutes eventually married these lovers and one "success story" married her Cornish pimp and migrated to a new boomtown in eastern Nevada after final depression set in on the Lode. They managed a brothel together and invested in other irregular enterprises, along with legitimate businesses. After three generations, however, her wealthy descendants are still penalized by their family's association with the fast life.[1]

Madam Rose Benjamin married her lover shortly before she left the Lode; and a beer-slinger, Lizzie Berlindo, was courted by a stalwart Cornishman.[2] The most dramatic public manifestation of a lover's commitment to a prostitute occurred at a miner's ball in Gold Hill when Mr. Callahan drew a gun and grazed Mr. Boyle after Boyle and his wife refused to join in a quadrille. Callahan believed that they were insulting his partner, a prostitute, although Boyle later insisted that he and his spouse merely thought the set was full.[3]

By 1880, Cad Truckee a well-known prostitute, had moved out of the brothel district to live with an unemployed Frenchman; and other women probably also left prostitution to engage in long-term affairs with men from the disreputable community or from the regular working class.[4] There is no clear evidence, however, that any Comstock prostitute left the bawdy quarters to become a pillar of the community, although one observer of life on the Lode, Mary McNair Mathews, remarked:

Sometimes a good citizen, wealthy and respectable, marries his wife from one of these corrupt houses, and he seldom ever regrets his choice. He builds her up to be respected and respectable. I have heard of several cases.[5]

Mrs. Mathews's hearing of several men who had uplifted prostitutes sounds like a common story-telling strategy. Everyone may know someone whose best friend's brother-in-law saw a ghost or visited a whore with a heart of gold or knew someone who had uplifted a prostitute, but no one has actually had that particular experience. Many Comstock prostitutes *could* have sustained romantic liaisons, but they probably didn't, because almost any man involved with an ordinary prostitute

exploited her to some degree. Either a lover was economically independent and could use his greater social and economic power to control the
relationship or he was economically dependent. If that dependence was
more than temporary, the lover was really a pimp.

Pimps

Since the nineteenth century the term "pimp" has usually been regarded
as a despicable epithet because the role combines explicit manipulation
of women with dependence on their earning power. The prostitute-pimp
relationship is antithetical to the cultural ideal of a strong, self-reliant
male protecting a woman from pitfalls and predators.

People on the Comstock rarely used the word "pimp," but instead
substituted "sport," "no-account," and "gentleman of leisure." Pimps
were visible enough to provoke a local ordinance outlawing "all lewd and
dissolute persons who live in and about houses of ill fame."[6] They were
seldom punished by the prescribed jail sentence of up to sixty days or the
fine of from $5 to $300, because few, if any, prostitutes would testify
against their men.

Newspapers rarely mentioned pimps except in the context of prostitutes' suicides. One woman poisoned herself because her pimp left her,
while another, who was Chinese, killed herself after her man gambled
away thirty dollars.[7] Seven other suicide stories mentioned prostitutes'
jealousy over men, or their abandonment by them, but those reports did
not differentiate pimps from lovers, merely identifying "her man" or
"her lover."

The 1875 census listed 81 men as speculators and an additional 25 as
gamblers, sports, or gentlemen of leisure. There were also 531 white
males between eighteen and sixty-five years of age with no occupation
listed. With few exceptions, the pimps enumerated in the census belonged to those categories. Many speculators took chances on mining
stocks and real estate rather than women and some gamblers and sports
focused their attention on cards or dice, but other men in those
categories lived off prostitutes' earnings, as did some men who listed no
occupation.

There were thirty-eight men in the 1875 census who could clearly be
identified as pimps because they resided in brothels or with individual
prostitutes. In 1880 there appeared to be fewer pimps, and only nine
could be identified clearly. Most of the Comstock pimps in 1875,
twenty-one, were between thirty-five and forty-five years old. Eight
others were between twenty-five and thirty-four, seven were between

forty-five and fifty-five, and two supplied no information about their ages. The range of these men's ages suggests that experience with women and other aspects of the fast life were important to successful pimping.

Only seven of those pimps were foreign-born—one in Ireland and six in Germany. Two did not list their birthplaces, and the rest came from the United States. Seventeen were born in the northeastern region, eleven in southern or border states, and one in the Midwest. Like the information on age, the information on pimps' birthplaces indicates that men's ability to live by their wits and manipulate women was probably enhanced by complete familiarity with American culture.[8]

Pimping involved few concrete obligations, and fancy men rarely assisted prostitutes with business, although they were probably available to protect their women from violent customers or bail them out of jail. The absence of any laws prohibiting men from soliciting for prostitutes in contrast to a number of ordinances restricting women suggest that informal customs effectively limited male solicitation. Pimps encouraged tumultuous one-sided relationships based on emotional manipulation rather than mutual services or extreme coercion. Their principal function was to provide prostitutes with an illusion of romance which women could rarely find with those who did not share in the social world of commercial sex.[9]

Unlike their modern counterparts who commonly exercise control over two or three women at the same time, most Comstock pimps were only involved with one prostitute during a given period.[10] They accompanied their prostitutes to masquerade balls, music halls, and opium dens. One sport was unjustly accused of introducing the demon poppy to the white population of Virginia City.

Opium smoking had been entirely confined to the Chinese up to and before the autumn of 1876, when the practice was introduced by a sporting character who had lived in China. . . . He spread the practice amongst his class, and his mistress, "a woman of the town," introduced it among her *demimonde* acquaintances, and it was not long before it had widely spread amongst the people mentioned, and then amongst the younger class of boys and girls, many of the latter of the more respected families.[11]

The tale that a pimp was responsible for whites' opium smoking illustrates the way in which many respectable people defined those men as totally evil. Their explicit exploitation of prostitutes, however, was seldom discussed in books or newspapers, but one unusual newspaper article at once described part of a pimp's evening rounds and also reviled him.

About 11 o'clock last night happening to be passing along B Street, near the Post Office; we overheard a row between two colored prostitutes; which for vileness of expression exceeded anything we ever heard before and *a thing that appeared like a white man* [emphasis added] whom one of the pair supports, was exceedingly anxious lest his black diamond should get her beautiful face damaged in the mess.[12]

No charges of coercion or entrapment were ever leveled against Comstock pimps. One newspaper story exposed a gang of sports who lured reputable men into "prostitutes' dens" and then blackmailed them. This same gang was also accused of attempting to compromise young engaged ladies but it was unclear whether they were compromising the women for purposes of blackmail or of prostitution.[13]

Pimps on the Comstock were all but ignored by newspaper reporters, perhaps in the hope that they would disappear or perhaps because fancy men were considered to be unprintably bad. In any case, there is no surviving physical description of a gentleman of leisure on the Lode, but San Francisco's history includes detailed, albeit conflicting, portraits of Charles Cora, a professional gambler who consorted with Belle Cora, a very successful madam in the mid-1850s. He was from New Orleans, and he was tall and swarthy. While there is debate over whether he lived primarily on Belle's earnings, Cora's dress on the day of his trial for murdering a United States marshal was in the classic manner of gentlemen of leisure. He wore a richly figured velvet vest, a pleated shirt, and kid gloves.[14]

Certainly the Comstock had resources to supply sporting men with finery. At the height of the boom in the mid-seventies, there were jewelry emporiums offering men watches, chains, studs, rings, and stickpins. Both male and female residents of D Street were distinguished by their sartorial splendor when they could afford it, and it is probable that Comstock pimps were as gaudily outfitted as their San Francisco competitors.

Some fancy men were more lovers than pimps to prostitutes, and they may have been honest, loyal, and true to their women. However, there were few public or private reports of such graceful behavior on the part of the pimps. Instead, newspapers printed stories about the gentlemen of leisure who took painted women's money, abused them, and eventually left. These stories probably represent a fraction of their misdeeds, since even pimps who beat prostitutes continued to be protected by their women.[15] Some men who pimped were forced off the Comstock during campaigns against habitual vagrants and outlaws, but most probably drifted on to the fast life in other towns, some taking their women and others leaving them behind.[16]

Profiteers

The men who owned buildings leased to prostitutes or owned or managed bawdy saloons, hurdy houses, melodeons, or Chinese brothels did not belong to the same category as fancy men. Although these profiteers earned money through prostitutes, their relationship was based primarily on economic exchange rather than sexual or emotional intimacy. In some cases the men who profited from prostitution barely knew the names of women occupying their buildings, while in others the men stayed on the premises during working hours. Whatever the relationship between a prostitute and an owner or manager, financial obligations and mutual economic profit were key in defining their interaction.

Men owned and managed most bawdy saloons, and the 1875 census shows 113 men owning or managing saloons or melodeons on the Comstock. An additional 90 men were employed in them. Many of the saloons were respectable, catering to a clientele ill-disposed toward prostitutes in the establishment, but others either tolerated prostitutes' presence or actually thrived on sexual commerce.[17]

It is impossible to use census data to determine exactly which saloons or lodging houses were or were not reputable, but the overwhelmingly male ownership of all such establishments supports the assertion that men were the major owners of bawdy saloons and melodeons, and brothels were the only irregular institutions which were nearly always operated by women. A few women did own small bawdy saloons on the Barbary Coast, but men owned and managed most places serving liquor or lager from a bar. Men stood behind the bar to break up drunken customers' fights and to oversee the play in saloons featuring faro, roulette, poker, keno, euchre, or pedro. While women could manage intimate saloons and brothels, they could not enforce order in larger establishments with high potential for group rowdiness or violence.

The major melodeons, Macguire's, Dick Bermann's Alhambra Theater, and Piper's Opera House (during certain periods), employed men to keep order, as did large saloons featuring waiter girls, such as A. C. Scott's Crystal Peak. Sometimes, however, male employees generated more violence than they quelled. At the Grecian Bend the bartender threatened to kill a beer-jerker named Annie Warren; and at another saloon, the barkeep habitually grew violent when customers sought out his favorite waiter girl.[18] It was often difficult for men to avoid entanglements when they worked alongside prostitutes.

Three Barbary Coast saloon owners discussed in the preceding chapter formed the romantic triangle which exploded when Peter Larkin, owner of the saloon at 146 South C, killed Daniel Corcoran, owner of the Union

Saloon, as he lay in bed with Nellie Sayers in her saloon at 146 1/2 South C.[19] It was also easy for owners to become emotionally involved as they worked in neighboring establishments and had common occupational interests.

According to local ordinances owners assumed some responsibility for prostitution on their premises, although they were seldom penalized. Nellie Sayers, *Mrs.* Corcoran, and Pat Gould were eventually denied saloon licenses and run off the Barbary Coast because of the disorderly character of their houses and the "riotous proceedings" within them.[20] They were the only recorded victims, however, of the ordinances punishing owners of unlicensed saloons and brothels located outside the legal limits of the vice districts. One attraction of working in a theater, bar, or brothel was that the owner or manager acted as an informal buffer between prostitutes and lawmen, but even so, few prostitutes escaped contact with the law's long arms.

The Lawmen

From the mid-1860s through the 1880s, Virginia City contained three levels of law enforcement personnel: a federal marshal and his staff, the Storey County sheriff and his deputies, and the municipal police chief and his force. The municipal police had the most regular contact with prostitutes, as they were required to keep the daily peace and arrest violators of local ordinances, as well as assist at fires, hangings, and elections.[21]

The major qualifications for being a Comstock policeman were nerve, talent with a gun, and political influence. The police chief was elected and his force was appointed shortly after annual elections by the partisan Board of Police Commissioners.[22] During the 1870s the regular force ranged from ten to fifteen members, supplemented by two or three special policemen who received their pay from private individuals but operated under rules and regulations governing regular officers.[23] For the great bonanza decade the ratio of police to residents was about 1 to 1,000, compared with 1 to 540 in New York City and 1 to 524 in Boston during the same period.[24]

The Virginia City police were both understaffed and underfunded. Salaries ranged from $100 to $125 a month, slightly more than miners' wages; but police work was at least as dangerous as mining on the Comstock. Men competed fiercely for the available police positions, and while some probably applied from a sense of duty, others undoubtedly recognized lucrative illegal possibilities in law enforcement.

All but four of twenty policemen sampled in Virginia City between 1866 and 1877 had previously engaged in working-class occupations. Eight had been miners, and most of the others had worked in different capacities in the mines and ore mills.[25] Two of the nonlaboring men had been saloonkeepers and another policeman had worked in a saloon. These four officers had clear attachments to the disreputable community— attachments which were not idiosyncratic but which instead mirrored the overall organization of criminal justice on the Comstock.

Throughout the American West, the line separating lawmen from outlaws was often fuzzy, because men on the fringes of the disreputable communities had both contacts and skills necessary to do police work in the mining boomtowns. In fact, in frontier cities where formal professional training was unknown, a criminal career might have been the best possible preparation for someone who

has a load of responsibility on his head which is never dreamt of by the uninitiated. In addition to knowing every rascal in the community, he has to familiarize himself with the description of escaped and discharged convicts, not only in this state, but from others, particularly California.[26]

The close contact between some police and criminals was reinforced by low police pay and also by the custom of hiring special policemen in Virignia City. Those special police were most often assigned to the second ward and to Chinatown, both of which housed bawdy saloons, brothels, and individual prostitutes.

Most of the local legislation regulating sexual traffic indirectly encouraged police corruption in their interaction with prostitutes. There were seldom complaints or direct harm caused by prostitutes' lewd language or residence outside the brothel district or violation of other ordinances. Police had the option of enforcing the law at their own discretion, and a friendship or a bribe could shut their eyes to misdeeds, while a rebuff might open them.[27]

Police corruption was a recognized fact of Comstock life, as it was in many other American cities during the same period. There were formal investigations of the Virginia City police force in 1866, 1869, and 1876, as well as a major trial of a special policeman in 1878.[28] The investigation of 1876 and the trial of 1878 also dramatically revealed the character and extent of policemen's ties to prostitutes.

The ties were based less on friendship than on expediency, and police took prostitutes' money and returned even less to them than fancy men. The 1876 hearings brought up charges of general brutality and debasement of women in the city jail, as well as Rose Benjamin's specific accusation that Officer Walker took twenty dollars from her purse in her brothel.[29]

A month later, new allegations were made against Officer Iby. Frankie Jordan, a prostitute at Rose's house, swore that she gave him forty dollars to avoid arrest. Lena Hunter, another madam, was even more damning as she testified to seeing Iby in a private melodeon box with one of her prostitutes. To cap it off, Ada, the prostitute, had unpinned the officer's star and attached it conspicuously to her breast.[30] No respectable man commented on that testimony, since hardly anyone respectable wished to become involved in the trial, but the prostitutes' testimony was convincing enough to bring about Iby's dismissal.[31]

In October of 1877 another round of publicity began when Special Officer William B. Davis shot a sometime miner named Louis Ash in the back at 2:30 in the morning during a prostitutes' dance on D Street. Although Davis claimed self-defense, he was indicted by a coroner's jury and brought to trial the following February.[32] The testimony in both the hearing and the trial brought more publicity to the relationships between lawmen and lawbreakers than any other event.

Davis, a former prizefighter and merchant marine, listed his occupation as saloon worker in the 1875 census and claimed a personal estate of seventy-five dollars. He was a forty-two-year-old Irishman married to a nineteen-year-old Japanese whom he met in Yokohama and by whom he had a son at sea.[33] He was installed as a special policeman for the second ward in May, 1877, and had served less than six months before the shooting.[34]

Nettie Bowen, a prostitute who lived with Ash, testified against the policeman, claiming that Davis followed Ash and killed him without provocation. In order to discredit her testimony, the defense attorney cast aspersions on her character eliciting information that her real name was Abby, not Nettie, and that she had come from San Francisco to work alone in Virginia City.[35] This was a rather strange tactic for the defense attorney to employ, since one of his key witnesses, Belle West, was also a prostitute. Belle, a hurdy girl who had come from the Colorado boomtowns, swore that Ash had threatened the officer before he drew his gun. On cross-examination, the prosecution forced her to admit her occupation, and she simply stated, "I go to bed with men for money."[36]

Both sides called a number of other witnesses, most of whom worked in the main red-light district. Conviction hinged on which case appeared more realistic and also on whether the twelve men believed ubiquitous rumors that Davis had offered a number of prostitutes money and future favors if they testified on his behalf.[37] The jurors opted in favor of Davis, acquitting him on February 7. How or why they judged him innocent is questionable, however, since his stupidity and gall were revealed when he swore that a reliable source had warned him of Ash's murderous intent. That "reliable" source was madam Rose Benjamin whom the policeman identified as "a respectable lady."[38]

Officer Davis was an extreme example of a policeman who appeared to have his closest ties with prostitutes. Unlike Iby or Walker he was accused of giving rather than taking prostitutes' bribes, but Davis's case still illustrates the callous exchange relationships policemen had with prostitutes. Bribery was so common that unknown men could simply pose as policemen and receive forty dollars hush money from a prostitute.[39]

To be sure, some policemen had no close associations with prostitutes or other members of the disreputable community. For example, Officer George Downey was a terror to "stage robbers, footpads, and burglars."[40] Another officer refused to accept part of a fine paid by a convicted prostitute, Anna Kelly, because he wanted no part of a woman's ill-gotten gains in his pocket.[41] Finally, in another case, Officer Taylor turned in fellow Officer Farnsworth for allowing Nellie Grunner, the Carson Banger, to wear his uniform and star into a saloon. Taylor and Farnsworth must have been enemies of long standing, for a few months before the uniform incident, Taylor accompanied Mrs. Farnsworth while she searched for her wayward husband in a D Street brothel.[42]

No matter how intimate they were with prostitutes, policemen were agents of the respectable community who always held the power to betray and arrest them. Comstock policemen who were close to prostitutes consistently misused their power, but they may have received less than they realized. So long as their relationships with fancy women were defined by the impersonal barter of favors, they were simply another variety of patron.

Customers

On the Comstock, as elsewhere, most customers and prostitutes had peculiar relationships with one another. Each group tried to fool the other, squeezing the bargain for a little bit extra. Customers and prostitutes sometimes hated and mistrusted each other, but ultimately they needed each other. Their transactions were filled with tensions that helped make the Comstock's bawdy districts among the rowdiest in the West. Patrons could be classified on a continuum from regular to occasional. Some men on the loose probably frequented the same prostitutes over a relatively long period of time, while others may have visited many prostitutes once or twice each, and still others might never have strayed into the bawdy districts.

Customers supplied prostitutes with tangible material rewards, such as money, jewelry, or mining stocks, and the bargains prostitutes arranged with them were both the most essential to subsistence and also the crudest of the many transactions they had with men. For the most part, the intimate details of sexual commerce on the Comstock are lost, but surviving information indicates that the variety of customers on the Lode matched the variety of prostitutes.

Unattached men formed the bulk of Julia Bulette's and other cottage prostitutes' patrons, and they were probably the most common type of customer for other prostitutes as well, but they were by no means the only patrons. They alone could not have supported the fancy brothels and stylish melodeons that made the D Street district come alive with laughter and music every night. Prostitution was so central to economic and social life on the Comstock that it is hard to imagine an adult male being immune to its lures, and gaudy masquerades and prostitutes' balls were practically irresistible. Newspaper reports and Alf Doten's diaries indicate that such entertainments were frequent, attracting men from every walk of life. Some of the balls were not grand events, but were instead small parties given during the Christmas holidays at brothels such as Bow Windows or Mary Blane's.[43] Other balls and masquerades were conducted on a much larger scale, filling the Armory Hall, the Summer Pavilion, or the Great Republic Saloon.[44]

Aside from the size of some of these entertainments, another indication of their plentiful, indiscriminate patronage were warnings to respectable townsmen advising them to stay away. One Saturday night ball at Macguire's melodeon included all the fast men and women of the town, "besides many others who had better be at home."[45] At one point during that ball there was a fight and weapons were drawn, but no charges were pressed because one of the participants was a married man with children. A ball given at the Armory to honor Juarez and Mexico included "some decent women," although "the women were principally whores."[46] The decent women soon departed, leaving men to mingle with prostitutes.

Husbands' and fathers' exposure to prostitutes was considered to be a minor problem compared with sons', and a local ordinance was proposed to enforce an 8:00 P.M. curfew on all Virginia City boys under sixteen years of age.[47] The ordinance was rejected on the grounds that boys of almost sixteen were too old for such supervision and also on the grounds that the real problem was not customers but rather the "soiled doves which at night come out from their retreats to lure men."[48] Two years later, the same issue was raised in the context of adolescent boys visiting the Alhambra Theater. The editorial allowed that grown men who went there might find even worse alternatives if the Alhambra were closed. At the same time, however, the writer admonished parents to keep their impressionable sons away from the theater—lest they turn into hoodlums.[49]

Theaters, large saloons, balls, and masquerades were the largest, most public places where patrons and prostitutes gathered. Not all men who visited them went to bed with prostitutes on the same or any other day or night, but every guest subsidized prostitution by paying entrance fees or by buying drinks at exorbitant prices or by simply adding to the general atmosphere of convivial chaos. Where patronage began is not easily determined. It certainly meant more and less than simple genital contact between prostitute and customer. People on the Comstock distinguished between being a spectator and an active participant in sexual commerce, but that distinction was hardly precise. Some men visited prostitutes' celebrations, bars, and brothels for companionship instead of sex, and they were more patrons of establishments than of individual women.

Most Comstock prostitutes' quarters were ugly and uncomfortable and at least as unpleasant as those occupied by lone miners, but the madams of better brothels offered men salons of sorts, with piano music and good liquor. Those could also be found in some small bawdy saloons and D Street cottages. Alf Doten's diary revealed the importance of prostitutes to his social life from late 1864 through the advent of his liaison with Mrs. Morton. Entries in his diary describe weekly, sometimes nightly, visits to the main bawdy district and to Chinatown, and Alf and his cronies often visited brothels, saloons, and individual prostitutes for cards, conversation, or drinks rather than sex.

Alf was an atypical man—a liberal bachelor who possessed few familial obligations, extra cash, and sharp curiosity. However, his convivial visits to prostitutes, often accompanied by friends, were so routine to him that it is possible to generalize that other men were similarly drawn to brothels and bawdy saloons for laughter and music. Under some circumstances, feminine companionship not regulated by the hidden rules of courtship or adultery was probably more attractive than brief, impersonal sex.

From 1865 to 1867 Alf was a steady customer at the Crystal Peak Dance Hall and Saloon, Max Walter's Music Hall, Macguire's melodeon, Bow Windows Brothel, and Tom Poo's Chinatown saloon and opium den. Some nights he visited a number of these sporting resorts.

> After theater Dan [a fellow reporter] and I cruised about together, went through Brick [Cad Thompson's], Bow Windows, and I left him at Chinatown—bed at 2—[50]

> after I got through I went with Sam Glassner down to Chinatown—drank at Tom Poo's—went to Mary's house—we were in her room with her—she gave us each a cake left from the holiday of yesterday—filled with nuts and sweetmeats—we laid on a bed with her & smoked opium with her—a little boy some 2 years old sleeping there, belonging to one of her women—long and interesting chat with her—came up to the office—On my way home I stopped at the Great Republic Saloon—big whore ball going on—bed [at home] at 2—[51]

On other nights, Alf might have visited Belle Neal's on B Street and then proceeded on to "one or two other little Spanish shindigs" or he might have stopped by Jenny Tyler's Bow Windows, where there was "lots of music, songs, wine, etc."[52] Like other men, he indirectly paid for prostitutes' companionship through exorbitant drink prices and surcharges on entertainment, but Alf's observations on the evenings he passed in barrooms and bagnios indicate that he considered himself to be a genuine friend of several prostitutes.

"Friendship" with a prostitute made it possible for customers to feel that they were backstage actors in the fast life, more knowledgeable and sophisticated than ordinary men. Such "friendships" also affirmed men's liberality and largesse in temporarily overlooking the traditional dichotomy between ladies and whores, and some Comstock prostitutes probably offered "friends" unquestioning emotional support. Many folktales about frontier prostitution describe the friendship between good-hearted prostitutes and good-timing men.[53] True friendship, however, rests on equality and spontaneous mutuality, rather than calculated transactions, and the foundation of economic exchange and the difference in social power between prostitutes and customers mitigated the possibility of deep, lasting friendship.

In the aftermath of Julia Bulette's murder, a number of contemporary observers remarked on the great generosity of respectable men who had marched in her funeral procession or refused to serve as jurors because of their vehement hatred of her alleged murderer.[54] None of those men, however, risked his reputation by stepping forward to pay her burial expenses or testify formally about her character.[55] Even customers of long standing maintained freedom from emotional or social obligations to a prostitute. Alf Doten went to view Julia's body and accompanied a friend to visit Jessie Lester after she had been shot by an unknown man.[56] Yet when a favorite music hall performer whom he regularly slept with at Bow Windows Brothel killed herself with an overdose of chloroform, he could only comment:

> Little Ida that I used to————some two years ago was found dead in her bed at the "Bow Windows" (Jenny Tyler's) this morning—She has been rather dissipated for some time past and latterly had taken to opium—Ida Vernon was her name—About 32 years old—a man was sleeping with her & found her dead in the morning—*rest in peace Ida* [original emphasis]—she was her worst enemy—.[57]

The subsequent news story about Ida's suicide left out the fact that a customer had awakened by her side and found her dead.[58] No matter how intimate a man's relationship with a prostitute, he was always able to leave her without facing formal sanctions. Sometimes men articulated their ambivalence toward prostitutes more cruelly, and embarrassing and sometimes hurtful pranks were fairly common, as were painful beatings and even murder.

Violence Against Prostitutes

Perhaps the most famous practical joke on Comstock prostitutes was delivered on Cad Thompson's Brick House in 1866. As she and her prostitutes went about their work, a group of rowdies stole the fire engine from Virginia Engine Company No. 1 and set it up on the corner of Sutton and D Streets. For realism, the men set fire to a small pile of straw and proceeded to flood the downstairs of Cad's brothel with fire hoses, annoy the women, disturb the customers, frighten the piano player, and damage the piano. The *Enterprise* asserted, "Nothing can justify this damage," but the reporter was protesting the temporary theft of a fire engine rather than the trouble caused Cad and her women.[59]

None of the men participating in the fire engine incident was punished, but another time, four men were arrested and fined for throwing stones and raw eggs at a row of D Street brothels.[60] Other pranks included customers' jumping from the upper boxes to the stage of Max Walter's Music Hall or "playing" with a derringer in a prostitute's room on South C Street.[61] Practical jokes were not always accompanied by the danger of physical harm from flood, flying objects, firearms, or clumsy feet, and Lizzie Berlindo, the aging, festive beer-slinger at the Crystal Fountain Saloon was terribly hurt by misrepresentation. A Cornishman offered to marry her and arranged a ceremony in the saloon itself. The parson proved to be an imposter, and the couple brought their case against him to court, where it was promptly thrown out. False promises to respectable women were treated seriously, but a prostitute's striving for the sanctity of marriage was considered to be only slightly less absurd than a man willing to join her in it.[62]

Other abuse of prostitutes could not be dismissed as mere foolishness and all prostitutes worked in danger of physical attacks, although those working alone were the most vulnerable to violence. Some women wore little whistles around their necks in order to summon police and ward off harm, but prostitutes had far less legal and informal protection than respectable women.[63] They feared reprisals if they reported men to the authorities, and they also faced the possibility of police indifference. Insurance companies routinely refused to insure prostitutes or their property because of their individual vulnerability and also because of the threat of arson in the D Street area.[64] They had to be alone with customers, and the nature of their work made them tempting targets for individuals bent on violence to their property or persons.

Belief in prostitutes' venality allowed men to rationalize stealing from them, and women working in dance houses or melodeons were particularly open to burglary. They left their quarters at fixed times during the evening, their whereabouts could be checked easily, and men seen entering and leaving their rooms were seldom questioned.[65] Lone, high-status prostitutes were also enticing targets for thieves or robbers, since they often kept cash and other valuable items about them. Julia Bulette's murderer stole her diamond pin, coral earbobs, gold charms, sables, and other costly items.[66] Other prostitutes stayed alive but lost money, jewelry, and other belongings.[67] Robbery was frequently associated with violence, although it usually stopped short of murder. Thus, a music professor stole a lone prostitute's watch and assaulted her before attempting suicide himself. In another case, three men, two of whom were miners, beat Rose Wilson and robbed her of $3,000 in coin.[68] On a few occasions, men randomly destroyed prostitutes' property without apparent provocation. For example, a drunken stranger entered the Irish Blond's cottage and used a quart bottle to smash mirrors, spitoons, pitchers, and every other breakable in his sight.[69]

Sometimes murder was the outcome of random or purposeful violence. Julia Bulette was exceptional in her death as well as her life, because she was the only murdered Comstock prostitute whose assailant was brought to trial, convicted, and punished, and few serious efforts were made to discover the murderers of five other prostitutes. A witness saw men shoot

Mit Raymond in the small Barbary Coast saloon she kept, but no one was ever arrested in that case.[70] Jessie Lester remained silent about the man who fatally shot her, and Carmen Julio's murderer killed himself before he could be brought to justice.[71] Two anonymous Chinese prostitutes were also murdered, but the coroner declared them dead by "causes unknown."[72] Other prostitutes were also threatened with murder and had attempts made on their lives.[73]

Men were implicated in almost every assault and murder recorded. Not all of those men were customers of the prostitutes whom they attacked, but most were, and some were patrons of other prostitutes. The popular ideology characterizing prostitutes as low human types made it easy for men to make them objects for hostility and aggression, and the lines between "normal" use of a woman and abuse of her were often blurred. Thus, Alf Doten could matter-of-factly describe activities in Summit City, near a new California gold strike: "4 hurdies arrived this PM from Downieville—hurdy houses started this evening—boys used girls very rough—".[74]

Newspapers warned men to "beware of the dives," urging them to avoid small bawdy saloons where female owners and employees often drugged drinks and rolled customers.[75] One man lost his breastpin, watch and chain to Kate Kelly of the Crown Point House in Gold Hill, and another was rolled for $395 in gold outside of Miss Daisy's saloon at 244 South C Street in Virginia City.[76] Chinese prostitutes were notorious for robbing customers.[77] A detailed article about the dangers of Chinatown described a man "ashamed to tell his name" who had lost $50 and ten shares of Sierra Nevada mining stock to the two Asian prostitutes whom he had engaged. Although the customer swore out a complaint, he was to embarrassed to appear in court against the women. A reporter from the *Enterprise* drew the following moral from the tale: "A fool and his money are soon parted and those who carry rich mining stock in their pockets should keep clear of Chinese female stock."[78]

The article about the man too ashamed to help prosecute the prostitutes illustrates the few advantages held by women who quietly robbed their customers. While people seldom condemned patronage, men living with their respectable wives, mothers, or sisters probably would have suffered if their visits became publicized. Moreover, a man was something of a fool if he permitted a prostitute to dupe him. So long as customers did not receive grave harm at prostitutes' hands, their desire to protect their reputations probably outweighed their hopes of bringing prostitutes to justice. Saving face not only stopped men from reporting crimes, but also halted their attempts to avenge robberies or other slights informally. Prostitutes had scarcely any reputations to preserve, while respectable men did.

Sometimes it was hard to distinguish between outright robbery and reasonable deception. Trinidad Ortes, a Spanish prostitute who lived on Taylor Street, coaxed a customer to give her his gold watch, valued at $140. The next day, the man regretted his gift and had her arrested. The judge dismissed the case, ruling the watch was initially given freely in a private transaction.[79]

Occasionally women resorted to violence while attempting to rob a customer. Usually, however, when prostitutes struck at men, they did so without thought of material gain. Thus, a waiter girl at the Bon Ton Saloon became so annoyed with a customer that she smashed his head with a champagne bottle, hence becoming known as a "striking beauty."[80] Big Bonanza and Catherine Cavanaugh were lone prostitutes involved in fights with men. The most spectacular prostitute's attack on a customer occurred in a brothel. During the period of the Franco-Prussian War, a Bow Windows prostitute fondly known as "The German Muscle Woman" lashed a patron with one of her large collection of whips because he staunchly supported the French.[81]

Prostitutes' Friends

In a social world where men were either predators or fools, prostitutes turned to other women for comfort and support, establishing lasting bonds under conditions which hardly encouraged friendship. These friendships were seldom publicly reported because they were not newsworthy and also because they contradicted widespread beliefs about women's constant competition for men, but many fragments of information show that women of ill repute remarkably loved one another amidst the cruel conditions of the Comstock's irregular marketplace.

Many middle-class women in nineteenth-century America participated in a female world of love and ritual.[82] Deep, mutual friendships between women lasted from their adolescence through their old age, surviving lengthy geographic separations. Social arrangements segregating boys and girls and men and women fortified those relationships. The home was women's sphere, and feminine support networks were essential to every event in a woman's life cycle from her birth to her death. Such women, whether kin or simply close friends, assumed an emotional centrality in one anothers' lives. In their diaries and letters, women in these pairs described the contentment and joy they felt in each others' company and their sense of isolation and despair when they were apart.

The regularity of their correspondence underlies the sincerity of their words.[83]

The special intimacy and affection that some nineteenth-century women shared is well-documented for the American upper and middle classes, but less is known about working- and lower-class women, many of whom could not write. To the extent that there was sex segregation within and outside those families, that males and females participated in different social worlds with different activities and meanings to their actions, it is probable that girls established special relationships with one another and with adult women. Poor women's lives, of course, were quite different from those of more affluent women, and the conditions under which they lived were less predictable. No one could be sure that she would remain in the same place all her life or be able to renew a friendship with regular visits or even have the time or skills to correspond over long distances. During childhood, many women from those classes probably learned special ways of relating to some other women such as their mothers, and they may also have established deep emotional ties with some female of their own generation.[84] The exigencies of daily life may have destroyed particular early relationships, although women retained the ability and need to form such ties with female friends.

Three aspects of prostitution on the Comstock made the idea of friendships among the women laughable, although other aspects clearly encouraged mutual interdependence. The degradation intrinsic to sexual commerce could have been internalized by the women, creating hatred for one another and for themselves; the need to find customers might have led to cutthroat competition; and jealousy over pimps or lovers may have contributed to feuds.[85] Comstock prostitutes were not immune to emotional and material strains, and newspapers reported nine different violent public fights among prostitutes. They brawled in the middle of C Street, on D Street, and on G Street.[86] Other scrimmages occurred near the post office, in front of the International Hotel, and by the Masonic House.[87] In some cases, prostitutes were dead drunk, as they used "filthy language" and hit one another.[88] In other cases, they were stone sober, as they scratched, kicked, bit, and tore one another's clothes.

While the competition and objectification that were part of Comstock prostitution undoubtedly contributed to hostility among some women, other structural aspects of prostitution supported their ability to make and retain intimate female friends. Women in brothels, small bawdy saloons and other situations worked and lived together, and cooperation if not friendship was essential to those establishments' success and to prostitutes' continued employment within them. In some small saloons,

women shared the same rooms and sometimes the same beds. Nellie
Sayers's Barbary Coast dive had two bedrooms housing Nellie, Susie
Brown, Kate Shay, Mrs. Mellon, and Mrs. McCarthy.[89] Sometimes two
or three women shared the same quarters, but worked independently,
and other independent prostitutes occupied rooms in the same lodging
houses or resided near one another in single dwellings. Some prostitutes
lived together and also traveled together from boomtown to boomtown
and parlor house to parlor house.[90]

Frontier prostitutes' living and traveling arrangements both reflected
and added to their mutual intimacy, and most other aspects of work
organization in prostitution also promoted solidarity. Even competition
could encourage friendship within informal groups of prostitutes while
generating rivalry with others, and women within a group could refer
customers to one another and also help in other ways.[91] Prostitutes'
isolation from the respectable community created a bond among them,
as did their antagonistic economic relationships to customers. They
shared a set of customs and an argot which distanced patrons and defined
the social reality which they experienced.[92] No one who was not a
prostitute could participate fully in the backstage social world of
brothels, bawdy saloons, or disreputable lodging houses.[93]

The hearing and trial following Julia Bulette's murder provided rare
public testimony about the positive feelings prostitutes had for one
another, the texture of their relationships, and the web of mutual obligations supporting their intimacy. Although Julia had lived on the Comstock for about four years, she regularly journeyed down the mountain to
visit Annie Smith and Mollie Livingston in parlor houses in Carson
City.[94] Another high-status prostitute, Lucy Smith, had first met Julia
in Carson but also saw her in Gold Hill, where Lucy owned a house.[95]

The communication network between Julia and her friends was
cemented by small favors. Annie Smith introduced Julia to a sympa-
thetic jeweler, Henry Monk; in turn, Julia took Annie's watch to be
mended by a fine craftsman in Virginia City.[96] Although Julia had
friends in Carson her closest relationships were with women on the
Comstock, such as her next-door neighbor, Gertrude Holmes of 6 North
D Street. Gertrude and Julia visited one another during the day and also
at night while waiting for men who had appointments. The two women
often breakfasted together and shared other meals at Gertrude's, because
her cottage had a kitchen while Julia's did not. They exchanged keep-
sakes, such as the little silver drinking cup Gertrude gave to Julia, and
they also helped one another with mending and advice about fashions.
Gertrude said of her dead friend, "We were like sisters."[97]

Of the many Comstock prostitutes whose deaths were reported in the newspapers between 1860 and 1880, only four had enough property to be probated. Mit Raymond, who owned a Barbary Coast saloon, left her property to her husband, and Jessie Lester, the madam, willed her estate to charity; but the two active prostitutes whose wills were probated relied upon other women to carry out their last wishes, although they had few resources with which to reward them.[98] Both Julia Bulette and Susan Ballard, who died after a long illness in 1871, appointed women to execute their estates. Julia had no known heirs or relatives, and she named Mary Jane Minirie as her chief executor. Lizzie Moore and Eliza Lawson also worked to organize Julia's effects for auction and to pay off claims against the estate. Eliza must have assumed a secondary role, however, since she was illiterate and could only sign papers eith an X. She was a laundress, while the other two women were prostitutes. All three would have shared Julia's estate, but nothing was left after they paid her debts.[99]

Susan Ballard left less than $1,000 to her infant daughter, Mary. She made her will as she lay dying and named Mary Ann Phillips and Peter Fitzgerald as her principal executors. She listed two other prostitutes, Catherine O'Connor and J. J. Cooper, as extra executors.[100] It was appropriate that both women name other prostitutes to carry out their last wishes, since prostitutes tried to protect one another from fatal harm and honored each other when they died.

Julia was instrumental in the conviction of the man who brutally beat Lizzie Hayes with his six-shooter; and other prostitutes worked to find and bring Julia's murderer to justice.[101] When Julia and Jessie Lester had grand funerals with flowers, fancy coffins, and touching eulogies, "the sisterhood" turned out in full force.[102] Julia's funeral included the fire department and more than a dozen carriages of mourners, while Jessie's included "some half dozen carriages filled with whores [who] followed her to the Catholic burial ground."[103] Other less affluent or renowned prostitutes were buried simply; but prior to burial they were sometimes laid out in their coffins as other prostitutes and friends paid their respects.[104]

When brothel prostitutes discovered other inmates' attempts to poison themselves, they rushed to call doctors, and in the meantime, they administered home antidotes such as mustard and olive oil.[105] Although some of those women might have had economic rather than altruistic reasons for attempted rescues, since death in a brothel would probably slow business for several days at least, the strength and romanticism of a few relationships were illustrated clearly by suicide pacts. Two sets of prostitutes made pacts in the summer of 1872, and the earlier suicide might have been a model for the later attempt. In July of that year, two fashionably dressed young women were found dead in a solitary cabin on B Street. Their names were not mentioned in the newspaper, but the article noted that their skins had the "rosy hue" of arsenic eaters'.[106] About five weeks later, another suicide pact caused a far greater uproar—in part because it had a "happy" ending and the two prostitutes survived.

Hattie Willis, age sixteen, and Katie Thompson, age twenty-one, took a combination of morphine and laudanum together. The other women staying at Rose Benjamin's summoned three doctors who pumped Hattie's and Katie's stomachs, while men gathered outside the brothel and a number of women from neighboring houses waited inside. The two women had known each other for less than two weeks, since the day Katie left her husband and entered prostitution. They became friends immediately, spending spare time together, planning their suicide, and deliberately skylarking around the parlor during dinner on the night of their attempt.[107]

Prostitutes lived together, traveled together, visited each other, fought and reconciled, exchanged gifts and favors, protected each other and, in two cases, even tried to die together. The full nature and extent of their intimacy remains unknown. Probably some of them loved one another; and probably love, closeness, or loneliness were sometimes manifested in sexual activity.

Lesbian sexual relationships were a part of frontier prostitution, and a famous, although probably apocryphal, tale describes the night that Calamity Jane was ejected from a brothel in Bozeman, Montana, because she was corrupting the other inmates. No event on the Comstock resembled her escapade, but once a male audience enjoying the pretty entertainers at Macguire's discovered that an outrageously flirtatious "gentleman" was really a woman and chased him/her away.[108]

There were no other reports of incidents associated with lesbianism, and no local laws prohibited women's sexual relationships. There was some regulation of women's publicly wearing male attire, although an ordinance outlawing women in trousers failed to pass.[109] Mary Dolan forfeited twenty dollars in justice court because she dressed as a man in public, but the board of aldermen and the police chief gave Marie Susie, a liquor store owner, permission to continue wearing breeches, and she also petitioned the Virginia City board of aldermen to allow her to dress as a man in public.[110] Her novel request was engendered by a recent brush with the law in San Francisco, where she was fined five dollars and ordered to stop wearing men's clothes, although she stated that she had been wearing them for more than twenty years. She justified her petition in Virginia City on the grounds that she and other female "sole traders" or merchants wanted to dress efficiently while working. She was divorced, but she produced documents from the district court clerk of Amador County, California, stating that she was virtuous, industrious, and prosperous. The document further noted that she was a major real estate owner in that county, and her own statement emphasized her virtue, asserting that she had no desire to be a prostitute.[111] It would be interesting to know why Marie Susie felt it necessary to add the last statement and whether her reasons had anything to do with a popular association of lesbianism with prostitution.

Prostitutes' lesbian activities were analyzed by several students of "sexual inversion" around the turn of the century.[112] One of the most famous of these scholars, Ceasare Lombroso, suggested that prostitutes were likely to be lesbians because of their close quarters in brothels and jails, their bad experiences with men, and their atavistic natures.[113] Only twenty years before Lombroso's contributions, lesbianism was seldom mentioned by anyone at all, except in sex manuals which hastily passed over mutual displays of affection between women.[114]

On the Comstock, the whole topic of lesbianism was so assiduously avoided that it was either nonexistent or unmentionable. The latter is probably the case, since love between women contradicted every aspect of sexual ideology on the Lode. On the whole the question of whether Comstock prostitutes had genital or other physical contact with one another is as unimportant as it is unanswerable. Twentieth-century conceptions which absolutely dichotomize platonic and romantic love distort the rich emotional relationships which occurred between many nineteenth-century women.[115] Surviving evidence indicates that some Comstock prostitutes created their own social worlds of love and mutuality, although the scope of those worlds remained and remain private matters for the friends who shared them.

Theoretical Implications

The variety of prostitutes' relationships with men and the complicated texture of each of their interactions reflected the dynamics of power within sexual commerce. Men did not monopolize power, although they usually had more economic and social options than women. Those options allowed them to dominate their relationships with prostitutes and to escape from those relationships when they chose, but prostitutes sometimes developed covert sources of power to give themselves some control in their daily lives.

The clearest exploitation in organized commercial sex involved prostitutes and the owners of land, buildings, or bawdy establishments in the vice districts. Their capital investment allowed owners to share prostitutes' profits, while they avoided most of the risks common to sexual barter. Profiteers had few obligations to prostitutes, if they routinely maintained sexual and emotional distance from them. They received a high rate of return for their expenditures, and owners were almost the only people to make great profits from sexual commerce.

Once they became sexually or emotionally tied to prostitutes, however, men gave up some of their power over the women. A pimp usually received most of a woman's earnings in exchange for providing an illusion of romantic love. They exploited prostitutes' emotions, but pimps suffered an enormous loss of social esteem because of their occupation. Their economic dependence on prostitutes and their questionable moral and legal status mitigated pimps' power over their women, but they usually dominated their relationships because of prostitutes' emotional dependence.

Lawmen provided prostitutes with services by exchanging freedom from arrest for sexual or financial bribes. The men patrolling the vice districts regularly associated with prostitutes, but they seldom developed truly intimate relationships with them. Police were among the auxiliary personnel associated with prostitution, but their differential power and routine exchanges simply made them a special type of steady customer.

Customers came to the bawdy districts to purchase feminine sexual contact and sometimes emotional solace as well. Because money is far less personal than sexuality, customers usually gave less than they received and they maintained freedom from social or emotional obligations to prostitutes. Sexual ideology, custom, and law permitted them to avoid most responsibility for prostitution, and they could engage in pranks or violence against prostitutes with little fear of punishment. The customers' power, however, was tempered by prostitutes' superior knowledge and control of the nuances of sexual commerce. Once men entered the bawdy quarters they were on prostitutes' turf, bound by a set of conventions and argot they seldom entirely understood. Moreover, customers sought out prostitutes because of socially molded needs they could not meet elsewhere; many men were lonely and uprooted, living in cramped rooms, working in danger, and searching for a few of life's pleasures.

Women sometimes stole from customers or blindly struck out at them with violence. The best defense which prostitutes had, however, was their own world of mutual friendship. An invisible wall built of daily confidences and common experiences separated prostitutes from men, and the loving friendships they managed to nurture protected them from utter brutalization.

With the exception of a handful of profiteers, no one really benefited from prostitution. Almost everyone associated with sexual commerce suffered some loss of human dignity in the manipulative interaction between prostitutes and the men in their lives. Although men benefited more than prostitutes, they were also trapped in the strange dynamics emerging from situations in which sexuality was transformed into work.

Hazards of the Game

They laid her out in her cocaine clothes
In her snowbird hat with its crimson rose;
On her headstone you'll find this refrain:
"She died as she lived, sniffing cocaine."
Traditional ballad from
Storeyville, New Orleans

PHYSICAL AND emotional damage were built into the organization of commercial sex on the Comstock. Birth control and childbearing were problematic and sometimes dangerous to prostitutes who had many sexual contacts but few resources to deal with children. Large numbers of sexual contacts also increased prostitutes' exposure to venereal disease and to harm from popular quack remedies for them. Those problems, the general harshness of life in the bawdy quarters, and the availability of alcohol and opiates in the irregular marketplace made it likely that women would turn to drugs to ease their pain. Sometimes, however, they found solace only in suicide.

The larger community and prostitutes themselves treated all of these hazards as individual, isolated misfortunes; but they are more accurately viewed as collective dangers intrinsic to prostitution. No prostitute could entirely escape the risks of pregnancy or disease, nor could she avoid the brisk drug traffic associated with the bawdy quarters. Individual problems increased the chance that a woman might abuse drugs or commit suicide, but most of the physical damage that was part of prostitution was a social phenomenon, reflecting the structure of sexual commerce and the material hardships and social stigma women experienced.

Almost every respectable married women on the Comstock endured difficulties from faulty birth control and difficult childbirth and risked contracting venereal disease from their husbands. Prostitutes, however, seldom had support from kinship networks or the wider community which could make pregnancy, childbirth, or illness easier. Moreover, prostitutes risked losing their livelihood if they were visibly pregnant or diseased. The material conditions and ideology surrounding prostitution enormously amplified the difficulties of just being female on the Comstock, and most of the hazards of the game were the ultimate extension of problems every woman faced.

Birth Control and Babies

Birth control may be defined as women's many efforts to limit their own reproduction, and it can range from contraception to abortion to infanticide.[1] No nineteenth-century birth control method was sure and many were suppressed by law in the United States, including the famous federal statute of 1873 prohibiting the mailing of contraceptive information or other "obscene" materials sometimes known as "Comstock Laws."[2] Anthony Comstock, the obstinate moral crusader, had nothing to do with the Lode, other than to make women's lives there and elsewhere a bit more difficult.

Prostitutes' friendship networks and business contacts facilitated their access to a wide variety of contraceptives regardless of legal constraints. Birth control opponents recognized this and sometimes referred to contraceptives as the devices of street prostitutes, noting that their use by married couples could produce impotence, uterine disorders, or monstrous children.[3] Whatever the consequences, however, birth control was essential to women who had multiple daily sexual contacts and who could seldom earn a living if they were obviously pregnant. There are no records of the techniques Comstock prostitutes preferred, but it is probable that they tried everything available at the time.

Some form of almost every modern birth control technique was used in the United States by 1860, and Dr. Edward Bliss Foote described them in his two controversial best-sellers which nationally sold more than seven hundred thousand total copies from the times they were first published in 1852 and 1872.[4] Some of those methods have been improved over the past century, but only the FHS hormone-suppressing pill can be considered as a full innovation.[5] Nevertheless, prostitutes could not avail themselves of many types of birth control because they involved intrusions upon their customers' wishes, and were thus economically unfeasible.

The popular rhythm method was hardly suitable for prostitutes because they would lose too much worktime by abstaining during their fertile periods. Moreover, during the nineteenth century, that method was unreliable because the human fertile period was not identified precisely until 1924.[6] Other common techniques requiring men's cooperation were also too limiting to prostitutes who could not trust their patrons to withdraw prematurely or use condoms. *Coitus interruptus,* male withdrawal prior to ejaculation, the most common method of contraception after abstinence, was obviously unsuitable for commercial sex because it was usually dissatisfying to men—decreasing their pleasure while increasing their responsibility.[7] Sexual frustration and social responsibility had no place in the ideotypic patron-prostitute relationship, and patrons shied away from using condoms for the same reasons that they rejected the withdrawal technique. Mme. de Stael offered the last word on condoms' drawbacks, describing the condom as "a breastplate against pleasure and a cobweb against danger."[8] Some men did rely on condoms as protection against venereal disease, but this was a matter of individual preference, and others used nothing or relied on preventive salves containing vaseline and boric acid.[9]

Prostitutes could seldom use three of the most popular contraceptive methods: rhythm, premature withdrawal, and condoms; but they still had alternatives, such as pessaries, vaginal sponges, cotton tampons, suppositories, and douches. Douches were the most widely used female contraceptive, and folk knowledge and physicians advocated a bewildering variety of them. Alum, zinc sulfate, perlash, infusions of white oak bark or red rose leaves, and plain water were all popular. Dependence on douching for contraception was dangerous, however, because it was ineffective and also because it could be physically harmful. Caustic carbolic acid, for example, was as much a fad among brothel inmates of the 1880s as shaken bottles of Coca-Cola were among prostitutes in the 1950s.[10]

No contraceptive method was entirely effective, and prostitutes sometimes had to choose between abortion and full-term pregnancy. An 1881 Michigan Board of Health survey estimated that one hundred thousand abortions were performed yearly in the United States, although post–Civil War moralists and legislators vehemently attacked the practice.[11] The American Medical Association offered a prize for the best antiabortion tract in 1864 and the *New York Times* called abortion "the Evil of the Age."[12] Antiabortion legislation passed in every state and, in 1869, the Nevada legislature enacted a law prohibiting the selling, administering or taking of abortifacients or the use of instruments to induce miscarriages. Physicians, however, were exempted by law when a mother's life was endangered.[13]

Even though mechanical abortions done with rudimentary catheters were both painful and gory, they were less dangerous than abortions through internal medicines. Failed mechanical abortions were most likely to be disclosed, but many women who died of "unknown causes" did so while attempting to abort, because chemical substances only produced abortion as a result of very harsh treatment to the body.[14] Abortifacients ranged from patent products like Sir James Clark's Pills (aloes, hellebore, powdered savin, ergot, quinine, iron, and solid extracts of tansy and rue) to simple quinine or iodine.[15] None of these was advertised, but the *Enterprise* and the *News* routinely carried items addressed "To the Ladies" regarding people like "Doctress" Hoffman, who offered strictly confidential treatment of "female complaints."[16] Another "specialist," Dr. Lefevre, supplemented his income by importing French perfume.[17]

Throughout the United States, chemical abortions, successful or lethal, were hidden; and the high national estimates of one hundred thousand yearly abortions were probably low. Most illegal abortions were disclosed only when a women died or became very ill as the result of an identifiable abortion attempt. Identification was usually made because of the presence of visible mechanical devices—coat hangers, knitting needles, or catheters.

Comstock newspapers reported only three abortions over the twenty-year boom. Spanish Lize (Gabriella Campo) died in a D Street brothel when a failed abortion produced peritonitis.[18] Three years earlier another prostitute had died while attempting to abort by means of an improvised catheter.[19] Both women's deaths were viewed as commonplace accidents involving women of ill repute, but another death of a respectable widow who kept a boardinghouse created a major scandal. Strange circumstances and a variety of conjectures about murder surrounded Mrs. Wicks's death in March of 1877, but the autopsy revealed that she had died attempting to abort a three-month-old fetus. Mrs. M. M. Cowan, a visiting female physician, was brought before a coroner's jury because she had examined Mrs. Wicks and her medical bag contained a syringe and a speculum with a vaginal tube. Charges were dropped, however, when the doctor testified that she was in town to nurse Mrs. Warren, a very respectable butcher's wife.[20]

There was a double standard for abortions for "good" and "bad" women, just as there was for almost everything else on the Comstock. Illegality made both chemical and mechanical processes more expensive and dangerous for everyone. Prostitutes, who usually had very little money, faced acute physical danger because they could seldom afford a skilled abortionist's services, and some of them chose to bear children.

When prostitutes became pregnant or had children, the responsibility was theirs alone. Even a rich man's mistress would have had a hard time demanding child support and proving paternity, since her questionable moral status could be used to refute her claims. A mistress's dubious assertions, however, were ironclad compared to those of a lower-status, more promiscuous woman. Ordinary patrons had no moral or legal obligations to children to whom they had no clearly proven blood ties. Impoverished prostitutes had the choice of raising their children in bleak circumstances and perhaps killing them slowly or deliberately murdering them soon after their birth.

A few women resorted to infanticide, an almost unthinkable crime, yet one which occurred with some frequency in nineteenth-century Europe and the United States.[21] Mothers were usually the criminals in these cases, and poverty and fear of the label of illegitimacy on themselves and their children motivated many murders. Some nineteenth-century investigators believed infanticide to be more common than the public thought, giving examples of babies who were intentionally poisoned with laudanum laced "soothing elixirs" sold for the purpose of preventing too much crying.[22]

Nevada had a statute against infanticide, punishing the concealment of a bastard's death and also making the criminal indictable for murder.[23] Like many other people, legislators assumed that unmarried women were the only ones with high enough incentive and low enough scruples to kill their babies—thus the infanticide law referred only to bastards. Their assumption, however, could not be weighed empirically because most Comstock infanticides were anonymous. While she was intoxicated, English Gussie, a notorious prostitute, confessed to killing her baby by throwing him into a privy, but after she sobered up Gussie denied it and no evidence was found.[24] Rose Bingham, a thirteen-year-old girl from a poor family, was discovered as she threw her baby from a window; but she was not prosecuted because she was so young.[25] The five other known infanticides could not be linked to any adult, and the criminals remained anonymous. Dead babies were found on B Street, near the Ophir mine, and in a variety of other hiding places on the Lode, while other babies and toddlers were abandoned or left at the orphan asylum in Virginia City.[26] Other infants were probably killed, but their deaths were attributed to different causes or their bodies were never found.

Infanticide was a viable alternative for prostitutes, but some women chose to raise their babies in the bawdy districts rather than kill them, abandon them, or put them up for adoption. In 1880, twenty-two prostitutes had children living with them. Most had only one child, but six had two children and three had three children living with them. At the time, two of the women were single, two divorced, nine married and abandoned, and nine widowed. The mothers were of many ages and ethnicities, although no Chinese babies were reported to the census takers. These children could be found at every point in the status structure of prostitution. Henry Thompson was raised amid the perfumes and piano music of his mother Cad's plush brothel while Mollie Malone's children played in her small one-prostitute bawdy saloon at 418 South Union. Farther down the mountain, Mary Durant's child lived in her tiny one-room crib on South E Street.

No one knows how or if those children survived psychologically. Their existence was hidden from the public much of the time and most of them left the Comstock before becoming adults. Two of the prostitutes' children, however, were barely traceable. In 1878, Henry Thompson committed suicide.[27] Another child led a long life, becoming rich from her prostitute-pimp parents' investments, but she never forgave her mother for sending her to stay at the state orphan asylum where gangrene set into a neglected injury necessitating the amputation of her arm.[28] These two cases may have been atypical, but they probably weren't, because few prostitutes could protect their children from emotional brutality, just as few could protect themselves. Some children, no one knows how many, must also have suffered because their mothers carried venereal diseases.

The Occupational Disease

Syphilis, gonorrhea, and other venereal diseases reached epidemic proportions after the Civil War. There were 2,626 active cases of venereal disease reported in the United States Army alone in 1875. A year earlier, in a report read before the American Public Health Association, Fredrick R. Sturges claimed that 1 out of every 18½ people in New York City was syphilitic.[29] Physicians throughout the world were concerned with both causes and cures for venereal diseases, but it was not until 1905 that Albert Von Wasserman developed diagnostic blood tests for syphilis.

Prostitutes and customers alike were well aware of the ways in which syphilis, soft chancre, venereal warts, gonorrhea, and herpes spread. Despite precautionary condoms, salves, or washing, men still contracted venereal diseases and blamed prostitutes alone for their infection. Acton in England and Sanger in the United States were among the pioneering reformers who assumed female culpability and suggested that prostitutes submit to registration, regular medical examinations, and involuntary hospitalization in venereal clinics. Customers, of course, were spared this degradation.[30] The St. Louis city council legislated regulated prostitution in 1870 by means of a loophole in state law, but an immediate coalition of religionists and women emerged to argue in favor of a single standard—regulation for both patrons and prostitutes or none at all.[31] Four years later, the Missouri state legislature changed the constitution and outlawed regulation. Unsuccessful attempts at formal regulation in Illinois, Pennsylvania, and New York also indicated that a large segment of the public favored holding prostitutes, not customers, responsible for venereal diseases.

The international debate over whether prostitution should be regulated to control venereal disease scarcely touched the Comstock where unregulated, legal prostitution was the norm. Except for advertisements for patent medicines and medical specialists, newspapers hardly discussed venereal disease. County hospital records never mentioned syphilis or gonorrhea, although they did list a number of deaths from rather vague "cancer of the brain," and witnesses at hearings on the hospital in 1876 stated that many of its inmates were men and women of ill repute whom prostitutes visited for nightly revels.[32] Although the original hospital had an "insane asylum" in its basement, it could not accommodate chronic patients, and three prostitutes had to be sent to the California state asylum because of their "mental debilitation by unknown causes"—probably syphilis.[33] Dr. C. C. Green, a hard-drinking man who attended Julia Bulette and other prostitutes, died by one of the diseases he had treated.[34] In 1875 he was sent to the asylum at Woodbridge, California, because he had slowly become an idiot and "he seemed to be attacked by a general and gradual wearing away of both body and mind."[35]

No one talked openly about venereal diseases, but Comstock residents had countless remedies available to them. Red Drops and Unfortunate's Friend were among the most popular drugstore potions in the country, and Pine Knot Bitters were conveniently available in liquor stores.[36] Local newspapers carried explicit advertisements for a variety of cures, and physicians also offered their services. Dr. Thomas promised *Enterprise* readers that his fine training at the Royal College in London had prepared him to provide "discrete cures" for venereal disease.[37] Dr. Price's Dispensary put Dr. Thomas's claims to shame by insisting on "Infallible Remedies" rather than discrete cures. Dr. Price's potions were "Surest and Quickest known for all private diseases of both sexes, young and old. Chronic venereal disease quickly relieved. No mercury used."[38]

The latter claim was appealing because the mercury treatment's side effects including frothing at the mouth, necrosis of the jaw bones, bleeding gums, ulcerated cheeks, gangrene, and, occasionally, strangulation. Until the introduction of Salvarsan in 1910, mercury cures were most common and most effective, but even the worst dysfunctions of mercury could not match the gruesome possibilities of surgery. Alf Doten assisted Dr. Hiller with such an operation.

At 3 I went with Dr. Hiller up to a house near Summit Mill—assisted in a surgical operation on Patrick _____ an Irishman some 35 years old—cut off about 2 inches of his penis—the head all rotten with pox [syphilitic chancre]—awful sight—took 1/2 an hour—[39]

Placed in the context of national venereal epidemics, fragments of information about illness and the hundreds of advertisements for venereal disease specialists and cures leave little doubt that syphilis and gonorrhea were major problems on the Comstock. Prostitutes' many sexual contacts made them likely victims and carriers of the disease, and the bawdy districts were probably infested with the pox. Infection may have been so feared that it was never mentioned in local intentional sources, but whatever the reason for people's silence, prostitutes were surely exposed to venereal infections, just as they were exposed to violence and pregnancy. Disease was another hazard of sexual commerce, drawing women toward the dangerous illusion of safety created by alcohol and opiates.

Invisible Enemies

Virtually all prostitutes used drugs. There were fewer grocery stores in Virginia City than saloons, not to mention liquor stores and wine merchants.[40] Prostitutes drank with customers in saloons, dance halls, brothels, and their own cottages, for liquor sales were a profitable part of their work.[41] They commonly supplemented alcohol with opiates, traded in pharmacies or Chinese opium dens. Raw gum opium, laudanum (tincture of opium), and morphine were cheaply available to customers. Addiction was also developed and maintained through the consumption of many opiate-laden patent medicines, such as Godfrey's Cordial, McMunn's Elixir, and Mrs. Winslow's Soothing Syrup, as well as soft drinks and cigarettes laced with morphine to stimulate repurchasing.[42]

Few if any women became prostitutes in order to obtain liquor or opiates, since they were cheap and readily available on the free market.

Perhaps a few women entered prostitution while they were drugged, but a great many perfect ladies remained respectable while dulling their senses with patent medicines containing alcohol or opium. There is considerable evidence that a large proportion of middle-class American women in the late nineteenth century stayed stoned for most of their adult lives.[43] Prostitutes had special reasons for consuming drugs, and synthetic euphoria allowed them to keep at their work. While drug abuse did not drive women to prostitution, drugs sustained them in dangerous, degrading daily routines.

Visions of dance hall girls tippling with customers seem benign compared with images of addict-prostitutes writhing in agony. Alcohol abuse, however, was at least as problematic as opiate abuse, although the current legal status of alcohol makes that hard to believe.[44] Comstock prostitutes surely suffered from narcotic abuse and a number died because of opiate poisoning; but alcoholism caused as much physical suffering and contributed to public violence in ways that opiates did not.

Until the mid-seventies when anti-Chinese sentiment led to the passage of opium regulations, many people on the Comstock defined liquor as the greater evil. Thus, Mary Parker, who habitually drank and sang at the top of her lungs, pleaded not guilty to charges of disturbing the peace on the grounds that she had reformed and no longer touched liquor. Her defense rested on her assertion that she only took opium, but the *Territorial Enterprise* noted this was a common ploy and "the opium dodge was no good."[45] Mary, the "Creole Warbler," was sentenced to an unusually long one-month jail term for disturbing the peace.

Comstock prostitutes were often arrested on charges of being drunk and disorderly, and while some police may have defined prostitution itself as "disorderly," the details surrounding the cases indicate that the defendants did indeed drink too much.[46] English Gussie emerged unruffled after she fell from an upper box in Macguire's melodeon and broke a hole in the floor.[47] Another inebriated prostitute broke out of the jail by knocking down wall panels.[48] Other ostensibly invulnerable prostitutes managed to weave down C Street carrying $1,000 in gold coin or pass out on Sutton while decked out in diamonds.[49] All four of these women's tales were recounted with ironic humor to prove that prostitutes might be stupid and drunken, but they were also lucky.

Liquor, however, more often led to violence than to luck. "Drunken amazons" fought with each other and with men. Most of those brawls were street fights, since no successful madam or barkeeper would tolerate such breaches of discipline.[50] Minor injuries and torn clothing usually stopped the fights, but black eyes and torn dresses were not the only consequences of intoxication. Cad Truckee, a Gold Hill prostitute, had both feet amputated because of frostbite that she contracted after passing out in the February snow.[51] Thirty-eight-year-old Irish Mary died of "natural causes" of drinking and exposure to the cold.[52] The death of Julia White, an affluent prostitute with her own cottage and $1,500 in savings, was also brought before a coroner's jury which ruled her death natural because "she had been drinking of late."[53] Lizzie Hayes, the owner of a bawdy saloon on C Street, and Florence Dunworth, a waiter girl, died of similar causes.[54] These four prostitutes surely died of alcohol abuse, but alcohol contributed to the deaths and debilitation of scores of others. Alcoholism was an addiction as powerful as opium addiction, but intoxication led to public misbehavior while narcotic consumption produced quiet stupors.

The Virginia City board of aldermen passed an ordinance declaring opium dens a nuisance, and a Nevada statute also outlawed them. The statute passed in 1877 required for the first time that druggists obtain a physician's permission before dispensing opium.[55] Neither law stemmed the brisk trade in opiates. They merely validated Caucasian moral ascendancy and facilitated police harassment of the Chinese.[56] People could always find disreputable physicians to write prescriptions, and once prescriptions were obtained they could be refilled far in excess of their legitimate therapeutic use.

By the mid-1870s a number of national medical authorities deplored the growth and spread of opium addiction among respectable people. Charlatans and quacks peddled nostrums to hapless addicts attempting to cure themselves, but many cures contained substantially more narcotics than consumers had used previously.[57] To discover if these growing fears about middle-class addiction were grounded in reality, Dr. Charles Warrington Earle conducted one of the first empirical studies of opiate use. He interviewed fifty Chicago druggists about their "best" customers. He found that of 235 identified addicts, 169 were women, and prostitutes were by far the largest group of opium addicts in the study (56) followed by "housewives" (45).[58]

Comstock prostitutes used all types of opiates, alone or together. Frankie Norton and Big Mouthed Annie frequented Chinese dens, but most other women had solitary habits.[59] The information about prostitutes' drug use comes primarily from suicide reports of twenty-two women who poisoned themselves with opiates, for drug use was so common it was seldom noted in other contexts. For example, Capriana Avila took morphine every day and English Ida used both opium and chloral to sleep.[60] Easy access to laudanum, morphine, and opium made suicide fairly simple; but at least one habitual addict, Frankie Norton, was saved because of the tolerance she built up from years of drug consumption.[61] Like Frankie, most prostitutes slowly poisoned themselves with alcohol and opiates, while some eventually used them to commit suicide.

Sudden Death

The Comstock's general suicide rates were high, and they were almost unbelievable for prostitutes. An exact computation of rates is unfeasible, because of class biases in reports and dramatic population fluctuation. A low estimate based on official records placed the Nevada rate for the 1870s at twice the national average and that rate was grossly underestimated.[62]

From 1863 through 1880, Comstock newspapers reported that 20 different prostitutes had attempted suicide and an additional 19 prostitutes successfully killed themselves. Like other suicide rates, these figures were low because of unreported deaths and also because of prostitutes' suicides in other places on the boomtown circuit. Moreover, newspaper records were not available for some months.[63] Despite these problems, newspaper articles furnish a rude profile of prostitutes' suicides and attempts, indicating that they occurred at rates of one to two a year throughout most of those eighteen years. There were no prostitutes' suicides, however, in 1870, 1877, 1879, and 1880; and there were seven, seven, and four in 1872, 1875, and 1876 respectively. To get some idea of the magnitude of the problem, imagine the peak year of 1875 when 7 out of 307 prostitutes, more than 2 percent, killed themselves.[64]

Prostitutes' suicides were so common that the *Enterprise* referred to one victim as merely "one more unfortunate," and poked fun at an attempt when another poisoned prostitute "got out a distance from shore but failed to cross the river."[65] Suicides were diverting items which allowed newspaper readers to feel better about their own lives, and at times they became active entertainment, as men gathered on D Street to await news of the doctors' success in pumping stomachs or administering antidotes.[66] Poison was by far the most common method used by prostitutes and also used by the four respectable women whose suicides were publicly reported.[67] Eleven prostitutes used laudanum, six opium, five morphine, two chloral, two arsenic, and twelve used unspecified poison. In contrast to women, most men shot themselves or occasionally slit their own throats.[68]

Some prostitutes' suicides were motivated by ostensibly trivial incidents; a madam wouldn't allow one of her women to go horseback riding in the afternoon; a customer used abusive language and threw beer. These accounts rarely mentioned the many troubles prostitutes experienced prior to the precipitating incidents. One case, however, illustrates some of the problems left unmentioned in most others. Capriana Avila, the target of the beer, had been planning suicide for a long time, and she often spoke of her plans while taking her daily doses of morphine. Before taking an overdose, she made arrangements to pay her funeral expenses by selling her personal property. Still, her feelings were mixed, because she told another inmate of Rose Benjamin's brothel that she wanted to fake suicide in order to bring back her reprobate pimp.[69]

If newspaper reporters noted the reasons for suicide at all, they used glossy generalizations. Sometimes they classified suicides as efforts to gain attention; as in the case of the Spring Chicken, who tried to hang herself with a hanky while she was in jail and Blanche De Maude, who made so many lurid trys she became known as "Suicide Frenchy."[70] Reporters more often blamed women's pimps or lovers for their deaths, crying a half-hearted, *"Cherchez l'homme."* Those articles never mentioned the general problems of material deprivation and social stigmatization which made suicide an appealing alternative to life.

Prostitutes of almost every age, nationality, race, and status within the irregular marketplace killed themselves. At age twenty-two, Laura Steele, a beautiful black-haired Scotswoman, took lethal laudanum at Rose's fancy brothel; Nellie Davis, a down-and-out thirty-three-year-old prostitute, overdosed on morphine in her solitary room at Mrs. Gray's B Street lodging house; and an anonymous Chinawoman who had cost her owner $800 suicided by means of laudanum in back of Stern's store in Gold Hill.[71] She was one of the six Chinese women who chose death over a life of hopeless slavery.

Suicide was a last resort of women who endured abortions, venereal diseases, alcoholism, narcotics abuse, and interpersonal violence. Sometimes caprice, but more often careful planning, lay behind their intentional deaths. Prostitutes closed the circle of their lives with suicides, and their decisions to die were often more farsighted than some of their earlier choices. The many hazards of the game were part of being a woman, and they were also part of the special cost of living outside of traditional moral boundaries. Despite the visible damage to them, many respectable people felt that prostitutes were not punished enough by the dreadful lives they led, and they developed an intricate ideology, set of customs, and body of laws which further punished disreputable women.

7

Separating Good Women and Bad: Sexual Ideology, Custom, and Law

I may die out in the ocean,
Be shot down in a gambling house brawl;
But if you follow me to the end of my story
You'll find a blonde was the cause of it all.
Traditional Cowboy Song

A VAST, VAGUE ideology hung over the Comstock like a fog, legitimating prostitutes' activities, wives' obligations, and working women's labors. Sexual ideology was an inclusive system of ideas defining men's and women's innate capacities for love and work and delineating male and female spheres and the appropriate behavior within them. Although it was rooted in material relationships, sexual ideology had a life of its own, influencing the short-run development of the family and the labor force. It survived because it allowed people to make sense of their social worlds and shape their day-to-day actions.[1] Much of the logic and content of sexual ideology was submerged in taken-for-granted reality, but the problematic nature of social life on the Comstock sometimes caused people to reveal their basic assumptions and commonsense beliefs about men and women.[2]

Sexual ideology never developed into a full-blown moral code, and it was seldom discussed unless challenged. It reinforced women's subordination in the home and in the regular and irregular marketplaces, emerging in greatest strength when traditional male-female relationships were threatened. The major ideological elements were: (1) women are physically inferior to men, (2) women are intellectually inferior to men, and (3) women are morally superior to men because they are at once closer to nature and farther from sexual desire.

Prostitution was a major ideological problem on the Lode, since it stood as a blatant contradiction to traditional ideals of womanhood, morality, and family life. Customs and laws labeling prostitutes aberrant and unfeminine and separating them from respectable women were rooted in more general sexual ideology. So long as those labels were enforced, prostitutes could be physically and morally segregated from the respectable community and their problematic presence could be ignored or rationalized. Antiprostitution customs and laws served a number of social functions clarifying rules about feminine social and sexual behavior, emphasizing the respectable community's behavioral boundaries, and heightening solidarity among respectable women.[3] Commercial sex on the Comstock was so bound up with other aspects of social life that it could not be eliminated, but it could be condemned and contained through ideology, custom, and law.

Sexual Ideology

Strands of sexual ideology appeared everywhere on the Lode, in casual jokes, in mass media, in scientific texts, and in every institution and sphere of social life where women were assumed to be men's physical and intellectual inferiors and their moral superiors. The doctrine of female physical weakness went unchallenged on the Comstock and was the element in sexual ideology least questioned by most American feminists. Women were generally weaker than most men, but the dominant ideology emphasized that weakness and depicted it as related to feminine reproductive capacities. The belief in womanly weakness implicitly legitimated their exclusion from employment in the mines, ore mills, building trades, and other traditionally male occupations. Of course most working women's jobs demanded physical exertion, but their stamina was tested in the service of traditionally feminine prerogatives such as cooking, cleaning, and child care. Moreover, women's paid labor was usually organized in single units or small shops and few others observed the difficulty or complexity of their work, so their physical exertion could either be denied or justified as a natural sacrifice to womanly goals.

The Comstock women who publicly demonstrated their strength in domestic labor or other occupations were defined as a lower social type than ladies. Leisured ladies submitted to cumbersome costumes causing headaches, fainting, nausea, vomiting, and damage to their vital organs.[4] Both crinoline skirts and padded bustles required wearers to be tightly harnessed in corsets, and these costumes enhanced the illusion of feminine fragility, while making it difficult for women to do physical work. Fashion held its own self-fulfilling prophecy which implied that women were weak and then contributed to debilitating illnesses serving as evidence of female physical inferiority.

When women were not imprisoned in corsets and padding they were considered to be unfeminine or at least unladylike. Thus, according to some Comstock writers, true ladies were simply too fragile to vote, let alone take on the other burdens in the public sector.[5] The reality of women's physical inferiority to men bolstered those arguments, but women's intellectual abilities were too visible to be similarly ridiculed, rationalized, or ignored.

After the Civil War, upper- and middle-class women throughout the United States vigorously demonstrated their intellectual skills and campaigned for improved female education, while retaining their own ladylike demeanor.[6] The popular ideology of feminine intellectual inferiority, however, denied the full meaning of their achievements. Sometimes exceptional women were described as anomalies so different from other women that they proved the rule that most women belonged in the family circle, and at other times intellectually superior women were condemned because they had sacrificed their femininity for their achievements. Many late-nineteenth-century physicians even blamed the configuration of symptoms known as "neurasthenia" on women's overtaxing their brains and straining against their natural place within the home.[7]

Beliefs about women's intellectual inferiority supported a great deal of antisuffrage sentiment on the Comstock. When suffrage speakers like Susan B. Anthony, Anna E. Dickenson, and Elizabeth Cady Stanton visited the Lode to lecture, public comments on their dress and demeanor usually overshadowed discussions of their arguments.[8] The attention to appearance devalued the suffragists' intellectual appeals while it emphasized the price they paid for their beliefs. Susan B. Anthony was privately described as a "thin, rather longspanned old maid" and another suffrage speaker elicited extensive newspaper notations on the style of her bloomers but no mention of the nature of her lectures.[9]

The question of women's suffrage in Nevada sparked public debate in 1869 when Storey County Assemblyman Curtis J. Hillyer proposed a resolution to strike the word "male" from the voting article in the state constitution.[10] That resolution failed as did other attempts in 1871, 1873, and 1883. The roots of a small suffrage society were sunk in Virginia City in 1870, when sixteen liberal middle-class men and women met to organize, but little occurred after their initial meeting.[11] The Nevada Equal Suffrage Association was not established until the late nineties and in 1914 Nevada was one of the last western states to enfranchise women.

If Comstock women spoke quietly they were seldom heard and if they turned intellectual cartwheels to attract public attention to women's rights they were castigated for destroying their womanliness. Laura DeForce Gordon, a local doctor's wife who was also a spiritualist and a feminist, was attacked for having the audacity to advise the state legislature on the suffrage question. At the same time she was accused of adultery and other misconduct.[12] Suffragists were usually portrayed as a strange group of "intellectual Amazons."[13] If possible their arguments were publicly dismissed as "entertaining, but not very profound."[14] The highest compliment ever bestowed on a feminist in the pages of the *Enterprise* was given to Elizabeth Cady Stanton, when the editor asserted that "her reasoning is manly."[15]

The belief in women's lack of intelligence combined with the belief in their physical weakness to legitimate their exclusion from full participation in political life, as well as in the labor force. The belief in feminine intellectual and physical weakness supported the assertion that women needed men's protection and implicitly supported marriage. If men were to entrust their homes and children to women, however, the fair sex had to have some good qualities and while they had many weaknesses, women were considered to possess greater moral strength than men. The belief in women's moral superiority affirmed their worthiness as matrimonial partners and also made women primarily culpable in adultery and prostitution. The myth of women's moral superiority included both a belief in mysterious womanly qualities of spirituality, innocence, and maternal instinct and a belief in minimal feminine sexuality. Belief in these two patterns of traits combined to make women responsible for men's and children's morality, as well as their own. The ideal of women's moral strength was also used to justify their exclusion from the public sphere where they might become contaminated by rough politics or rude commerce. One major argument against suffrage was that it degraded respectable women, and the ideal, refined, maternal wife was held up in contrast to "suffrage shriekers."[16] According to some Comstock antisuffragists, a good woman had all the political rights she desired because of the overwhelming moral influence she exerted on her husband: "She is the presiding priestess of the home and if she is gifted, and beautiful, and womanly, her influence is immeasurable."[17]

Suffrage advocates sometimes attempted to transform the theme of women's moral superiority into a telling argument in favor of increased political and economic participation. Thus, Elizabeth Cady Stanton urged a special audience of 125 Comstock ladies to be "natural, virtuous, and industrious."[18] Curtis J. Hillyer told the Nevada State Assembly that women's distinctive influence would change politics into a "social institution," since natural feminine morality made women potential saviors of corrupt political life.[19] This political assumption about women's innate morality had conservative implications and sometimes led to proposals for suffrage compromises. One such proposal on the Comstock offered women the vote on educational and temperance issues but on nothing else.[20]

The ideology of women's moral superiority widened the gulf between respectable and disreputable women. Good women were expected to uplift and guide men, and men were expected to protect ladies from contact with degrading individuals like prostitutes or sporting men. A young lady wrote the *Enterprise* to request police to clear C Street of "leering blackguards and bummers" because "We ladies have few rights to claim of the police in the absence of our husbands or other natural protectors, and one of them is protection from the insulting stare of these miserable things."[21]

Women merited protection when they stayed within their family circles, but they forfeited many of their claims when they became independent or aggressive. The ideal woman was passive, modest, retiring, moral, and instinctively maternal. Virtue was not only its own reward, but it was also an extension of femininity, for good women were both moral and asexual. The affirmation of feminine goodness and the denial of feminine sexuality produced a convoluted ideology which held prostitutes solely responsible for commercial sex.

Most medical and sexual advisors assumed that women entered marriage for maternal rather than conjugal reasons and sexual abstinence was often defined as a morally superior form of birth control. Wives were admonished to remain cold and indifferent in order to restrain their husbands' natural aggressiveness.[22] At the same time, prostitutes were often portrayed as unnaturally passionate nymphomaniacs. (In an interesting ideological shift, the current emphasis on women's naturally strong sexuality has produced widespread discussion of prostitutes' frigidity and unwillingness to show affection to customers.)

Groups in St. Louis, Chicago, Washington, D.C., Philadelphia, and New York City campaigned for regulated prostitution districts like those in France in the early 1870s. They argued that a system of registration and medical examination for prostitutes would allow patrons to find safe objects for their naturally volcanic passions. Social purity advocates and feminists successfully fought these efforts on the grounds that men should restrain their sexuality and elevate their characters as women had. Both groups, however, accepted the belief that men's sexuality was stronger than women's.[23]

Prostitution on the Comstock was supported by tacit acceptance of the belief in volcanic male sexuality, and that conception of sexuality legitimated prostitution because it implied that women had sexual choices which men did not have. Sexual behavior was one of the few areas in which women supposedly had the innate capacity to make more reasonable decisions than men. Women had the power to preserve their purity, to yield to seduction, or to overtly tempt, while men were helpless before their own sexual vitality. If they abandoned their natural morality to choose prostitution or other illicit sexual activities, women had betrayed their true natures.

Women who became prostitutes were blamed for either bending to unnatural sexual urges or bowing to unfeminine avarice. In either case, they were held accountable for prostitution and sometimes for other ills as well. Thus the Great Fire of 1875 which razed most of Virginia City was said to have been caused by a drunken prostitute who overturned an oil lamp. Common conceptions of prostitutes not only blamed them for their own downfall but also denied them any hope of redemption because "when a poor woman, to procure the necessities of life, sells her body for money we say she is lost."[24] These lost women were considered to be potentially polluting to others, and the people of Virginia City developed a whole set of customs to separate good and bad women.

Customs of Segregation

The customs segregating prostitutes and respectable women clearly signaled that ladies were better and different from prostitutes, reinforcing beliefs in respectable women's general superiority. Most of the customs regulated behavior in public places where prostitutes and wives might accidentally meet, and the customs had the latent function of protecting some patrons from embarrassing confrontations between their wives and their paramours. Similar customs can still be found in some places in Nevada where prostitutes refrain from speaking to respectable men in public.[25]

Custom was an invisible barrier between the respectable and disreputable communities on the Comstock. Respectable people took pride in constructing that barrier, asserting that their own moral and social control of the Comstock was evidence of the community's growing sophistication and stability. Louise M. Palmer was pleased to note, "Ladies of the *demi-monde* no longer expect to eat the dinners, and grace the parties of the *haute ton*."[26]

The financial rewards or deference granted to some prostitutes affronted respectable women who viewed themselves as inherently better than prostitutes. Mary McNair Mathews complained:

Many of the men support more women than the law allows them. They live after the Salt Lake style, only they are not so honorable as old Brigham [Young] was, for he married all his wives according to his religion. Here they marry but one, and the unmarried ones are always dressed the richest.[27]

When John Milleain, Julia Bulette's convicted assassin, was about to be hanged, he directed the following words to the ladies of the Comstock: "in Virginia City it is different; the public women are more respected than ladies."[28]

Milleain exaggerated the amount of respect prostitutes received, for women went to great lengths to avoid being labeled disreputable. Castellana Morales, who lived in the middle of the main bawdy district, swore in court that she was merely nursing a sick madam and repeatedly asserted, "I am not leading a life of prostitution, I swear positively."[29] Kitty Shea, who ran a lodging house on A Street, took out a notice in the *Enterprise* to announce that she was not the Kate Shea currently held in the county jail. However, those women's efforts to protect their reputations were negligible compared with those of Deborah Ann Phillips, who shot a man because he publicly called her "a damned whore."[30] The jury returned a verdict of justifiable homicide and she was fully pardoned by Governor Nye after a number of prominent Comstock residents petitioned him.[31]

The women involved in those incidents were especially vulnerable to the label of "prostitute," as they were all unattached and involved in regular public interaction with men, but even women of irreproachable virtue initiated and conformed to customs separating them from women of ill repute. The symbolic contrast between respectable women and prostitutes increased the general social value of the former group. More practically, in excluding prostitutes from social events, respectable women monopolized men's attention at those gatherings. The separation of prostitutes, however, had more obvious material grounds as well as status goals. Many bawdy women were offensive, nasty, and occasionally violent and the sporting men and ragged customers whom they attracted were even worse. These men made shopping and public walks miserable for "ladies of ordinary modesty" who were startled by their "insolent staring and offensive remarks."[32]

In order to avoid unpleasant incidents respectable people often barred prostitutes and their consorts from public dances.[33] The Horrible Club informed *Enterprise* readers that security guards would permit no disreputable characters at the group's Independence Day masquerade.[34] Ladies were requested to purchase tickets in advance because the Turn Verein wanted to turn away all objectionable characters from its annual ball.[35] The elite December Twenty-Eighth Carnival Committee attempted to exclude disreputables by issuing tickets by invitation, making them nontransferable, and posting a committee at the door to ask guests to unmask before they entered.[36] Some organizations, however, were more lenient because their membership included a number of unattached males, and the Young American Engine Company No. 2 kept its picnic and dance entirely respectable, but allowed more merriment at the grand masquerade ball as the organizers announced:

Heretofore no ladies but those of known respectability have been admitted, but to-night [*sic*] the doorkeepers will not seek to look beneath masks worn either in or upon the face.
This allows all who want to amuse themselves to do so.[37]

Prostitutes and ladies were also separated at the theater where people complained about "the many loose women parading on the stage," and theater owners made efforts to shield ladies from unsavory actresses and audiences.[38] Piper's Opera House held special ladies' nights of legitimate drama or light entertainment and ladies' and childrens' matinees. At ladies' nights Piper allowed no smoking, no drinking, and nothing "said or done of a nature to shock the feelings of any that might attend."[39] When ladies attended the theater they usually sat in the dress circle, and on those evenings prostitutes were ushered into the gallery.[40] On the night of her death Julia Bulette was not permitted to enter Piper's Opera House by the front door and she chose to return home rather than sit in the gallery.[41]

Some separation of prostitutes and respectable women was based on specific behaviors. Prostitutes smoked cigarettes and ladies not only eschewed tobacco but on occasion also requested that no one smoke in their presence.[42] Prostitutes played billiards in public and ladies did not.[43] Some ladies were even offended when the Presbyterian minister mentioned prostitution in a Sunday sermon.[44]

In a burst of inspired animosity some delicate ladies revealed their full

fear and hatred of prostitutes by supporting Julia Bulette's alleged murderer. They made no speeches in Milleain's behalf, but they quietly
aided him while most Comstock men clamored for his hanging. Respectable women circulated a petition to the governor to commute Milleain's sentence from death to life imprisonment, visited him in jail, and
made sure that he drank wine and ate omelettes during the days following his conviction.[45] In his scaffold speech Milleain said:

I also thank the ladies of Virginia who came to see me in my cell and brought
with them consolation that only they could find for the circumstances.[46]

Prostitutes were ostracized from the respectable community's social
life and from respectable lodging and boardinghouses. Landlords advertised for tenants "recommended as being respectable."[47] Mary McNair
Mathews described how she treated dubious lodgers:

When I lived on A Street, I rented a suite of rooms to a couple of ladies, as I
supposed, but I soon found that they were actresses in a melodeon theater. I
told them I could not keep them any longer. Their month was only half up and I
refunded them the balance of their money. They asked permission to leave their
trunks until the next day.[48]

The issue of prostitutes' segregation involved more than ladies'
avoidance of unpleasant situations or ladies' assertions of social prerogatives. Their separation from the respectable community also articulated a
definition of morality and indicated who had the power to formulate it.
Residential segregation of most prostitutes in the bawdy districts was as
close as the respectable people of Virginia City could come to banning
prostitution. "Therefore, D Street was the condemned part of the
city."[49]

Legislating Prostitution

Attempts to limit and regulate prostitution on the Comstock were not
directly linked to any international or American social movements concerned with commercial sex, but the efforts of moral reformers in other
parts of the world undoubtedly influenced their activity on the Lode.
During the last half of the nineteenth century prostitution was considered to be *the* social evil in Great Britain and the United States, and the
traffic in women embodied the major social problems of urban poverty,
crime, disease, and exploitation.[50]

British reformers organized in reaction to the Contagious Disease Acts
which called for police to take prostitutes into custody and incarcerate

them in government hospitals if they were suspected of carrying venereal diseases. According to the reformers, that system deprived women of their constitutional rights under Magna Charta and habeas corpus, involved a presumption of guilt rather than innocence, led to possible degradation of pure but poor women, punished prostitutes alone and not customers, and facilitated police corruption.[51] After militant campaigns the acts in Britain were finally revoked in 1885. St. Louis was the only American city to enact legislation similar to the Contagious Disease Acts or the French regulation system, and the successful campaigns to repeal regulation contributed to a national climate in which prostitution could be publicly mentioned and debated.[52]

Although there was no formal antiregulationist movement in Nevada, both conservative arguments against government regulation and radical arguments against state support of the social evil were used to defeat bill which came before the state senate in 1873. It called for registration of all houses of ill fame and their inmates, appointment of a local physician to examine prostitutes weekly, and creation of a special prostitutes' hospital to be funded by a monthly six-dollar tax on prostitutes and a ten-dollar tax on brothel keepers. Under the bill's provisions prostitutes working alone were classified as brothel keepers.[53] Conservative antiregulationists opposed the bill because it was to explicit and because it would be too hard for small towns to enforce registration and finance regular physical examinations, and radicals argued against it because it "gives licentiousness an intolerable license and protection."[54]

In 1877, a year of antiprostitution agitation on the Comstock, the state passed a new vagrancy law which included prostitution in its provisions. The statute extended previous legislation to include a penalty of up to ninety days for

> every lewd and dissolute male person who lives in and about houses of ill fame [pimps], also every lewd and dissolute female person known as a "street walker" or common prostitute, who shall upon the public streets or any saloon, barroom, club room, or any place of resort for men, or anywhere within the sight or hearing of ladies or children, conduct herself in an immodest, drunken, indecent, profane, or abusive manner, either by actions, language, or improper exposure of her person.[55]

If that law had been strictly enforced it could have wiped out most of the Comstock's lone prostitutes, waiter girls, melodeon entertainers, and brothel employees. By the time that statute was passed, however, the Comstock was slipping into its final depression and the police in the disintegrating community could do little to enforce morality. The new statute was so general and so widely applicable that it was impractical, and many of its provisions appeared in earlier Virginia City ordinances which were equally difficult to enforce where prostitution was an integral part of social life.

The Virginia City board of aldermen regulated most prostitution on the Lode because of their jurisdiction over the major bawdy districts. They passed three interdependent categories of ordinances affecting prostitution. One category stipulated licensing conditions for hurdy houses, melodeons, and saloons employing waiter girls. The second set regulated the public conduct of prostitutes and their likely customers. Finally, the most debated ordinances limited the location of houses of ill fame.

When the first local licensing law for dance houses was passed in 1863 the lone men who dominated the Lode scoffed at it, and when an unlicensed house on C Street was shut down the *Gold Hill News* commented that the sheriff was "always putting one or another of his big feet into it and spoiling other people's fun."[56] The license fee for dance houses was sustained and a new licensing ordinance for melodeons was modeled on the dance house ordinance.[57] In 1867 the board of aldermen extended licensing provisions to all saloons with waiter girls, requiring owners to pay a quarterly license fee for each woman they employed.[58]

The licensing ordinances were designed to generate revenue, but they could also be used to regulate prostitution and shut down enterprises which disturbed respectable neighborhoods or which were unusually disorderly. If a hurdy house, melodeon, or bawdy saloon owner were convicted of running a disorderly house the aldermen could revoke his or her license, as they finally did in Nellie Sayers's case.[59] Usually proprietors were only charged with disorderly conduct after a number of taxpayers had formally petitioned the police or the board of aldermen.[60] However, even if the police acted on a complaint and an owner were convicted, the conviction would be necessary but not sufficient for license revocation.

Licensing ordinances were directed at the owners of sporting resorts rather than the women working for them. In 1878, however, a new ordinance was passed to regulate conduct within saloons and it directed penalties at employers and employees alike. In order to make saloons less rowdy during the day and allow respectable women and men to pass them without harrassment, waiter girls were prohibited from working between the hours of six in the morning and six in the evening, and only the wives and daughters of saloon proprietors could work in them during the day.[61] This ordinance also made it easier for the overextended police force to focus its efforts to keep order during the evening, by prohibiting some situations likely to lead to disorderly behavior.

Disorderly conduct, the second category under which Comstock prostitution was regulated, became an early focus for the original Virginia City board of trustees, who were mandated to legislate against public drunkenness and fighting.[62] The early disorderly conduct ordinance was soon amended to prohibit publicly exposing one's person, making lewd and indecent gestures, and voicing profane or lewd noises in public.[63] Prostitutes were often guilty of some of those behaviors when they solicited customers in public places, as were men consorting with prostitutes or harassing respectable women.

Other ordinances regulated types of disorderly conduct common to prostitutes alone. It was an offense for women of ill repute to entice patrons by displaying themselves, wearing provocative clothing, or calling to them in loud voices.[64] Regulations passed in 1875 also required prostitutes to hang curtains or blinds in their windows, making it more difficult for women in cribs, single rooms, or small houses to advertise themselves.[65]

Disorderly conduct ordinances could theoretically affect both women and men, but occasional arrest reports published in newspapers suggest that the ordinances were most often enforced against prostitutes.[66] The ordinances limiting vulgar public behavior were biased against working-class prostitutes who routinely solicited customers in public places, and they had little long-term influence on prostitutes of upper and middle rank. Those women were more likely to be affected by a third set of ordinances formally limiting the location of houses of ill fame and the residences of individual prostitutes. Those regulations at once condoned and condemned prostitution, implicitly acknowledging its necessary place in social life and explicitly isolating it in special parts of the city.

The bawdy quarters were zoned and rezoned throughout the boom years, yet like Virginia City itself their contours remained fundamentally the same. The corner of Union and D streets was always the heart of the main bawdy district and Chinatown was fixed at the city's northwest end. The first location ordinance, passed in 1865 nine months after Virginia City was officially incorporated, called for fines against property owners whose premises were used by prostitutes outside a restricted area west of D Street, south of Sutton Avenue, and north of Mill Avenue.[67] There are no records of fines being levied, although the main bawdy district and the Barbary Coast both extended well south of Union Street.

The city directory for 1868–1869 listed even tighter, less realistic limitations, confining prostitution to a two-block area and stipulating fines against prostitutes dwelling outside the tiny restricted district. That ordinance also provided that half of all fine money would go to informants, but the law was far too strict to effectively control the actual location of prostitution.[68] In 1875 a more realistic ordinance enlarged the boundaries to include the area between D and F streets from Union Street to Mill Avenue.[69] Those red-light district boundaries stood through 1880, with slight modifications in 1878.[70]

Of all the local ordinances dealing with prostitution, those regulating prostitutes' residential patterns were the most blatantly ignored. Although prostitutes were concentrated in the D Street quarter and in Chinatown, which was regulated under separate ordinances, they could be found in many other neighborhoods. The ordinances' primary functions were symbolic rather than practical. They affirmed the respectable community's power to pass laws supporting its moral world view, although the actual effect of the ordinances indicated that community's relative powerlessness to shape the city in its image. None of the three categories of ordinances did much to eliminate prostitution, but each ordinance testified to the material and moral fissures crosscutting the Comstock.

Social Conflict and Prostitution Ordinances

It is somewhat surprising that people on the Comstock tried to control prostitution at all, since most of them accepted it as a necessary if annoying evil. Why would anyone bother interfering with consensual sex when people were dying in mine disasters, shooting each other in the streets, and misbehaving in every imaginable way? Prostitution certainly troubled respectable people, but it only became a public issue because they felt they could control relatively defenseless women of ill repute by means of formal legislation. Most citizens' complaints about sexual commerce were voiced at times when there were enough social control resources to regulate prostitution minimally and when the Comstock had some semblance of basic civic order.[71]

Custom and law testified to the negative attitudes respectable people held toward prostitutes, but despite their often vehement attitudes, few respectable citizens engaged in overt activities against women of ill repute. There was only one incident of collective violence against prostitutes when men and women living in the neighborhood smashed and gutted a dive on the Divide during the depression of 1870.[72] Their

action foreshadowed the vigilantes of 1871 who focused on male outlaws, and both groups acted during the trough of a local and national
depression when there were few social control resources on the Lode. In
spite of "the talk . . . that several more of the chebangs will be cleaned
out unless the owners of them mend their ways," there were no other
incidents of collective violence against prostitutes on the Comstock.[73]

Opposing economic interests embedded in the Lode's social structure
modulated attacks on prostitution. The fights to limit the location of
prostitutes and control disorderly drinking establishments involved two
different sets of businessmen. Merchants, craftsmen, and proprietors
bent on preserving order in the commercial districts were in conflict with
investors who leased land or buildings to bawdy enterprises or who were
silent partners in them. Members of both groups usually maintained
respectable facades, and it would be useful to characterize them as orderlies and investors rather than as respectables and disreputables.

The individuals dedicated to maintaining order by and large gave up
on D Street and concentrated their efforts on cleaning up C Street. A list
of signers of one petition to remove the "noisey nuisance" of the Eureka
Saloon and summaries of other petitions indicate that most of the campaigners for order were men whose businesses were adversely affected by
the presence of nearby brothels and bawdy saloons.[74] In 1867, the board
of aldermen received a petition clearly articulating those businessmen's
needs, as they requested the aldermen to direct police to remove prostitutes from C Street because it was the city's principal business
thoroughfare and ladies (customers) were compelled to pass prostitutes
while doing their shopping. The presence of prostitutes cut down the
flow of customers.[75]

When vagrancy and location ordinances were enforced more strictly
near C and Union streets, the businessmen's campaign shifted to the
Barbary Coast on South C Street. Crusaders for order petitioned the
aldermen either to close the disorderly dens on the Barbary Coast or to
keep them within "the bounds of propriety," because they hurt
neighboring respectable businesses.[76] After the Fourth Ward School
opened nearby, orderly businessmen again attempted to take over the
Barbary district, bolstering their arguments by pointing out the proximity of prostitutes to innocent schoolchildren. Citizens' complaints
finally led to three saloonkeepers' convictions for disorderly conduct, and
by the summer of 1877 respectable businesses had replaced almost all of
the saloons on the Coast.[77]

Although there was little public reaction against attempts to outlaw
prostitution from reputable commercial districts, private opposition im-

peded the aldermen's ability to revoke licenses or call for strict enforcement of bawdy district boundaries. Most aldermen depended on both respectable and disreputable constituents, and they probably were reluctant to side entirely with one or the other group. The men and women with real estate holdings or investments in dubious enterprises worked behind the scenes to defeat ordinances limiting the location of prostitution. In 1877 the *Chronicle* exposed State Senator and former Alderman John Piper's conflict of interest in owning land and buildings housing brothels and his arguing publicly against the enforcement of location ordinances on the grounds that the limitations inflicted hardships on property owners.[78] Other property owners warded off citizens' requests that a grand jury be convened to investigate individuals owning or in the process of building houses for prostitutes located outside of the restricted districts.[79]

Small businessmen were most likely to petition to limit the location of houses of ill fame, but working-class people residing near brothels and bawdy saloons sometimes complained publicly about the disruption of neighborhood peace.[80] The complaints of both groups, however, seldom resulted in the containment of prostitution. Organized commercial sex was too profitable and too necessary to the community's social structure to be seriously regulated. The earnest attempts to legally control prostitution on the Comstock in part represented class interests, but they also symbolized more ephemeral status interests.

Antiprostitution activity on the Comstock was most likely to occur during periods of consolidation when the chaos following a bonanza strike had died down and during periods of recession prior to the onset of full depression. Almost all local ordinances, citizens' complaints, and newspaper campaigns against the social evil occurred in 1863 and in 1874 and the first half of 1875 when the Lode was consolidating after great ore strikes, and from 1867 through early 1869, and 1877 through mid-1878, when recession in the mining economy suddenly reversed general prosperity. These were the only eight years of twenty in which there was much public activity of any kind designed to control prostitution. During those years minimal social control resources were still available, but the respectable middle class was losing its feeble grip on civic order. Public activities against prostitution were an attempt by respectables to symbolically reassert their moral authority over everyone else on the Comstock.

Prostitution negated the general values which affirmed the social status of the respectable middle class. Order, hard work, reticence, religion, and concern for family life had no place in the teeming bawdy community.[81] When the Comstock's economic organization was in extraordinary flux and no single group had consolidated its social status or political power, segments of the respectable community battled prostitution in an attempt to control their own lives. Structured nuclear families were a key underpinning of respectable middle-class life, and antiprostitution activists sought to segregate prostitutes from their pure wives and innocent children.

The ideology, customs, and laws stigmatizing prostitutes did not mirror a unified "collective consciousness" on the Comstock, but they instead reflected competing social values and material concerns. Although prostitutes were far less harmful to the community than violent male outlaws or stock manipulators who caused the great crashes on the San Francisco stock exchange, women of ill repute became targets for social action because they were among the few symbols of the Lode's social chaos which respectable people believed they could control. In attempting to control prostitution people affirmed their own ideal of an orderly way of life and also created a sense of solidarity among themselves. Prostitutes became scapegoats for the uncertainty and social disorganization that were part of the social life on the mining frontier.

8

Lessons from the Lode:
Theoretical Considerations

"It Wasn't God Who Made Honky Tonk Angels"
J. D. Miller

THE VARIED LYRICS from folk songs and ballads quoted at the beginning of each chapter suggest the diverse images of prostitution which have combined to become a clear thread in the fabric of American culture. Those images are with us today in "Honky Tonk Woman," "The Queen of the Silver Dollar," and other contemporary songs, stories, and legends. Prostitution is so compelling a topic because it combines nothing more and nothing less than the most basic elements of life—work and sexuality. Our social identities and self-conceptions are organized around the daily projects at which we labor and the web of emotions drawing us to other people (sexuality in the broadest sense).

Ideally, work in the public sphere is separated from conscious sexuality, but in prostitution sex and work are one. The money customers have earned allows them to purchase sexual contact from prostitutes who live by bartering their own sexuality. Sex is transformed into work, and prostitution is at once so fascinating and so frightening because it represents the fusion of two necessarily differentiated parts of human experience. The stigma associated with Comstock prostitution is still visible today because sexual commerce violates the boundaries separating public work from private sexuality. Prostitutes were and are public women because they offer a deeply personal part of themselves in exchange for financial remuneration.

A full theory of prostitution must be a theory of human society itself, for sexual commerce is rooted in fundamental material and ideological structures. Prostitution represents the extraordinarily complex interactions of sexuality, sex roles, and social structure at every level of social organization—psychodynamic, face-to-face interaction, community, societal, and work system. No single theoretical framework has offered an adequate synthesis of those levels, and probably no single theory can. This concluding chapter will draw from the case of the Comstock to sketch some theoretical considerations about prostitution in terms of several different sociological paradigms. While the theoretical implications presented at the end of various other chapters have been specifically linked to the mining frontier, those discussed here have wider significance, and are suggested, but not necessarily demonstrated, by the extreme case of the Comstock Lode.

Defining Prostitution

The legend of the frontier prostitute focuses on female prostitutes alone, and all of the identifiable sellers of commercial sex on the Comstock were women. Throughout this book the term "prostitution" has referred to female-male transactions, but while most prostitutes in the United States were and are women, it should be noted that for more than a century a significant amount of sexual commerce has involved male or child sellers and male customers.[1] Homosexual and child prostitution are special cases since they are offenses against social definitions of appropriate sexual orientation and object choice, as well as violations of norms condemning commercial sex. The existence of those special forms of prostitution, however, must be considered in any definition or discussion of commercial sex. It is important to develop a full sociological definition of prostitution which can encompass all its forms in order to use the case of the Comstock Lode to frame general theoretical issues about sexual commerce.

Different cultures and subcultures have defined and responded to prostitution in different ways, and a useful definition must be historically specific. Since the post–Civil War period of the Comstock boom, almost all prostitution in the United States has involved the same general activities and social meanings and this definition will deal with prostitution in the modern United States. Of course premarital chastity is now less important than it was in the late nineteenth century, and it is now far easier for prostitutes to change occupations, but the women of D Street would probably feel at home today in New York's Times Square or San Francisco's Tenderloin. Prostitution then and now involves directly communicated sexual barter characterized by promiscuity, impersonality, and affective neutrality.[2]

Directly communicated exchange of sexual contact for financial consideration is the central element defining American prostitution. Customers may also visit prostitutes for companionship or enhancement of their own social status, but unless their formal goal is sexual release they are involved in something other than prostitution. Although they were supporting prostitutes, the men who visited Cad Thompson's parlor to chat and listen to the piano or trouped to the Alhambra Theater to ogle the shapely performers were not directly engaged in prostitution. Even those patrons who found solitary release while watching bawdy stage shows were not immediately involved in transactions with prostitutes, because they did not communicate with them in order to find satisfaction. Prostitution need not include genital contact, but it necessarily involves both the customer's goal of sexual release and direct, face-to-face interaction with a prostitute to facilitate it.

Prostitutes exchange sexual compliance for financial considerations, and much of the transaction's appeal for each party rests on its promiscuity, impersonality, and affective neutrality. (I am assuming the familiar two-party form of prostitution, although I am aware that some prostitution includes several customers and/or prostitutes in interaction.) On the Lode customers and prostitutes alike were ideally free to engage in sexual activity with as many partners as they wished. Promiscuity, however, is often tempered by patrons' desires for lengthy or exclusive access to particular prostitutes, and they may want any combination of extended sexual contact, peusdo-intimacy, or increased control over the relationship. When exclusivity supplants promiscuity, kept prostitutes like Laura Fair gain temporary financial security and social anonymity at the risk of financial and emotional dependence on one patron. Emotional investment is diminished by promiscuity combined with impersonality and affective neutrality.

The impersonality associated with prostitution permits both parties to present superficial facades to one another and to mitigate their own potential feelings of shame. Impersonality separates prostitution from everyday life, allowing it to be rationalized as just another personal service in which each party has limited, immediate claims.[3] It protects prostitutes and customers from revealing too much of themselves and makes it easier for each of them to deny that their "real" selves are engaged in sexual barter. Impersonality was the source of Comstock prostitutes' using a number of false "working names" or modern prostitutes referring to all of their customers as "johns."

Affective neutrality, the lack of emotional involvement, is deeply intertwined with promiscuity and impersonality. In an ideotypic transaction neither prostitute nor customer partakes of emotional intimacy and their mutual obligations end with each exchange. The customer pays for a commodity, sexual contact, and nothing more. Prostitutes or madams usually request advance payment to emphasize the limits of the exchange and also to make sure that the customer will not shift the transaction after the fact and refuse to pay.

The three neutralizing mechanisms are never absolutely found in actual prostitution, for it involves people who can seldom dehumanize themselves or one another by totally denying their own predispositions and emotional responses. Instead, promiscuity, impersonality, and affective neutrality are definitional characteristics which must exist to some extent within any exchange we now call prostitution in the United States. They are the mechanisms separating sexual and emotional intimacy in prostitution and making it a form of service work within the irregular marketplace rather than a labor of love. Those characteristics, however, are camouflaged and mixed with real or pseudo-intimacy in high-status forms of prostitution. The stratification system within prostitution on the Comstock and elsewhere reflects customers' willingness to pay more for exclusivity, companionship, charm, or talent, as well as the fact that visible, blatant forms of prostitution are common targets of public condemnation.

Stigmatization is an essential aspect of modern American prostitution. Some scholars have stretched general definitions of sexual commerce to include ancient religious prostitution and North African ritual prostitution to earn a dowry, but those customs could not be defined as prostitution in modern America because they are socially encouraged and sellers are motivated by a collective goal. Prostitution in the United States is necessarily outside the moral boundaries of the dominant social order, and prostitutes and sometimes customers as well always suffer some social degradation.

Prostitution is socially functional to the community in which it exists because it is set apart from approved relationships such as marriage. The invisible boundary between acceptable behavior and prostitution provided respectable people on the Comstock with an affirmation of their own morality and right to define what was right and wrong. Its very deviance is part of the psychic lure of prostitution for prostitutes and patrons alike. Prostitutes, moreover, provide sexual services which are often hard to find because of normative or legal prohibitions, ranging from sex without social or emotional obligation to sadism to homosexuality. So long as prostitutes are at once tolerated and stigmatized they can serve as social safety valves offering those services while indicating the activities' inherent deviance. Acts of prostitution are not intrinsically "abnormal," but they must be labeled deviant in order to remain socially functional. A full sociological definition of prostitution includes all of those considerations and reads: *Prostitution is directly communicated sexual barter characterized by varying degrees of promiscuity, impersonality, and affective neutrality leading to informal or formal stigmatization of the seller and sometimes of the buyer as well.*

Social Class, Economic Organization, and Prostitution

The stigma of prostitution usually rests more heavily on sellers than on buyers, because prostitutes must earn their livings and organize much of their lives around sexual commerce. Prostitutes on the Lode seldom transcended public labels because of the clear social distinctions between respectable and disreputable women and because of the absence of available job alternatives to prostitution. So long as they remained on the Lode most prostitutes were virtually trapped in the fast life, but with the exception of Chinese women indentured or sold as slaves, Comstock prostitutes *chose* to be involved in sexual commerce.[4] Their choices, however, were shaped by the constraints of social class and women's marginality to the labor force.

Stratification within the fast life was so intricate and so far-reaching that it sometimes masked all prostitutes' shared relationship to the larger society. Despite their obvious class and status differences, prostitutes from madams to outcasts occupied a common vulnerable sexual status compared to respectable women and men on the Comstock. Prostitutes were public women with few rights to privacy because they were not identified with one lawful protector, they worked in a public sphere, and they were often objects of gossip or notoriety. Because the Lode was an isolated, densely populated community in which it was hard to conceal secrets, most women engaging in frequent acts of prostitution were publicly labeled as prostitutes and they probably came to act on those labels. Not everyone selling sexual contact, however, became or becomes a public person, receiving and internalizing the label "prostitute."

People gain the feeling and knowledge of who they are from others around them, and prostitutes take on their self-definitions from other people's responses.[5] They may be punished as prostitutes by legal authorities or rewarded and confirmed by their peers in prostitution. By and large, however, people who adopt prostitution as a central deviant identity and come to see themselves as prostitutes pass through some formal or informal degradation ceremony, an occasion on which an individual's total public identity is transformed into something lower in the scheme of human types.[6] Someone's whole self is devalued because of some achieved or ascribed nonconformity, and people who become prostitutes are often penalized for sexual misconduct. Their degradation ceremonies could range from arrest for homosexuality to imprisonment for solicitation to being publicly fired from a job or expelled from school because of unwed pregnancy. Other private, less formal ceremonies could involve ostracism from a group or family because of promiscuity or the violation of other sexual codes.

Not everyone who passes through a degradation ceremony accepts a devalued social identity, and whether or not the labels take hold depend in part on individuals' social and psychic resources. The social resources to resist negative labels are related to social class. For example, working-class and poor people have little recourse to professionals or alternative living arrangements which help more affluent people avoid formal degradation ceremonies of arrest, trial or hearing, or imprisonment. Once they have been formally labeled, moreover, most working-class people have few skills or financial resources to allow them to conceal their lowered moral status or seek out a viable new way of life. The ability to resist degradation ceremonies, especially formal ones, rests on a combination of self-esteem and social class.[7] Both social class and self-image influence decisions to become prostitutes, and so do more abstract aspects of economic organization: women's marginality and sex segregation in the labor force, the quality of working life, and demographic conditions.

Most Comstock prostitutes came from immigrant groups and from the working and lower classes, although representatives of every social group could be found in the bawdy districts. Because conditions of women's employment were so limited and so bad compared with those of today it is possible that a higher percentage of middle-class women became prostitutes on the Lode than do so currently. The supply side of female prostitution reflected the amount and type of legitimate employment open to women along with the quality of their working lives, and women's options for labor force participation are always key structural elements shaping overall prostitution rates. The few jobs available to Comstock women were menial, underpaid, and difficult, and some occupations like domestic service also held possibilities of unwelcome sexual advances from employers. Prostitution must have been a rational choice in comparison to many jobs or to unemployment.

Social critics writing on prostitution almost unfailingly mention the lack of employment opportunities for women as a central cause of female prostitution.[8] Female prostitution would not disappear if women and men were entirely equal in labor force participation, because the price of sexual services would undoubtedly climb with their scarcity and some women would probably retain emotional desires to become prostitutes. The supply of available prostitutes would probably decline, however, as it has in noncapitalist countries like Cuba, China, and the Soviet Union, where programs of full employment, state intervention, and rehabilitation have razed bawdy districts and produced extremely low reported prostitution rates. (The decline in prostitution in these countries has probably been overestimated by government sources. Nevertheless, skeptical foreign observers frequently comment on the new puritanism in cities like Havana, Shanghai, and Leningrad.)

The quantitative aspects of women's employment affect supply of prostitution, but so do the more qualitative aspects of working life, and the internal organization of labor on the Comstock undoubtedly affected both the supply and demand for prostitutes.

Women working in menial jobs were generally treated as unworthy of the respect accorded ladies, and some of them accepted the labels facilitating their entrance into the degrading life of prostitution. Working men were also often treated like interchangeable parts in the machines of the mines and ore mills, and miners labored under inhuman conditions, facing heat and danger of fatal accident. Danger at work and boredom in cramped lodging houses created tensions which were partially dissipated in the bawdy districts. The quality of work everywhere affects both the supply and demand for prostitution; for as people are treated like objects rather than individuals in their daily labor they learn to think of themselves and others that way, and they can more easily reduce personal, individual sexual interaction to an objective exchange of physical contact for remuneration.[9]

Labor force composition and the quality of work were not the only structural features sustaining supply and demand for prostitution on the Lode, and the large number of unattached men combined with the scarcity of single women to contribute to the high rate of prostitution. The imbalanced sex ratio reflected wider economic trends spurring migration and immigration to the boomtowns promising riches or at least offering jobs. Because geographic mobility is such an essential part of American life, the economic causes of prostitution cannot be isolated within a single community.

The irregular marketplace was another aspect of economic organization on the Comstock encouraging prostitution, and the vice districts were tangible representations of the trade in illegal or morally questionable goods and services. Organized irregular markets made it possible for prostitutes to travel from city to city and easily locate themselves within irregular enterprises in the disreputable communities where men and women provided one another with social support for their marginality. Even on the Lode, the irregular marketplace was linked to worldwide trade in illegal or immoral goods and services, as prostitutes immigrated from China and South America, opium traveled from the Far East, and dubious investment schemes were touted in the European countryside. The irregular marketplace integrated prostitution into a system of differentiated, usually complementary criminal activities and channeled investments between illegitimate and legitimate economic sectors.

The supply side of female prostitution is affected by degradation ceremonies involving sexual conduct and by women's role in the labor force, but other economic factors influence both the supply and demand for commercial sex. They include the quality of working life, imbalanced sex ratios reflecting labor force composition, and organized, worldwide irregular markets. Most of those factors also affect other areas of social life in highly stratified, complex societies. When a society is stratified by class and also by reputability or disreputability, prostitution is merely an extreme form of stigmatized dirty work.

Prostitution as Dirty Work

Prostitution was the single largest female occupational category on the Comstock, and it shared common properties with some predominantly male occupations which also involved contact with people, objects, or activities which had no acknowledged place in respectable life. Dirty work, a term originating in the sociology of occupations, categorizes and explains labor which most people prefer to avoid, ignore, or forget.[10] It can be employed to place prostitution in a larger context, connecting it with respectable jobs sharing common characteristics. Those jobs are also stigmatized, because like prostitutes other dirty workers trade social esteem for remuneration and sell their moral sensibilities along with their labor power. A stratification system supporting a strict division of labor among social classes and between the sexes encourages the development of separate occupational dirty work in both the regular and irregular marketplaces.

Despite personal preferences almost everyone does some dirty work from cleaning toilets to informing on lax coworkers, although people with financial resources usually hire someone else to do as much of their dirty work as possible. Occasional dirty work, however, is quite different from the occupational dirty work which is a central aspect of its performers' lives. Just as not everyone selling sex is a prostitute, not everyone doing dirty work is a dirty worker.

Society has no place for the people and objects with whom dirty workers have routine contact. Dirty workers' jobs always involve waste, whether it is the human waste of habitual criminals or loathsome johns or the material waste of excrement, garbage, or dead bodies.[11] Occupational groups like criminal attorneys, plumbers, physicians, or sex therapists also come into contact with socially discredited people or things, but they attempt to *transform* the discredited objects of their work into something or someone which is socially valued, while dirty workers simply dispose of unredeemable waste.

There are two theoretically separable types of dirty work, each of which contains some elements of the other. Social control dirty work involves the use or threat of sanctioned violence, and dirty workers routinely performing control-oriented labor include hangmen, uniformed police, mental ward orderlies, and other low-level workers in total institutions. Social maintenance dirty work covers a broader range of workers from janitors to undertakers to prostitutes. Power and discretion are found in social control and it may also be a prelude to later redemption, although that transformation is not part of the dirty worker's job. Maintenance dirty work, however, is without power or discretion or the possibility of transformation and it is the dirtier of the two types.

All dirty work requires few intellectual skills, and is relatively low in pay and status.[12] Jokes, nervous laughter, or quick attempts to switch conversational lines usually characterize outsiders' discussions of it, for all kinds of dirty work are generally impolite, socially veiled topics; although the basic objects of dirty work—shameful waste, death, and sex—are central to human experience. Prostitution is dirty work since it involves material and human waste. Prostitutes are receptacles for "wasteful" semen not associated with procreation or mutual pleasure. Also, all but very high status prostitutes deal with human waste in the form of customers who are visibly unattractive or who expect them to perform sexual acts generally considered offensive or perverse. Prostitutes are socially isolated in their odd hours and physical separation in formal and informal vice districts, and respectable people can ignore sexual commerce most of the time.

The criminal or semicriminal status of prostitution is insufficient to define it as dirty work, for skilled criminal occupations are sometimes widely respected and admired. Instead, prostitution is dirty work because of its social invisibility, general lower pay and status, and constant association with human or material waste. While most other kinds of dirty work are obviously important to society, prostitution is more problematic. It is not necessary in the same ways as clean streets or orderly disposition of criminals are, but it appears to be as emotionally central as those services are materially essential. No other form of dirty work has generated as widespread and rich folklore and legends, and while commercial sex may not be needed in the same ways as other dirty work, it is clearly an important part of our present social organization.

Prostitution, Sexuality, and Psychic Structure

There were many reasons why miners thronged to the Comstock's D Street district night after night and men like the young Alf Doten embarked on compulsive quests for sexual satisfaction. They had money to spend and tensions to dissipate, but the release patrons found with prostitutes could not be explained by simply equating tension with sexual excitation with genital satisfaction. Male sexuality had been *socially* defined as far stronger than women's, requiring nearly immediate genital release. Conscious and unconscious symbolization are mechanisms by which individuals internalize socially appropriate sexual pressure, aim, and object, and the psychodynamic process of that structuring can best be understood in terms of Freudian theory.

Prostitution is absolutely bound to patriarchy and the structure of emotional life as we know it because of its connection to the oedipal crisis. Sexual commerce symbolizes the differentiation between sexuality and emotional intimacy, which is both a difficult and a necessary part of early childhood socialization.[13] Much of prostitution's fascination for so many people lies in this separation of erotic impulses from feelings of tenderness and intimacy, and it is the only systematic interaction reducing sexuality to a pure exchange in which personal commitment has no place. The customer receives sex and the prostitute receives remuneration as each isolates sexual contact from realistic emotional warmth.

Mature sexuality, according to Freud, is a fusion of affection and eroticism, but the path to that maturity includes a number of barriers. All children's initial erotic feelings focus on their mothers, but they painfully learn to identify with their sex-appropriate parent and assume a heterosexual object orientation. Unconscious, inappropriate sexual impulses continue to develop throughout childhood, however, and surface during adolescence when internalized incest barriers direct them toward appropriate others with whom Freud said "a real sexual life may be carried on."[14]

Prostitution recalls early situations in which it was necessary to separate sexuality and affection, providing sexual outlets to individuals who have difficulty reconnecting eroticism and emotional warmth. It is the ultimate extension of the incest barrier, ideotypically splitting sexuality and affection and involving partners who are by and large strangers to one another. Sexual commerce separates and specifies sex instead of making it a diffuse property of interpersonal relationships, and customers and prostitutes alike can compartmentalize sexuality, removing it from their affective attachments.

There is a wealth of psychoanalytic writing tying prostitution to the early oedipal crisis of incestuous desire, but case histories of individual sexual psychopathology are far less important than the general theory explaining the symbolic importance of prostitution.[15] A great deal of prostitution's general appeal in fact and fantasy is linked to normal heterosexual growth, as it is revealed through the examination of neurotic development.

In an early article on variations in the choice of love objects, Freud discussed the reasons why some men were consistently attracted to women of dubious virtue.[16] Individuals making that "special type of object choice" find that their jealousy of other men in a woman's life heightens their own intense erotic interest. They can at once express their anger toward other men by possessing a woman who they desire and identify with those men at the same time. In essence they are reproducing feelings which they had during the oedipal period, when they sought their mothers while hating and wanting to identify with their fathers.

The incestuous oedipal triangle in which sons must learn to restrict their sensual feelings toward their mothers was also the key to Freud's discussion of impotence. Men unsuccessful in resolving the oedipus complex may actively seek sexual partners undeserving of the admiration which they consciously bestow on their mothers. Some men are entirely impotent with any woman who elicits esteem or tenderness, and others only achieve potency when they have degraded those women. Those are neurotic responses, but most men have some residue of unresolved conflict encouraging them to dichotomize good and bad women.

In only very few people of culture are the two strains of tenderness and sensuality duly fused into one; the man almost always feels his sexual activity hampered by his respect for the woman and only develops full sexual potency when he finds himself in the presence of a lower type of sexual object.[17]

That passage was written in post-Victorian Vienna where sexual ideology dividing good and bad women and separating maternity from sexuality molded many people's emotions and behavior, but a comparable ideology supported prostitution on the Comstock and to the extent that it is still influential it contributes to prostitution today. Even though current ideology minimizes those dichotomies, they are still necessary to men's achievement of masculinity, and thus they are powerful unconscious foundations for the traffic in women.

The process of becoming female is more externally and internally complicated than that of becoming male, and neither Freud nor later psychoanalytic theorists have fully mapped the feminine oedipus complex, although they defined its successful outcome as genital heterosexuality.[18] Somehow girls learn to deflect the erotic impulses they feel toward their fathers and toward their mothers onto appropriate adult love objects. Thus, women must also learn to differentiate sexuality and affection and then reconnect them in suitable situations.

Freud believed that forbidden sex objects like men who were otherwise attached were attractive to some women in the same ways that prostitutes were to some men.[19] Unlike men, however, most women do not need to degrade their object choices, but sometimes they only find sexual satisfaction in situations fraught with secrecy and intrigue. The forbidden male and the importance of complicated concealment reproduce some of the intense emotion of the feminine oedipal conflict. The stigma and secrecy associated with sexual commerce may make prostitution fantasies or prostitution itself compelling to women seeking Freud's "necessary condition of forbiddenness."

Women and men alike are drawn to prostitution because of the implicit presence of others in the transaction. Just as men may be neurotically attracted to women connected to other men, women may be enticed by men linked to other women. Prostitutes symbolically compete with the respectable women who are legitimately related to their customers and they also directly vie with other prostitutes seeking business. The usually invisible presence of third and fourth parties in prostitution may replicate the intimate rivalry between mothers and daughters occurring in the relational triangle with fathers.[20]

Classical psychoanalytic theory defines the oedipus complex as the central force behind emotional health and also behind neurosis. While it may not be critical to all human experience, oedipal conflict appears to be essential to people raised in nuclear families with a distinct sex-based division of labor. The oedipal crisis is crucial to the production of socially appropriate sex role identity in cultures where women mother the young and fathers assume secondary roles in family organization. While the unconscious structuring of the oedipal configuration cannot be measured or viewed, its manifestations and consequences in everyday life affirm its critical presence.

The many powerful feelings associated with prostitution and patronage have some of their roots in unconscious forces. On the Comstock the rigid dichotomization of prostitutes and respectable women went far beyond rationality and social functionality. Surely Alf Doten's compulsive patronage and Laura Fair's intense love triangle cannot be understood solely in terms of social forces. Material conditions alone did not cause Comstock prostitutes' high suicide rates. Psychoanalytic theory adds to the understanding of the hidden dimensions of prostitution unexplained by structural considerations.

Comstock prostitution was not a cloudy episode in psychohistory, and extensive material evidence has survived to document the effects of structural factors on sexual commerce. Theories of social structure and interaction explain most about prostitution and its internal stratification system, but something else is necessary to account for the depth of positive and negative feeling about the traffic in women. The theory of the oedipus complex uncovers the roots of fantasies and fears surrounding sexual commerce and those compelling collective images interact with structural forces to generate and sustain commercial sex.

Class, Patriarchy, and Prostitution

This case study of sexual commerce in a short-lived frontier community has revealed the depth and scope of the relationship between prostitution and social structure. That relationship is so complex that it is tempting to label prostitution "the oldest profession," and dismiss it as an unchanging element of human experience. But the situation on the Comstock obviously demonstrates that prostitution can and does change in response to social organization, and both the rate and the texture of sexual commerce have changed over the past century because of changes in economic structure. Today there is no major American city where women are so tangential to the respectable labor force as they were on the Lode, where men are so directly endangered by their labor, and where prostitution is so central to community life.

Prostitution has psychic foundations along with economic roots and the social patterning of parenting also contributes to the supply and demand for prostitution. So long as children are raised by mother figures in patriarchal households, many men will seek out disreputable women and some women will desire to become degraded. Men comprise the vast majority of sexual buyers and women the majority of sellers because of the structured male-female differences in emotional needs and sex roles and the sex segregation and discrimination against women in the labor force.

Identifiable Comstock prostitutes were all women, and most of them were degraded by their profession. I have focused on the elements of degradation in sexual commerce because they have overwhelmingly dominated American prostitution for more than a century. While a few prostitutes may live the golden legend of luxury and sexual satisfaction, most exist in material and emotional poverty. Investors, irregular entrepreneurs, pimps, and corrupt law enforcement officials usually absorb the profits, while prostitutes bear the primary burdens of physical abuse and responsibility for disease prevention and birth control. Women also receive the majority of moral and legal blame for their transactions because of dominant sexual ideology and discrimination in the criminal justice system, reflecting our deep cultural belief that selling access to one's body involves selling something that should not be included in the market economy.

Theories of psychosexual development and material structure are equally salient to a full understanding of sexual commerce, for prostitution reaches from the individual unconscious to the world economy. Material forces shaped the supply of prostitutes and the internal organization of prostitution on the Comstock, while psychodynamic motivation drew men to the bawdy districts and contributed to some individual women's decisions to enter prostitution. The symbolic dichotomization of good and bad women and of clean and dirty work are a bridge linking unconscious life to the material world in which prostitution is a crucial part of social life.

Appendixes

Appendix 1

I USED EVERY important primary and secondary source of data for the Comstock boom years from 1860 through 1880 in this study. Many sources were available because the community was unusually self-conscious of its own historical importance, and writers like Dan De Quille, Mark Twain, and Wells Drury entertained their contemporaries throughout the world with embellished anecdotes about the great silver boomtown. National interest in the Comstock undoubtedly facilitated the preservation of many documents, but it also made it necessary for me to sift truth from fiction and use as many types of data and kinds of analysis as possible. This strategy sometimes produced competing evidence which I usually weighed according to decision rules favoring unintentional sources.

The *Virginia City Territorial Enterprise* was a major resource for this study because it was the largest, best written, and most influential newspaper on the Lode. After I read an initial sample of thirty papers to obtain a sense of the newspaper's style and layout, I carefully noted the local news pages (two and three) in every surviving issue available at the Nevada Historical Society, Special Collections of the University of Nevada at Reno, and the Bancroft Collection at the University of California at Berkeley. An additional random sample of forty issues was later drawn to examine the advertising on page four in order to discover whether venereal disease cures or abortifacients were mentioned.

The *Enterprise* was founded in December, 1858, in Genoa, the seat of Carson County, Territory of Utah. Its publishers moved briefly to Carson City and then followed the early rush to the Comstock in November of that year. It began as a weekly, but became a daily on September 14, 1861, and was published every day in Virginia City until 1893.[1] Fires, natural disasters, and human carelessness have depleted the surviving *Enterprise* runs, and I could find only scattered issues of the paper until January, 1865 when consecutive issues were available. Daily issues were used from January, 1865 through December, 1880, with the exceptions of March, 1866; October 23 through December 31, 1867 and 1868; and January, 1869 and 1870.

The *Enterprise* was certainly biased, as a nationally circulating Republican paper with backers who had holdings in California banks and Comstock mines. Its tidbits of daily local news, however, seldom betrayed a systematic value orientation, and the regular filler items concerning prostitution were invaluable to this study. The newspaper had to be read issue by issue in order to capture the full weight of those brief notes on the fast life. It also published key public documents like city ordinances and weekly summaries of the meetings of the board of aldermen that have not survived anywhere else.

As a supplement to the *Enterprise*, I read the *Gold Hill Daily News* comprehensively from its first issue of October 12, 1863, through January, 1865, when complete issues of the *Enterprise* existed and whenever individual issues of the *Enterprise* were unavailable. Unlike the *Enterprise,* the *News* published few stories dealing with national or international events, and its editors concentrated on local stories. Even its local section, however, was less detailed than the *Enterprise* and almost half of the four-page *News* was filled with advertisements.

The *Gold Hill News* was an important paper because of its continuous publication from 1863 through 1882 and because Alf Doten was its associate editor for much of that time. There was a great deal of similarity between the *News* and the *Enterprise* because reporters for the two papers often worked and relaxed together. Mark Twain discussed how slow news periods forced reporters for the *News* and the *Enterprise* into joyous collaboration over exaggerated or invented stories, implicitly indicating the need to check most items against as many different sources as possible.[2]

Two other Virginia City newspapers were also important to add information about major events involving prostitutes. The *Virginia Daily Union* was the *Enterprise's* rival from 1862 through 1866. The *Virginia Evening Chronicle* was the other real competition, and it was published daily except Sunday from 1872 through August, 1927. I read those papers the same day, the day before, and the day after the *Enterprise* carried a long story about a prostitute's death or a scandal in the bawdy district or published a new local ordinance.

I used the *New York Times Index* from 1863 through 1880, and found that most of the nationally circulated reports of the Comstock were brief versions of those which had already appeared in local newspapers. The *Times* and two other national periodicals, *Harper's* and the *Overland Monthly*, contained far less news of the Nevada mining frontier than I had expected. They tend to cast some doubt on the popular belief that the Comstock remained in the forefront of the national consciousness throughout its boom years.

Newspapers were the major intentional source I used. There was also valuable, detailed information in contemporary magazine articles and in Mark Twain's *Roughing It*, Dan De Quille's *The Big Bonanza*, Thompson and West's *History of Nevada, 1881*, and Mary McNair Mathews' *Ten Years in Nevada*. I used other books as well, but found those to be the most useful contemporary accounts of social life on the Lode.

Important published unintentional sources included business and mining directories and journals of the Nevada State Assembly and Senate from 1864 through 1881. Government documents supplied no transcriptions of floor debates, but they reported on the introduction and subsequent fate of bills relevant to women and to prostitution. For almost twenty years Storey County *was* Nevada. It was the richest, most powerful, and most populated part of the state, and state legislative records were particularly relevant to social conditions on the Comstock.

The United States censuses and the special Nevada state census of 1875 were the central unpublished sources for this study. They provided a check against intentional sources and also yielded a gold mine of data on their own. Although I only skimmed the manuscripts of the territorial censuses for 1860 and 1861 and the United States census for 1870, I coded individual cases and used the Statistical Package for the Social Sciences for the 1875 Nevada state census and the 1880 United States census for Storey County. The 1875 census was a transcribed manuscript recorded in 1875, just before the largest of all fires swept the Comstock. I chose it because it was the only census taken during a bonanza period when there was a large general population, a maximum of prostitutes, and an established albeit flexible class structure. Moreover, the census was printed and it was easier to decipher than the flowery nineteenth-century handwriting found on the microfilmed manuscripts. I used the microfilmed manuscripts for 1880 because the Comstock's population was still fairly large at that time and it was the first census to list marital status and relationship to household head.

The manuscript censuses are superb sources of social science data that have just begun to be used, although they are now available at ten-year intervals from 1790 through 1900. They cannot be utilized without caution, however. The census consistently underrepresents poor people, recent immigrants, and others who fear the government.[3] In 1880 the *Enterprise* ran an editorial asking citizens to cooperate with census takers and not call them "Peeping Toms" or "Paul Prys."[4] Some prejudices, however, were rational, for census takers often secured their jobs through political patronage and hesitated to ask embarrassing questions, either leaving answers blank or making them up.[5] Figures on income in the Nevada state census, for example, must simply be ignored because they were so capriciously recorded. Another example of census takers' ineptitude occurred during the 1870s when it was customary for saloons and bawdy houses to invite them in for drinks, and in 1875 one census taker enumerated the same area of Virginia City's main red-light district twice—from either confusion or enjoyment.

These are a few examples of pitfalls in the census. The major one, however, is the slim possibility that people systematically lied to enumerators. This would have been difficult on the Comstock where enumerators were drawn from the community, but the only real checks against nonrandom dissimulation were the use of more than one census and the use of other data sources.

Prostitutes were identified if they were labeled by one of the many terms listed at the beginning of chapter 3; if they were given the euphemism of chambermaid, dressmaker, or housekeeper and lived beside identified prostitutes; or if they had no occupation listed and resided in the legally demarcated bawdy districts. Location was the key decision rule for unidentified prostitutes and it probably led to a slight underestimation of the total number. The use of this decision rule indicated the importance of collecting and assimilating qualitative data on a given population before using the census.

Census takers made their rounds in order, and the 1880 manuscripts listed street addresses although those of 1875 did not. The order was nonrandom, so it was best to collect data on the universe of women. I collected information about all Comstock women over eighteen years of age or listed as employed or married for 1875 and only on prostitutes for 1880.

I made decisions about women's relationship to household heads in 1875 according to decision rules developed by the Philadelphia Social

History Project at the University of Pennsylvania.[6] A woman was coded as married if she had the same surname as the man listed above her, if she were listed as a housekeeper or had no occupation listed, if she were no more than fifteen years older or younger than the identified household head, *and* if it were clear that she was not a child or sibling within a larger identifiable household unit. Other decisions were more obvious, requiring no clear rules.

A small but very important group of unpublished sources provided extraordinary information about daily life on the Lode. They included Alf Doten's diaries described in chapter 2, the three prostitutes' probates found in the Storey County courthouse, and photographs housed in Special Collections of the University of Nevada at Reno and the Nevada Historical Society. The Special Collections and the Historical Society also housed some valuable ephemera like theatrical handbills; menus; and cartes de visites, small cardboard mounted photographs used as visiting cards in the 1870s by respectable and disreputable people alike. I gained insights about the similarities and differences in past and present prostitution from a brief four-day fieldwork project in Ely, a modern Nevada mining town, and from conversations with various individuals in the San Francisco fast life.

Appendix 2
Roster of Comstock Prostitutes, 1880

Gold Hill

No.	Name	Probable Residence	Address
1.	Edith Francis	lodging house	29 Rayton
2.	E. Baden	crib	alley
3.	Lizzie Gladdings	crib	alley
4.	Angeline Swain	small house	1 Main St.
5.	Carrie R. Wood	small house	1 Main St.
6.	Annie Barbara	small house	452 Main St.
7.	Fannie Kent	small house	452 Main St.
8.	Myrna Harmon	shanty	none (near depot)
9.	Maggie Joyce	shanty	none (near depot)

Virginia City

No.	Name	Probable Residence	Address
1.	Fannie Ham	small house	95 N. Stewart
2.	Fannie Toye	small house	316 S. A St.
3.	Magdalena Gray	small house	40 S. B St.
4.	Sara W. Bartell	lodging house	24 S. B St.
5.	Kitty W. Vanderbilt	rooms above gambling hall	27 N. B St.
6.	Miss W. Montgomery	rooms above gambling hall	27 N. B St.

Virginia City—Continued

No.	Name	Probable Residence	Address
7.	Rose Sissa	owner's quarters of gambling hall	27 N. B St.
8.	Mary Conway	jail	N. B St.
9.	Emma Hall	jail	N. B St.
10.	Mary Orndorff	jail	N. B St.
11.	Lizzie Siles	jail	N. B St.
12.	Mrs. Ticle	jail	N. B St.
13.	H. M. Wall	jail	N. B St.
14.	Lizzie H. Cumasses	lodging house	57 N. B St.
15.	Mary Healy	lodging house	269 S. C St.
16.	Bessie Blum	lodging house	201 S. C St.
17.	Maggie McGivney	lodging house	194 S. C St.
18.	Fannie Palmer	lodging house	194 S. C St.
19.	Minerva Toforth	lodging house	194 S. C St.
20.	Sara Rodgers	lodging house	194 S. C St.
21.	Alice McMurray	lodging house	194 S. C St.
22.	Mary Skensen	rented rooms above saloon	174 S. C St.
23.	Alice Bryson	small house	106 S. C St.
24.	Annie B. Paddock	small house	106 S. C St.
25.	Rose Gigane	lodging house	103 S. C St.
26.	Alice Alston	lodging house	90 S. C St.
27.	Jennie Hamilton	crib	none (alley)
28.	Julia A. Drew	crib	none (alley)
29.	Rosa Cannen	lodging house	17 S. C St.
30.	Jenny Butler	lodging house	17 S. C St.
31.	Mary Sheehan	lodging house	17 S. C St.
32.	Mary Vernan	lodging house	17 S. C St.
33.	Maggie Johnson	lodging house	17 S. C St.
34.	Ida Maynard	rented rooms above saloon	37 N. C St.
35.	Sara Barnett	lodging house	67½ N. C St.
36.	Anna Graham	lodging house	67½ N. C St.
37.	Margaret Cluny	lodging house	141 N. C St.
38.	Mary Asberry	lodging house	141 N. C St.
39.	Nora Shay	lodging house	141 N. C St.
40.	Emma Mehennet	small house	250 S. D St.
41.	Emily Barnett	small house	250 S. D St.
42.	Julia Shay	brothel	197 S. D St.
43.	Louisa Stone	brothel	197 S. D St.

Virginia City—Continued

No.	Name	Probable Residence	Address
44.	Mary Larery	brothel	197 S. D St.
45.	Mary Manuel	rented room above saloon	61 S. D St.
46.	Emma Lacy	brothel	56 S. D St.
47.	Maud Raymond	brothel	56 S. D St.
48.	Nellie Peel	brothel	56 S. D St.
49.	Inez Leonard	brothel	56 S. D St.
50.	Mary Galarya	brothel	45 S. D St.
51.	Etta Stephens	brothel	45 S. D St.
52.	Katie Foster	brothel	45 S. D St.
53.	Sadie Severnay	crib	44½ S. D St.
54.	Amelia Sargent	crib	44 S. D St.
55.	Rose Duval	brothel	39 S. D St.
56.	Mamie Duffield	brothel	39 S. D St.
57.	Eliza Duffield	brothel	39 S. D St.
58.	Mary Allen	brothel	39 S. D St.
59.	Augusta Frost	crib	none (alley)
60.	Jane Robinson	brothel	34 S. D St.
61.	Hattie C. Robinson	brothel	34 S. D St.
62.	Tessa Goodwin	brothel	34 S. D St.
63.	Mary Browly	brothel	34 S. D St.
64.	Kate Amplar	lodging house	31 S. D St.
65.	Emma Henderson	rented room above saloon	27 S. D St.
66.	Gamil Valentine	small house	17 S. D St.
67.	Annie Wallace	small house	17 S. D St.
68.	Emma Wiler	crib	16 S. D St.
69.	Rocca Guppeace	crib	none (alley)
70.	Annie Miller	brothel	15 S. D St.
71.	Annie Burnett	brothel	15 S. D St.
72.	Kitty Caymont	brothel	15 S. D St.
73.	Emma Hall	brothel	15 S. D St.
74.	Caroline W. (Cad) Thompson	brothel	15 S. D St.
75.	Aimee Tousig	small house	14 S. D St.
76.	Mary Orndorff	small house	14 S. D St.
77.	Lena Baolis	cottage	13 S. D St.
78.	Annie Lake	cottage	12 S. D St.
79.	Emma Cuffman	cottage	9½ S. D St.
80.	Annie E. Higgens	cottage	7½ S. D St.
81.	Josie Mayfield	cottage	7 S. D St.
82.	Josephine Culave	lodging house	5 S. D St.

Virginia City—Continued

No.	Name	Probable Residence	Address
83.	Rebecca Collister	lodging house	5 S. D St.
84.	Maud Johnson	lodging house	5 S. D St.
85.	Sarrah Pottle	lodging house	5 S. D St.
86.	Mollie Wiston	brothel	1 N. D St.
87.	Jessie Winter	brothel	1 N. D St.
88.	Donnette Pomeroy	brothel	1 N. D St.
89.	Blanche Lebo	brothel	1 N. D St.
90.	Alice May	brothel	1 N. D St.
91.	Neattie Bassett	cottage	15 N. D St.
92.	Kittie Huff	small house	17½ N. D St.
93.	Kitty Mitchell	small house	17½ N. D St.
94.	Henrietta Gould	cottage	29 N. D St.
95.	Rose Pfonda	cottage	29 N. D St.
96.	Della Hitchcock	lodging house	134 S. E St.
97.	Lillie Barber	lodging house	47 S. E St.
98.	Mary Durant	crib	none (alley off E)
99.	Reinez Galino	crib	none (alley off E)
100.	Sophine Pinis	crib	none (alley off E)
101.	Camille Gimez	crib	none (alley off E)
102.	Mary McCloud	small house	44 S. F St.
103.	Alice Brison	small house	44 S. F St.
104.	Mary Dillard	lodging house	73 S. F St.
105.	Catherine Cain	shanty	none (alley off S. G)
106.	Bridget Cavanaugh	lodging house	11 S. G St.
107.	Jani Perry	boarding house	165 S. L St.
108.	Mollie Malone	rooms off saloon	418 Union St.
109.	Mary Doyle	rooms off saloon	418 Union St.
110.	Isabell Clark	small house	8 Taylor St.
111.	Mollie A. Farrell	small house	8 Taylor St.
112.	Ella Williams	small house	167 Noyes
113.	Lydia Newton	cottage	55 North St.
114.	Lyzetta Beaux	cottage	51 North St.
115.	W. F. McLaughlin	cottage	19 North St.
116.	Mary Dillard	shanty	none (outskirts)
117.	Johanna McDermot	shanty	none (outskirts)
118.	Sou Lee	opium den	67 Union St.
119.	Gee Ah	brothel	none (alley off I)
120.	Leu Ha	brothel	none (alley off I)
121.	Sing Ton	brothel	none (alley off I)

Virginia City—Continued

No.	Name	Probable Residence	Address
122.	Sing Ting	brothel	12 S. I St.
123.	Sing Haw	brothel	12 S. I St.
124.	Fin Lau	brothel	12 S. I St.
125.	Luh Chu	brothel	18 S. I St.
126.	Pau Gee	brothel	18 S. I St.
127.	Gow Gum	brothel	8 Chinatown
128.	Gow Gung	brothel	8 Chinatown
129.	Gun Choy	brothel	12 Chinatown
130.	Chung To	brothel	12 Chinatown
131.	Get Gu	brothel	12 Chinatown
132.	Sah Lin	brothel	20 Chinatown
133.	Ah You	brothel	20 Chinatown
134.	Ling Giu	brothel	20 Chinatown
135.	Cho Way Toy	brothel	20 Chinatown
136.	Ah Gin	brothel	none (Chinatown)
137.	Ah Choy	brothel	none (Chinatown)

Source: Information was gathered from the United States Census manuscripts of 1880.

Note: Types of residences were estimated from location and also from qualitative information in newspaper stories and probate records. Most of the dwellings are described in the text. Please note, lodging house refers only to those establishments in which prostitutes rented some rooms and disreputable men or working-class men rented others.

Notes

Introduction

1. *Virginia City Territorial Enterprise,* June 27, 1867.
2. For examples of the ways in which Julia Bulette was glorified see Zeke Daniels [Effie Mona Mack], *The Life and Death of Julia C. Bulette: Queen of the Redlights* (Virginia City, Nevada: Lamp Post Press, 1958); George D. Lyman, *The Saga of the Comstock Lode: Boom Days in Virginia City* (New York: Ballantine Books, 1971 [1934]), p. 208; and Warren Hinckle and Fredric Hobbs, *The Richest Place on Earth: The Story of Virginia City and the Heyday of the Comstock Lode* (Boston: Houghton Mifflin Co., 1978), pp. 53–54.
3. Doris Foley, *Lola Montez: The Divine Eccentric* (New York: Ballantine Books, 1973); Max Miller, *Holladay Street* (New York: New American Library, 1962); and Curt Gentry, *The Madams of San Francisco* (New York: Ballantine Books, 1971 [1964]), pp. 81–136.
4. Lucius Beebe and Charles Clegg, *Legends of the Comstock Lode* (Carson City, Nevada: Grahame H. Hardy, 1950), pp. 16–18.
5. *Gold Hill News,* January 21, 1867; and Papers Concerning the Estate of Julia Bulette, 1867–1868, Storey County Courthouse, Virginia City, Nevada.
6. Sigmund Freud, "A Special Type of Object Choice Made by Men" (1910) and "The Prevalent Form of Degradation in Erotic Life" (1912), collected in *Freud: Sexuality and the Psychology of Love,* ed. Phillip Reiff (New York: Collier Books, 1974), pp. 49–70; H. R. Hays, *The Dangerous Sex* (New

York: Pocket Books, 1972); and Wolfgang Lederer, *The Fear of Women* (New York: Greene and Stratton, 1968).

7. Zola Ross, *Bonanza Queen* (Indianapolis, Ind.: Bobbs-Merrill, 1949), p. 147.

8. Michael Carder [Vernon L. Fluharty], *Return of the Outlaw* (Philadelphia: Macrey Smity Co., 1954), p. 217.

9. Alf Doten's unedited diaries were an invaluable source for this book, and they are available in manuscript in the Special Collections of the library of the University of Nevada at Reno. An edited three-volume edition of the diaries published by the University of Nevada Press presents a unique, detailed picture of daily life on the Lode, but that edition omits some useful information about prostitution. Unless it is otherwise noted, all references to the Doten Diaries indicate the original manuscripts. Citations from the original manuscripts are by the date of each entry. Those dates are also included in the published edition, and researchers can easily compare the two sources. See Walter Van Tilburg Clark, ed., *The Journals of Alfred Doten: 1849–1903* (Reno: University of Nevada Press, 1973).

10. Kingsley Davis, "The Sociology of Prostitution," *American Sociological Review* 2 (October 1937):750.

11. For examples of the individualistic interpretation see Simone de Beauvoir, *The Second Sex* (New York: Alfred A. Knopf, 1962), chap. 19; Harold Greenwald, *The Elegant Prostitute: A Social and Psychoanalytic Study* (New York: Ballantine Books, 1970 [1958]); and William I. Thomas, *The Unadjusted Girl* (Boston: Little, Brown and Co., 1923).

12. The manuscript census for 1875 recorded more than nineteen thousand people living in Storey County. However, almost all observers estimated the population to be larger at the crest of the boom in 1873, 1874, and early 1875. See 1875 census manuscript transcribed in *Appendix to the Journals of the Senate and Assembly of the Eighth Session of the Legislature of the State of Nevada,* vol. 3 (Carson City, Nevada: John J. Hill State Printer, 1877), p. 615.

13. Some of the similarities between prostitution on the Comstock and in other American cities are apparent in William W. Sanger, M.D., *The History of Prostitution: Its Extent, Causes, and Effects Throughout the World* (New York: Eugenics Publishing Co., 1937 [1897]. A major section of this work deals with prostitution in New York City around 1858, when Sanger conducted interviews with 2,000 New York prostitutes. Another useful source is Gentry, *The Madams of San Francisco.*

14. Max Weber, *The Methodology of the Social Sciences,* trans. and ed. Edward Shils and Henry Finch (New York: Free Press, 1959), pp. 90–110.

15. Herbert Blumer, "Society as Symbolic Interaction," and "Attitudes and the Social Act," in *Symbolic Interactionism: Perspective and Method* (Englewood Cliffs, N.J.: Prentice-Hall, 1969), pp. 78–100.

16. E. P. Thompson, "Time, Work Discipline, and Capitalism," *Past and Present* 38 (December 1967):56–97. In this article Thompson superbly

describes the ways in which changing work organization led to changes in the temporal organization of daily life.

17. J. Wells Kelly, *First Directory of the Nevada Territory* (San Francisco: Valentine and Co., 1862), pp. 12–13. This gives the times of various state routes from San Francisco to Virginia City. For a sense of the fastest travel between the Comstock and Reno see W. Turrentine Jackson, "Racing from Reno to Virginia City by Wells Fargo and Pacific Union Express," *Nevada Historical Society Quarterly* (Summer 1977):75–91.

18. Barbara Ehrenreich and Deirdre English, "The Manufacture of Housework," *Socialist Revolution* 5 (October-December 1975):5–40.

19. Marc Bloch, *The Historian's Craft* (New York: Vintage Books, 1953), pp. 60–62.

20. Kai T. Erikson, "Sociology and the Historical Perspective," *American Sociologist* 5 (November 1970):332.

21. U.S. Bureau of the Census, *Historical Statistics of the United States, Colonial Times to 1957* (Washington, D.C.: Government Printing Office, 1960), p. 214. This is probably an underestimate of illiteracy. Literacy figures in Storey County were distorted in 1870 and 1875, when census takers counted all Chinese as literate—able to read and write English. This omission reflected anti-Chinese sentiment, as enumerators listed Asians as "Chinaman" or "Chinawoman" and seldom bothered to interview individuals. This may have been common throughout the western United States (Howard Zinn, *The Politics of History* [Boston: Beacon Press, 1970]).

22. For notes on problems about how records are saved and made available to the public, see Bloch, *The Historian's Craft,* pp. 69–78.

Chapter 1

1. *Gold Hill News,* October 31, 1963.

2. Thomas Harold Kinnersley, "Virginia, Nevada, 1859–1890: A Study of Police, Water, and Fire Problems" (Ph.D. diss. University of California at Los Angeles, 1974), p. 30.

3. Ibid., p. 31.

4. Mark Twain [Samuel Clemens], *Roughing It* (New York: Signet Classics, 1962 [1872]), pp. 228–29.

5. Louis Wirth, "Urbanism as a Way of Life," in *On Cities and Social Life,* ed. Albert Reiss, Jr. (Chicago: University of Chicago Press, 1964), pp. 62–66.

6. Ben J. Wattenberg, ed., *The Statistical History of the United States from Colonial Times to the Present* (New York: Basic Books, 1976), p. 2.

7. *Virginia City Territorial Enterprise,* February 25, 1875.

8. Louise M. Palmer, "How We Live in Nevada," *Overland Monthly* 2 (May 1869):459.

9. William R. Gillis, comp., *The Nevada Directory of 1868–69* (San Francisco: M. D. Carr and Co., 1868), p. 268. A number of city directories in the mid-nineteenth century also listed local ordinances.

10. *Territorial Enterprise,* August 1, 1868, January 6, 1874, and December 17, 1875.
11. Kinnersley, "Virginia, Nevada, 1859-1890," pp. 63-65.
12. Ibid., pp. 66-67.
13. Ibid., p. 43.
14. Dan De Quille [William Wright], *The Big Bonanza* (New York: Apollo Editions, 1969 [1876]), p. 297.
15. Russell R. Elliott, *History of Nevada* (Lincoln: University of Nebraska Press, 1973), pp. 125 and 133; Myron Angel, ed., *Reproduction of Thompson and West's "History of Nevada, 1881"* (Berkeley: Howell North, 1958), p. 620.
16. Elliott, *History of Nevada,* pp. 144-51.
17. Kinnersley, "Virginia, Nevada, 1859-1890," pp. 71-72.
18. Ibid., pp. 69-70.
19. Ibid., pp. 59-60.
20. Ibid.
21. Alfred Doten Diaries, Special Collections of the University of Nevada at Reno, April 18, 1868; and *Territorial Enterprise,* December 2, 1875.
22. *Territorial Enterprise,* June 1t, 1872.
23. Curt Gentry, *The Madams of San Francisco* (New York: Ballantine Books, 1971 [1964]), p. 51.
24. Richard G. Lillard, *Desert Challenge* (Lincoln: University of Nebraska Press, 1969 [1949]), p. 212.
25. Robert B. Merrifield, "Nevada, 1859-1881: The Impact of an Advanced Technological Society upon a Frontier Area" (Ph.D. diss., University of Chicago, 1958), p. 135.
26. Elliott, *History of Nevada,* pp. 123-25.
27. Kinnersley, "Virginia, Nevada, 1859-1890," p. 39.
28. Ibid., p. 42.
29. Elliott, *History of Nevada,* pp. 135-37.
30. Merrifield, "Nevada, 1859-1881," p. 181.
31. De Quille, *The Big Bonanza,* pp. 307-8.
32. Elliott, *History of Nevada,* pp. 134-35.
33. Ibid., pp. 134-7.
34. Merrifield, "Nevada, 1859-1881," p. 225.
35. Angel, *Reproduction of Thompson and West,* pp. 612a and 612b.
36. Kinnersley, "Virginia, Nevada, 1859-1890," p. 54.
37. Merrifield, "Nevada, 1859-1881," p. 33.
38. Ibid., p. 163; and *Territorial Enterprise,* September 11, 1977.
39. Merrifield, "Nevada, 1859-1881," p. 162.
40. Elliott, *History of Nevada,* pp. 142-44.
41. Merrifield, "Nevada, 1859-1881," p. 33.
42. Mary McNair Mathews, *Ten Years in Nevada or Life on the Pacific Coast* (Buffalo: Baker, Jones and Co., 1880), p. 171.

43. Helen L. Sumner, *Report on the Condition of Women and Child Wage Earners in the United States,* vol. 9, *History of Women in Industry in the United States* (Washington, D.C.: Government Printing Office, 1910), p. 11.

44. See Nevada Legislature, *Appendix to the Journals of the Senate and Assembly of the Eighth Session of the Legislature of the State of Nevada,* vol. 3 (Carson City, Nevada: John J. Hill State Printer, 1877). This volume is a transcription of the special state census of 1875. I cross-tabulated ethnicity with women's occupations, but with the exception of lodging and boardinghouse keepers, there was no strong relationship between respectable women's occupations and their ethnic origins.

45. *Territorial Enterprise,* March 9, 1879; Mathews, *Ten Years in Nevada,* p. 135; and Doten Diaries, October 12, 1874.

46. Sumner, *Report on the Condition of Women,* p. 183.

47. *Territorial Enterprise,* November 19, 1874.

48. Twain, *Roughing It,* p. 299.

49. *Territorial Enterprise,* June 24, 1876, and March 9, 1879.

50. Palmer, "How We Live in Nevada," p. 461.

51. *Territorial Enterprise,* April 6, 1866.

52. Mathews, *Ten Years in Nevada,* pp. 39–40.

53. Mathews, *Ten Years in Nevada,* p. 14.

54. *Territorial Enterprise,* April 4, 1863.

55. Ibid., November 2, 1877; and Mathews, *Ten Years in Nevada,* p. 137.

56. *Territorial Enterprise,* July 28, 1877.

57. Ibid., June 26, 1877.

58. Nevada Legislature, *Statutes of the State of Nevada Passed at the Third Session of the Legislature,* 1867 (Carson City, Nevada: Joseph E. Eckley State Printer, 1867), chap. 10.

59. For a discussion of current ownership of brothel land and buildings see Gail Sheehy, "The Landlords of Hell's Bedroom," *New York Magazine* 6 (November 20, 1972):67–80; E. Robbins, "Chinese Slave Girls," *Overland Monthly* n.s. (1908):100–102.

60. *Territorial Enterprise,* February 27, 1877; *Virginia Evening Chronicle,* February 21, 1877, and February 22, 1877.

61. *Virginia Evening Chronicle,* February 22, 1877.

62. Assessment Rolls for the City of Virginia, 1875, Storey County Courthouse; and Nevada State Census for 1875.

63. Angel, *Reproduction of Thompson and West,* p. 599.

64. *Territorial Enterprise,* March 14, 1871, March 26, 1871, and March 28, 1871; De Quille, *The Big Bonanza,* pp. 181–86.

65. Kinnersley, "Virginia, Nevada, 1859–1890," pp. 83–84, 94–95.

66. *Territorial Enterprise,* March 9, 1871; and Elliott, *History of Nevada,* pp. 123–24.

67. Angel, *Reproduction of Thompson and West,* p. 577.

68. *Territorial Enterprise,* December 7, 1876.

69. Charles Winick and Paul M. Kinsie, *The Lively Commerce: Prostitution in the United States* (Chicago: Quadrangle Books, 1971), pp. 131–84; Walter C. Reckless, "The Distribution of Commercialized Vice in the City, *American Journal of Sociology* 32 (July 1926):164–76; and William I. Thomas, *The Unadjusted Girl* (Boston: Little, Brown and Co., 1923).

70. Although it is quite dangerous to generalize from structural evidence to social psychological implications, I believe that some discussion of the broad emotional effects of industrialization and laissez faire capitalism is essential to an understanding of the development of prostitution from the last half of the nineteenth century to the present. I have based my discussion on Karl Marx, *The Economic and Philosophic Manuscripts of 1844* (New York: International Publishers, 1964).

71. Frances Finnegan, *Poverty and Prostitution: A Study of Victorian Prostitutes in York* (Cambridge: Cambridge University Press, 1979); and Winick and Kinsie, *The Lively Commerce,* pp. 245–68.

72. Sumner, *Report on the Condition of Women,* p. 245.

73. Hubert Howe Bancroft, *The Works of Hubert Howe Bancroft,* vol. 25, *History of Nevada, Colorado, and Wyoming* (San Francisco: History Company Publishers, 1890), pp. 171–72.

Chapter 2

1. Milton Rugoff, *Prudery and Passion: Sexuality in Victorian America* (New York: G. P. Putnam's Sons, 1971), p. 50.

2. Daniel Scott Smith, "The Dating of the American Sexual Revolution: Evidence and Interpretations," in *The American Family in Social Historical Perspective,* ed. Michael Gordon (New York: St. Martin's Press, 1973), pp. 109–10.

3. Carl N. Degler, "What Ought to Be and What Was: Women's Sexuality in the Nineteenth Century," *American Historical Review* 79 (December 1974):1467–90; and *At Odds: Women and the Family in America from the Revolution to the Present* (New York: Oxford University Press, 1980). pp. 249–78.

4. John S. Haller, Jr., and Robin M. Haller, *The Physician and Sexuality in Victorian America* (Urbana: University of Illinois Press, 1974), pp. 109–10.

5. Barbara Welter, "The Cult of True Womanhood; 1820–1860," in Gordon, *The American Family,* p. 227.

6. John D. West, M.D., *Maidenhood and Motherhood: Or Ten Phases of Woman's Life* (Chicago: Law, King, and Law Publishing House, 1887), pp. 346–48.

7. Carroll D. Wright, *Marriage and Divorce in the United States: 1867–1886* (Washington, D.C.: Government Printing Office, 1897), p. 353.

8. *Virginia City Territorial Enterprise,* July 8, 1866, March 1, 1869, and August 10, 1871; *Virginia Evening Bulletin,* September 10, 1863; Louise M. Palmer, "How We Live in Nevada," *Overland Monthly* 2 (May 1869):461.

9. Alfred Doten Diaries, Special Collections of the University of Nevada at Reno, October 2, 1872.

10. For examples of parents' fear, see *Gold Hill News,* April 3, 1864; *Territorial Enterprise,* April 29, 1869.

11. *Territorial Enterprise,* March 7, 1874.

12. Arthur W. Calhoun, *A Social History of the American Family,* vols. 2 and 3 (New York: Barnes and Noble, 1918); Eli Zaretsky, "Capitalism, the Family, and Personal Life," *Socialist Review* 15 (May-June 1973):20–21; Glen Elder, "Family History and the Life Course," *Journal of Family History* 2 (1977):279–304; and Frank Furstenburg, "Industrialization and the American Family," *American Sociological Review* 31 (1966):326–37.

13. Bernard Farber, *Family Organization and Interaction* (San Francisco: Chandler Publishing Co., 1964), pp. 104–11.

14. Mary McNair Mathews, *Ten Years in Nevada or Life on the Pacific Coast* (Buffalo: Baker, Jones and Co., 1880), p. 91.

15. Ibid., p. 195.

16. Susan Strasser, "Never Done: The Ideology and Technology of Household Work, 1850–1930" (Ph.D. diss., State University of New York at Stony Brook, 1977).

17. Thomas Harold Kinnersley, "Virginia, Nevada, 1859–1890: A Study of Police, Water, and Fire Problems" (Ph.D. diss., University of California at Los Angeles, 1974), pp. 147–49.

18. Ibid., pp. 150–4; and Mathews, *Ten Years in Nevada,* p. 183.

19. Ibid.; and Palmer, "How We Live in Nevada."

20. Mathews, *Ten Years in Nevada,* p. 92. Census figures also suggest that boarders supplemented household income.

21. *Territorial Enterprise,* September 7, 1868; Mathews, *Ten Years in Nevada,* p. 130.

22. Ellen Willis, "Consumerism and Women," *Socialist Review* 1 (May-June 1970):76–82.

23. Palmer, "How We Live in Nevada," p. 459; John Demos, *A Little Commonwealth: Family Life in Plymouth Colony* (New York: Oxford University Press, 1971), p. 53.

24. Thorstein Veblen, *The Theory of the Leisure Class: An Economic Study of Institutions* (New York: Modern Library, 1934), p. 59.

25. Palmer, "How We Live in Nevada," p. 461.

26. Joseph F. Kett, "Adolescence and Youth in Nineteenth Century America," in *Education in American History,* ed. Michael Katz (New York: Praeger Publishers, 1973), p. 62.

27. Haller and Haller, *The Physician and Sexuality,* p. 79.

28. *Virginia Evening Bulletin,* August 12, 1863.

29. Welter, "The Cult of True Womanhood," p. 239.

30. Farber, *Family Organization and Interaction,* pp. 104–20.

31. Welter, "The Cult of True Womanhood," p. 240.

32. Ibid.

33. *Territorial Enterprise,* July 10, 1877, and November 17, 1878.
34. *Gold Hill News,* May 29, 1864.
35. Nevada Legislature, *Statutes of the State of Nevada Passed at the First Session of the Legislature* (Carson City, Nevada: John Church State Printer, 1865), chap. 76.
36. Wright, *Marriage and Divorce,* pp. 708–11.
37. Nevada Legislature, *Statutes of the State of Nevada Passed at the Eighth Session of the Legislature* (Carson City, Nevada: John J. Hill State Printer, 1877), chap. 43.
38. *Territorial Enterprise,* March 16, 1877, April 14, 1877, and April 24, 1877.
39. Ibid., September 23, 1877, and March 11, 1877.
40. Ibid., October 6, 1977.
41. *Gold Hill News,* May 13, 1864.
42. See, for example, *Territorial Enterprise,* January 22, 1867, and July 6, 1865.
43. Mathews, *Ten Years in Nevada,* p. 193.
44. Haller and Haller, *The Physician and Sexuality,* pp. 97–102; and Degler, *At Odds,* pp. 247. Haller and Haller tend to overemphasize the supression of female sexuality, while Degler focuses too much attention on materials celebrating sexuality. For a balanced picture, both sources should be consulted.
45. Degler, *At Odds,* pp. 257–58.
46. Wright, *Marriage and Divorce,* pp. 708–11.
47. Emanie Sachs, *The Terrible Siren: Victoria Woodhull* (New York: Harper and Brothers, 1928), pp. 34–97.
48. Rugoff, *Prudery and Passion,* pp. 232–33; and *Territorial Enterprise,* May 13, 1874.
49. *Territorial Enterprise,* May 30, 1874.
50. Ibid., August 8, 1868, and March 14, 1871.
51. Doten Diaries, August 28, 1867.
52. Palmer, "How We Live in Nevada," p. 461.
53. Wright, *Marriage and Divorce,* pp. 352–53.
54. *Papers and Proceedings of the American Sociological Society,* vol. 3 (Chicago: University of Chicago Press, 1909).
55. See, for example, *Territorial Enterprise,* April 29, 1875.
56. *Virginia Evening Bulletin,* July 19, 1863.
57. Wright, *Marriage and Divorce,* pp. 708–11.
58. William W. Sanger, M.D., *The History of Prostitution: Its Extent, Causes, and Effects Throughout the World* (New York: Eugenics Publishing Company, 1937 [1897]), pp. 473–75, and *Territorial Enterprise,* December 7, 1877.
59. Wright, *Marriage and Divorce,* pp. 708–11.
60. These liaisons were seldom mentioned in public sources, and they first came to my attention through census data from 1880, in which relationships to household heads were listed.

61. This information was gathered from the United States manuscript census of 1880.
62. *Territorial Enterprise,* February 19, 1874, and March 12, 1874.
63. Notes on Alf's pre-Comstock life were taken from the preface to *The Journals of Alfred Doten: 1849–1903,* ed. Walter Van Tilburg Clark, vol. 1 (Reno: University of Nevada Press, 1973), pp. xi–xx. The other citations in this chapter refer to the original manuscript diaries.
64. Doten Diaries, December 23, 1866.
65. Ibid., September 19, 1865, and August 12, 1865.
66. Ibid., May 11, 1872, and September 29, 1875.
67. Ibid., September 10, 1867.
68. Ibid., September 20, 1867, and May 11, 1867.
69. Ibid., May 26, 1867.
70. Ibid., October 13, 1867.
71. Ibid., August 28, 1867, October 8, 1867, and November 5, 1867.
72. Ibid., September 29, 1867.
73. Ibid., March 31, 1872.
74. Ibid., July 15, 1873.
75. Ibid., August 18, 1873.
76. Emma Goldman, *The Traffic in Women and Other Essays on Feminism* (New York: Times Change Press, 1970 [1900]), p. 20.
77. For a theoretical discussion of housework and domestic service see Susan Strasser, "Mistress and Maid," *Marxist Perspectives* 1 (Winter 1978):52–67.

Chapter 3

1. Roger Brown, *Words and Things* (New York: Free Press, 1969), pp. 229–41.
2. Curt Gentry, *The Madams of San Francisco* (New York: Ballentine Books, 1971 [1964]), p. 112–13.
3. Ibid.; and Anonymous, *The Green Book, or, the Gentleman's Guide to New Orleans, Listing the Principal Maisons de Joie: Names of Madames, Angels, Nymphs, and Fairies, Color and Nationality* (New Orleans: 1895).
4. Robert B. Merrifield, "Nevada, 1859–1881: The Impact of an Advanced Technological Society upon a Frontier Area" (Ph.D. diss., University of Chicago, 1958), pp. 235–36; and Myron Angel, ed., *Reproduction of Thompson and West's "History of Nevada, 1881"* (Berkeley: Howell North, 1958), pp. 612a and 612b.
5. Merrifield, "Nevada, 1859–1881," p. 236; and Alfred Doten Diaries, Special Collections of the University of Nevada at Reno.
6. For a discussion of prostitutes' circuits see Gentry, *The Madams of San Francisco,* pp. 146–48.
7. *Virginia City Territorial Enterprise,* August 5, 1875.
8. Wells Drury, *An Editor on the Comstock Lode* (New York: Farrar and Rinehart, 1936), p. 229.

9. Ibid.

10. Among those women was Margie Rubens, who killed herself. See *Territorial Enterprise,* November 26, 1878.

11. Ibid., March 11, 1872, and July 20, 1879.

12. Ibid., June 15, 1872.

13. Drury, *An Editor on the Comstock Lode,* p. 121.

14. Ibid.

15. Angel, *Reproduction of Thompson and West,* p. 602.

16. Ibid., p. 571; and J. Wells Kelly, *First Directory of the Nevada Territory* (San Francisco: Valentine and Co., 1862), p. 137.

17. *Territorial Enterprise,* November 3, 1872.

18. For a note on the blue lights see *Gold Hill News,* January 14, 1864.

19. *Territorial Enterprise,* March 16, 1869, August 22, 1871, and October 7, 1873. See also Thomas Harold Kinnersley, "Virginia, Nevada, 1859–1890: A Study of Police, Water, and Fire Problems" (Ph.D. diss., University of California at Los Angeles, 1974), pp. 263–65.

20. *Territorial Enterprise,* July 15, 1871.

21. *Gold Hill News,* September 5, 1875.

22. Doten Diaries, July 4, 1867; and *Territorial Enterprise,* November 20, 1866.

23. *Territorial Enterprise,* August 17, 1872, and November 20, 1866.

24. Ibid., February 8, 1878.

25. For notes on cribs in other cities see Gentry, *The Madams of San Francisco,* p. 182; for pictures see E. J. Bellocq, *Storeyville Portraits: Photographs from the New Orleans Red Light District, Circa 1912* (New York: Museum of Modern Art, 1970); for Virginia City see *Gold Hill News,* September 15, 1875; and *Territorial Enterprise,* July 1, 1875.

26. David J. Pivar, *Purity Crusade: Sexual Morality and Social Control, 1868–1900* (Westport, Conn.: Greenwood Press, 1973), pp. 104–5.

27. Ibid., pp. 141–42. In 1895 the age of consent was lowered from fourteen to twelve.

28. *Territorial Enterprise,* August 6, 1875.

29. Ibid., June 7, 1877.

30. Ibid., July 10, 1877.

31. Ibid., August 30, 1876, September 15, 1876, April 7, 1877, and April 2, 1879.

32. William W. Sanger, M.D., *The History of Prostitution: Its Extent, Causes, and Effects Throughout the World* (New York: Eugenics Publishing Co., 1937 [1897]), pp. 453–54.

33. *Territorial Enterprise,* October 6, 1867.

34. Gentry, *The Madams of San Francisco,* p. 67.

35. Ibid., pp. 72–75, and Karl Marx, *The Eighteenth Brumaire of Louis Bonaparte* (New York: New York Labor News Co., 1951), pp. 107–8.

36. See Census manuscripts for 1875 and 1880.

37. William R. Gillis, comp., *The Nevada Directory for 1868–69* (San Francisco: M. D. Carr and Co., 1868), p. 268. This lists city ordinances along with addresses and advertisements.

38. *Territorial Enterprise,* July 1, 1868.

39. Lucie Cheng Hirata, "Free, Indentured, Enslaved: Chinese Prostitutes in Nineteenth Century America," *Signs: A Journal of Women in Culture and Society* 5 (Autumn 1979):8–16; and Stanford M. Lyman, *The Asian in the West* (Reno: University of Nevada Press, 1971), pp. 18–19.

40. Hirata, "Free, Indentured, Enslaved," p. 10.

41. Ibid., p. 9.

42. *Territorial Enterprise,* June 9, 1878.

43. Mark Twain [Samuel Clemens], *Roughing It* (New York: Signet Classics, 1962 [1872]), pp. 236–40.

44. For notes on blacks, see Doten Diaries, June 21, 1866; and *Territorial Enterprise,* May 2, 1866, and August 31, 1863.

45. Doten Diaries, June 1, 1867.

46. Ibid., June 2, 1867.

47. *Territorial Enterprise,* February 8, 1878.

48. Gentry, *The Madams of San Francisco,* pp. 27–32.

49. William S. McCallum quoted in Gentry, *The Madams of San Francisco,* p. 28.

50. Census takers did not fully record literacy. Most accounts note that Chinese women could barely speak English, yet columns headed "Cannot Read" and "Cannot Write" were seldom checked for them or anyone else in the 1875 and 1880 censuses.

51. Sanger, *The History of Prostitution,* pp. 473–77.

52. *Virginia Evening Bulletin,* April 16, 1863.

53. *Territorial Enterprise,* August 17, 1872.

54. Ibid., August 4, 1876.

Chapter 4

1. Curt Gentry, *The Madams of San Francisco* (New York: Ballantine Books, 1971 [1964]), p. 152.

2. Kingsley Davis, "The Sociology of Prostitution," *American Sociological Review* 2 (October 1937):746–48.

3. For a graphic illustration of manipulation of customers see Sara Kernochan, *Dry Hustle* (New York: William Morrow and Co., 1977).

4. Gale Miller, *Odd Jobs: The World of Deviant Work* (Englewood Cliffs, N.J.: Prentice-Hall, 1978), pp. 132–33.

5. *Virginia City Territorial Enterprise,* June 3, 1874, and June 6, 1874.

6. Ibid., June 7, 1877, and July 10, 1877.

7. Ibid., July 14, 1875.

8. Ibid., July 10, 1878, March 31, 1875, and July 1, 1875.

9. Ibid., August 6, 1875.

10. Ibid.; see also November 20, 1875, and June 7, 1877.

11. Ibid., June 6, 1877.

12. Nevada Supreme Court decision *The State of Nevada v. Peter Larkin, Reports of the Decisions of the Supreme Court of the State of Nevada,* vol. 11 (1876):314–33; *Territorial Enterprise,* August 30, 1875, January 20, 1877, and April 5, 1877; and Alfred Doten Diaries, Special Collections of the University of Nevada at Reno, January 19, 1877.

13. *The State of Nevada v. Peter Larkin,* p. 320.

14. Ibid., p. 329; and *Territorial Enterprise,* March 30, 1876.

15. *Territorial Enterprise,* April 7, 1877, and April 5, 1877.

16. See, for example, *Territorial Enterprise,* April 8, 1866.

17. Ibid., July 10, 1877.

18. Ibid., March 6, 1875.

19. Ibid., October 7, 1873, and January 12, 1877.

20. Ibid., January 5, 1878.

21. Ibid., August 4, 1875.

22. Ibid., February 8, 1878.

23. Ibid., June 28, 1873.

24. Ibid., August 29, 1876; and Assessment Rolls for Virginia City in 1875, Storey County Courthouse.

25. Doten Diaries, July 4, 1867 and July 27, 1867.

26. According to a source at the Nevada Historical Society, a gentleman living in Rhyolite, Nevada, currently has those letters in his possession and is considering publishing them privately. If he does not, I hope he places them in some public repository so that they are not lost to history.

27. Doten Diaries, December 27, 1864 and January 24, 1865; and Myron Angel, ed., *Reproduction of Thompson and West's "History of Nevada, 1881,"* (Berkeley: Howell North, 1958), p. 346.

28. Doten Diaries, December 26, 1864.

29. Papers Concerning the Estate of Jessie Lester, Deceased 1865, Storey County Courthouse.

30. Ibid. Quality of the furniture was estimated by pictures of Victorian interiors, general price lists, descriptions on the estate inventory, and prices which various items brought.

31. Harold L. Wilensky, "The Professionalization of Everyone?" in *The Sociology of Organizations: Basic Studies,* ed. Oscar Grusky and George A. Miller (New York: Free Press, 1970), pp. 483–501.

32. See, for examples, *Territorial Enterprise,* August 17, 1876; and *Gold Hill News,* March 2, 1864.

33. *Territorial Enterprise,* November 26, 1871.

34. Ibid., September 13, 1872, and February 13, 1879.

35. Gentry, *The Madams of San Francisco,* pp. 139–43.

36. *San Francisco Chronicle,* May 9, 1883.

37. Ibid.; and Gentry, *The Madams of San Francisco,* pp. 166–78.

38. *Territorial Enterprise,* September 24, 1871.

39. *Elko Independent* (Elko, Nevada), July 11, 1879.

40. Doten Diaries, September 7, 1871.

41. Ibid., February 5, 1865.

42. *Gold Hill News,* March 30, 1864.

43. Clipping from *Gold Hill News* in Doten Diaries, June 17, 1871.

44. Allen Lesser, *Enchanting Rebel: The Secret of Adah Issacs Menken* (Philadelphia: Ruttle, Shaw, and Whetherhill, 1947), p. 126; and Bernard Falk, *The Naked Lady: A Biography of Adah Issacs Menken* (London: Hutchinson & Co., 1952), p. 61.

45. Doten Diaries, August 29, 1867.

46. Kenneth Lamott, *Who Killed Mr. Crittenden?: Being a True Account of the Notorious Murder Trial that Stunned San Francisco, the Laura D. Fair Case* (New York: David McKay Co., 1963). This book was based on the detailed transcripts of the Fair case, as well as newspaper stories. Checks of the *Enterprise* coverage of the trial support the accuracy of this book, and it is the source for the section on Laura Fair.

47. Ibid., p. 287.

48. Ibid., p. 54.

49. Papers Concerning the Estate of Julia Bulette, 1867–1868, Storey County Courthouse. As in the case of Jessie Lester, descriptions were pieced together from inventories and auction prices of Julia's belongings, as well as general sources of fashions of the times.

50. *Gold Hill News,* January 31, 1867; and Doten Diaries, January 19, 1867, January 20, 1867, and January 21, 1867.

51. *Territorial Enterprise,* January 22, 1867.

52. *Gold Hill News,* January 22, 1867.

53. Ibid., January 21, 1867.

54. Doten Diaries, January 21, 1867.

55. *Territorial Enterprise,* April 26, 1868.

56. Ibid., May 25, 1867.

57. Papers Concerning the Estate of Julia Bulette.

58. Charlotte Gere, *Victorian Jewelry Design* (Chicago: Henry Regery Co., 1972), p. 92.

59. For the current examples see Kate Coleman, "Carnal Knowledge: A Portrait of Four Hookers," *Ramparts* 10 (December 1971):19–28.

60. *Territorial Enterprise,* January 21, 1867, January 22, 1867, and June 27, 1867; and Doten Diaries, December 13, 1865.

61. Dressing rooms sometimes became an issue for securing liquor licenses. See *Territorial Enterprise,* February 9, 1870.

62. Gentry, *The Madams of San Francisco,* p. 75.

63. Wilbur S. Shepperson, *Restless Stangers: Nevada's Immigrants and Their Interpreters* (Reno: University of Nevada Press, 1970), p. 103.

64. Doten Diaries, January 1, 1872; and *Territorial Enterprise,* August 17, 1872. See also Doten Diaries, February 5, 1865 and February 8, 1868.

65. *Territorial Enterprise,* April 18, 1871.
66. Ibid., January 14, 1873. This describes a fight between two customers who wanted to accompany the same hurdy girl.
67. Gentry, *The Madams of San Francisco,* p. 153.
68. Ibid., p. 184.
69. *Territorial Enterprise,* May 6, 1875, and May 7, 1875.
70. Ibid., February 8, 1878.
71. Gentry, *The Madams of San Francisco,* pp. 182-3.
72. *Territorial Enterprise,* August 17, 1873.
73. Ibid., August 17, 1878.
74. Ibid., July 19, 1866, and May 5, 1858.
75. Ibid., June 18, 1880.
76. Ibid., December 9, 1866.
77. Ibid.; see also November 21, 1866, and September 8, 1866.
78. Doten Diaries, January 21, 1867.
79. For a qualitative account of the Chinese leaving see *Territorial Enterprise,* December 19, 1877. See also U.S. Census, *Population of the United States at the Tenth Census: 1880,* p. 659.
80. Stanford M. Lyman, *The Asian in the West* (Reno: University of Nevada Press, 1971), pp. 18-19; and Lucie Cheng Hirata, "Free, Indentured, Enslaved: Prostitutes in Nineteenth Century America," *Signs: A Journal of Women in Culture and Society* 5 (Autumn 1979):6-7.
81. Lyman, *The Asian in the West,* pp. 18-19.
82. Mary McNair Mathews, *Ten Years in Nevada or Life on the Pacific Coast* (Buffalo: Baker, Jones and Co., 1880), p. 257.
83. John Helmer, *Drugs and Minority Oppression* (New York: Seabury Press, 1975), p. 23; and Hirata, "Free, Indentured, Enslaved," pp. 19-20.
84. *Territorial Enterprise,* June 9, 1872.
85. Thanks to David Milton for reviewing the list of Chinese names from the census and commenting on their provincial origins.
86. Lyman, *The Asian in the West,* pp. 18-19.
87. Hirata, "Free, Indentured, Enslaved," p. 16.
88. Gentry, *The Madams of San Francisco,* p. 63; and Carol Green Wilson, *Chinatown Quest: The Life Adventures of Donaldina Cameron* (Stanford: Stanford University Press, 1950), p. 9.
89. Gentry, *The Madams of San Francisco,* p. 150; and Hirata, "Free, Indentured, Enslaved," pp. 13-14.
90. Mark Twain [Samuel Clemens]; *Roughing It* (New York: Signet Classics, 1962 [1872]), p. 295.
91. See, for example, *Territorial Enterprise,* August 20, 1870.
92. Ibid., September 19, 1877.
93. Ibid., August 24, 1877.
94. *Virginia Evening Bulletin,* November 23, 1863.
95. Doten Diaries, February 13, 1866.

Chapter 5

1. Personal interview, 1973.
2. *Virginia City Territorial Enterprise,* January 5, 1878, and September 21, 1867.
3. Ibid., March 20, 1878.
4. Comparison of data from Nevada State Census of 1875 with data from United States Census of 1880 for Storey County, Nevada.
5. Mary McNair Mathews, *Ten Years in Nevada or Life on the Pacific Coast* (Buffalo: Baker, Jones and Co., 1880), p. 193.
6. William R. Gillis, comp., *The Nevada Directory for 1868–69* (San Francisco: M. D. Carr and Co., 1868), p. 263. This directory lists local ordinances, as well as home and business addresses.
7. *Territorial Enterprise,* August 29, 1876, and May 22, 1876.
8. A relatively scholarly current work discusses both some historical and some current requirements for pimps' roles. See Christina and Richard Milner, *Black Players: The Secret Life of Black Pimps* (Boston: Little, Brown and Co., 1972), pp. 51–117.
9. Ibid.
10. Ibid., p. 12; and qualitative data from Nevada State Census of 1875.
11. H. H. Kane, *Opium Smoking in America and China* (New York: G. P. Putnam's, 1882), p. 3.
12. *Virginia Evening Bulletin,* May 12, 1863.
13. *Territorial Enterprise,* September 7, 1879.
14. Curt Gentry, *The Madams of San Francisco* (New York: Ballantine Books, 1971 [1964]), pp. 83 and 96.
15. See, for example, *Territorial Enterprise,* June 21, 1866, and July 24, 1877.
16. See, for example, *Territorial Enterprise,* January 20, 1877. Sporadic periods of vigilante activities involved pressures on pimps to leave the Comstock. See April 4, 1871, for a report on such pressures. See also discussions of vagrants, March 11, 1872, and November 24, 1880.
17. Wells Drury, *An Editor on the Comstock Lode* (New York: Farrar and Reinhart, 1936), pp. 122–27.
18. *Territorial Enterprise,* July 11, 1869, and August 4, 1869.
19. Ibid., January 30, 1877, and August 6, 1875.
20. Ibid., April 5, 1877, April 6, 1877, and July 11, 1877.
21. Thomas Harold Kinnersley, "Virginia, Nevada, 1859–1890: A Study of Police, Water, and Fire Problems" (Ph.D. diss., University of California at Los Angeles, 1974), pp. 80–84.
22. Ibid., p. 95.
23. Ibid., pp. 85 and 97.
24. Ibid., p. 97.
25. Ibid., p. 324.

26. *Gold Hill News,* August 27, 1869.
27. Kinnersley, "Virginia, Nevada, 1859–1890," p. 94; and *Territorial Enterprise,* April 5, 1866, and April 7, 1876.
28. Gillis, *Nevada Directory,* pp. 256–7.
29. *Territorial Enterprise,* September 7, 1876, September 8, 1876, and September 9, 1876.
30. Ibid., October 18, 1876.
31. Ibid., October 25, 1876.
32. Ibid., October 9, 1877.
33. Nevada Legislature, *Appendix to the Journals of the Senate and Assembly of the Eighth Session of the Legislature of the State of Nevada,* vol. 3 (Carson City, Nevada: John J. Hill State Printer, 1877), p. 86.
34. *Territorial Enterprise,* October 4, 1877.
35. Ibid., February 6, 1878.
36. Ibid., February 8, 1878.
37. Ibid., February 6, 1868.
38. Ibid., February 8, 1878.
39. Ibid., February 9, 1868.
40. *Gold Hill News,* August 15, 1872.
41. *Territorial Enterprise,* August 20, 1876.
42. Ibid., August 16, 1878.
43. Alfred Doten Diaries, Special Collections of the University of Nevada at Reno, December 30, 1865.
44. Doten Diaries, June 1, 1867, September 20, 1865, October 4, 1865, and May 9, 1877.
45. *Gold Hill News,* February 24, 1864.
46. Doten Diaries, September 27, 1865.
47. *Territorial Enterprise,* November 29, 1876.
48. Ibid.
49. Ibid., November 7, 1878.
50. Doten Diaries, August 27, 1865.
51. Ibid., October 4, 1865.
52. Ibid., December 23, 1866, and November 5, 1865.
53. See, for example, Gentry, *The Madams of San Francisco;* and Zola Ross, *Bonanza Queen* (New York: Bobbs-Merrill, 1949). Perhaps the ultimate glorification of a prostitute's friendship was that between Kitty Russell and Matt Dillon on television's *Gunsmoke.*
54. Doten Diaries, January 21, 1867; and *Territorial Enterprise,* June 27, 1867.
55. Papers Concerning the Estate of Julia Bulette, 1867–1868, Storey County Courthouse, Virginia City, Nevada.
56. Doten Diaries, December 26, 1864, January 24, 1865, and January 21, 1867.
57. Ibid., February 6, 1868.
58. *Territorial Enterprise,* February 7, 1868.

59. Ibid., November 20, 1866; and Doten Diaries, November 18, 1866.

60. *Virginia Evening Bulletin,* May 14, 1864.

61. *Territorial Enterprise,* May 11, 1866; and *Virginia Evening Bulletin,* March 20, 1868.

62. *Territorial Enterprise,* September 21, 1867, and September 22, 1867.

63. Ibid., November 10, 1871. This article is one of several discussing prostitutes' whistles.

64. Ibid., February 2, 1871. This discusses the difficulties prostitutes had in obtaining insurance.

65. Ibid., April 4, 1873; and *Gold Hill News,* January 28, 1864.

66. *Territorial Enterprise,* May 25, 1867.

67. Ibid., February 29, 1868, and April 4, 1873; and *Gold Hill News,* January 28, 1864.

68. *Territorial Enterprise,* November 22, 1878, and January 3, 1874.

69. Ibid., August 21, 1871.

70. Ibid., June 6, 1874, and August 21, 1874.

71. Ibid., January 8, 1874; and Myron Angel, ed., *Reproduction of Thompson and West's "History of Nevada, 1881,"* (Berkeley: Howell North, 1958), p. 346.

72. *Virginia Evening Bulletin,* November 23, 1863; and *Territorial Enterprise,* August 17, 1873.

73. See, for example, *Gold Hill News,* May 3, 1867; and *Territorial Enterprise,* May 25, 1867, and June 21, 1866.

74. Doten Diaries, August 10, 1865.

75. *Territorial Enterprise,* December 15, 1874.

76. Ibid., August 7, 1872, and June 8, 1877.

77. See, for example, *Gold Hill News,* March 3, 1864; and *Territorial Enterprise,* February 12, 1874.

78. *Territorial Enterprise,* January 29, 1867.

79. Ibid., January 8, 1864.

80. Ibid., September 6, 1868.

81. Wilbur S. Shepperson, *Restless Strangers: Nevada's Immigrants and Their Interpreters* (Reno: University of Nevada Press, 1970), p. 102.

82. Carroll Smith-Rosenberg, "The Female World of Love and Ritual: Relations Between Women in Nineteenth-Century America," *Signs: A Journal of Women in Culture and Society* 1 (Autumn 1975):1–29.

83. Ibid., p. 13.

84. For a discussion of the mother-daughter bond and its importance to adult women's relationships see Nancy Chodorow, "Family Structure and Feminine Personality," in *Women, Culture and Society,* ed. Michelle Z. Rosaldo and Louise Lamphere (Stanford: Stanford University Press, 1974), pp. 43–66.

85. For reports of twentieth century pimps' use of jealousy to control their women, see Milner and Milner, *Black Players* and Bob Adelman and Susan Hall, *Gentlemen of Leisure* (New York: New American Library,

1974). For a discussion of self-hatred and internalization, see Franz Fanon, *The Wretched of the Earth* (New York: Grove Press, 1968).

86. *Territorial Enterprise,* April 14, 1870, and July 4, 1872; and *Virginia Evening Bulletin,* September 23, 1863.

87. *Virginia Evening Bulletin,* May 12, 1863; and *Territorial Enterprise,* September 20, 1866, and February 22, 1873.

88. *Virginia Evening Bulletin,* September 29, 1863. This article describes a fight in the afternoon on C Street between "two drunken amazons." It offers excellent pictures of a fight and also of righteous indignation against the participants.

89. *Territorial Enterprise,* August 6, 1875.

90. Gentry, *The Madams of San Francisco,* pp. 142–7.

91. William W. Sanger, M.D., *The History of Prostitution: Its Extent, Causes, and Effects Throughout the World* (New York: Eugenics Publishing Co., 1937 [1897]), pp. 57–58; and Judith Walkowitz, "Notes on the History of Victorian Prostitution," *Feminist Studies* 1 (Summer 1972):105–14.

92. James H. Bryan, "Apprenticeships in Prostitution," *Social Problems* 12 (Winter 1965):287–97.

93. For a description of frontstage and backstage and their symbolic meanings in everyday interaction, see Erving Goffman, *The Presentation of Self in Everyday Life* (New York: Anchor Books, 1959).

94. *Territorial Enterprise,* June 27, 1867.

95. Ibid.

96. Ibid.

97. Ibid.

98. Ibid., June 6, 1874; and Papers Concerning the Estate of Jessie Lester, 1865, Storey County Courthouse, Virginia City, Nevada.

99. Papers Concerning the Estate of Julia Bulette, 1867–1868, Storey County Courthouse, Virginia City, Nevada.

100. Papers Concerning the Estate of Susan Ballard, 1871, Storey County Courthouse, Virginia City, Nevada.

101. *Territorial Enterprise,* June 21, 1866, and January 22, 1867.

102. Doten Diaries, January 21, 1867; and *Territorial Enterprise,* January 22, 1867.

103. Ibid.; and Doten Diaries, January 24, 1865.

104. *Gold Hill News,* September 5, 1875; and *Territorial Enterprise,* May 16, 1875.

105. See, for example, *Territorial Enterprise,* April 12, 1873, June 22, 1876, July 10, 1874, January 2, 1875, and April 8, 1866.

106. Ibid., July 11, 1872.

107. Ibid., August 17, 1872.

108. *Virginia Evening Bulletin,* October 20, 1863.

109. *Territorial Enterprise,* March 6, 1873.

110. Ibid., September 11, 1870, April 21, 1871, and July 6, 1876.

111. Ibid.

112. J. Richardson Parke, *Human Sexuality* (Philadelphia: Professional Publishing Co., 1906), pp. 319–20.

113. Ceasare Lombroso, *LaDonna Delinquente,* cited in Parke, *Human Sexuality,* p. 320.

114. John S. Haller, Jr., and Robin M. Haller, *The Physician and Sexuality in Victorian America* (Urbana: University of Illinois Press, 1974), pp. 106–7.

115. Smith-Rosenberg, "The Female World of Love and Ritual," p. 8.

Chapter 6

1. Linda Gordon, *Woman's Body, Woman's Right: A Social History of Birth Control in America* (New York: Grossman Publishers, 1976), p. xiv.

2. Milton Rugoff, *Prudery and Passion: Sexuality in Victorian America* (New York: G. P. Putnam's Sons, 1971), pp. 123–31.

3. John S. Haller, Jr., and Robin M. Haller, *The Physician and Sexuality in Victorian America* (Urbana: University of Illinois Press, 1974), p. 114.

4. Foote also offered mail order supplies of the devices he advocated in his books.

5. Gordon, *Woman's Body,* p. 28.

6. Ibid., pp. 28 and 45.

7. Ibid., pp. 45 and 62; and Haller and Haller, *The Physician and Sexuality,* p. 115.

8. Haller and Haller, *The Physician and Sexuality,* p. 115.

9. Ibid., p. 262.

10. J. Kelly Webb, "One of the Abuses of Carbolic Acid," *Columbus Medical Journal* 1 (1883):433–66; and a personal interview with a San Francisco prostitute.

11. Gordon, *Woman's Body,* p. 63.

12. Ibid., pp. 52–60.

13. Nevada Legislature, *Statutes of the State of Nevada Passed at the Twelfth Session of the Legislature* (Carson City, Nevada: State Printing Office, 1885), p. 1020.

14. Gordon, *Woman's Body,* p. 53.

15. Haller and Haller, *The Physician and Sexuality,* pp. 216 and 284.

16. See for example, *Virginia City Territorial Enterprise,* February 12, 1866.

17. Wilbur S. Shepperson, *Restless Strangers: Nevada's Immigrants and Their Interpreters* (Reno: University of Nevada Press, 1970), p. 36.

18. *Territorial Enterprise,* October 12, 1880.

19. Ibid., January 3, 1877.

20. Ibid., March 11, 1877.

21. Gordon, *Woman's Body,* p. 51; and William Langer, "Infanticide: A Historical Survey," *History of Childhood Quarterly* 1 (1974):353–65.

22. Gordon, *Woman's Body,* p. 51.

23. State of Nevada, *Statutes of the Twelfth Legislature,* p. 1020.

24. *Territorial Enterprise,* February 7, 1868.

25. *Gold Hill News,* April 18, 1864.
26. For infanticides see *Territorial Enterprise,* August 26, 1868, September 16, 1868, January 15, 1874, January 16, 1874, and June 20, 1879. For examples of abandonments see *Virginia Evening Bulletin,* February 11, 1864, and *Territorial Enterprise,* September 12, 1877.
27. *Territorial Enterprise,* August 16, 1878.
28. Personal interview.
29. Haller and Haller, *The Physician and Sexuality,* pp. 258–59.
30. William Acton, *Prostitution* (New York: Frederick E. Praeger, 1969 [1857]), and William W. Sanger, M.D., *The History of Prostitution: Its Extent, Causes, and Effects Throughout the World* (New York: Eugenics Publishing Company, 1937 [1897]).
31. David J. Pivar, *Purity Crusade: Sexual Morality and Social Control, 1868–1900* (Westport, Conn.: Greenwood Press, 1973), pp. 52–56.
32. *Territorial Enterprise,* April 20, 1876, April 21, 1876, and March 5, 1876.
33. Ibid., February 13, 1869, September 4, 1873, and January 23, 1877.
34. Debts against the Estate of Julia Bulette, 1867–1878, Storey County Courthouse; and Alfred Doten Diaries, Special Collections of the University of Nevada at Reno, April 24, 1878.
35. *Territorial Enterprise,* June 6, 1875.
36. Sanger, *The History of Prostitution,* pp. 595–96; and Haller and Haller, *The Physician and Sexuality,* pp. 264–65.
37. *Territorial Enterprise,* August 22, 1876.
38. Ibid., April 17, 1872.
39. Doten Diaries, September 22, 1866.
40. Robert B. Merrifield, "Nevada, 1859–1881: The Impact of an Advanced Technological Society upon a Frontier Area," (Ph.D. diss., University of Chicago, 1958), p. 33.
41. Sanger, *The History of Prostitution,* pp. 561–4; and Curt Gentry, *The Madams of San Francisco* (New York: Ballantine Books, 1971 [1964]), pp. 75–80.
42. Haller and Haller, *The Physician and Sexuality,* pp. 273–303.
43. Ibid., pp. 279–89.
44. For a discussion of the myths surrounding narcotic abuse see John Helmer, *Drugs and Minority Oppression* (New York: Seabury Press, 1975), pp. 3–17.
45. *Territorial Enterprise,* February 19, 1870.
46. No complete arrest records were available for the boom years. However, most women whose arrests were reported in the *Virginia Evening Bulletin* and the *Territorial Enterprise* were charged with drunk and disorderly conduct.
47. *Territorial Enterprise,* February 2, 1868.
48. Ibid., September 19, 1872.
49. *Virginia Evening Bulletin,* August 24, 1863, and October 8, 1863.
50. For an example of this sort of fight, see *Virginia Evening Bulletin,* November 29, 1863.

51. *Territorial Enterprise,* February 3, 1877.
52. Ibid., March 5, 1868, and March 6, 1868.
53. Ibid., May 18, 1872.
54. Ibid., June 22, 1869; and Doten Diaries, July 19, 1867 and June 20, 1869.
55. Nevada Legislature, *Statutes of the State of Nevada Passed at the Eighth Session of the Legislature* (Carson City Nevada: John J. Hill State Printer, 1877) chap. 27; and *Territorial Enterprise,* September 13, 1876.
56. Helmer, *Drugs and Minority Oppression,* pp. 18–33.
57. Haller and Haller, *The Physician and Sexuality,* pp. 292–303.
58. C. W. Earle, "The Opium Habit," *Chicago Medical Review* 2 (1880):443–44.
59. *Territorial Enterprise,* April 22, 1877.
60. Ibid., August 29, 1876; and Doten Diaries, February 6, 1868.
61. *Territorial Enterprise,* June 22, 1876.
62. Shepperson, *Restless Strangers,* p. 151.
63. Few Comstock newspapers printed prior to 1863 have been preserved. Also, fires and other damage made it hard to obtain papers for some months. Thirteen months of newspapers published after 1863 were not available; July through December of 1864; January through March of 1866; January, November, and December of 1869; and January, November, and December of 1870.
64. Currently, a national suicide rate of 50 per 100,000 or one-fiftieth of one percent is considered to be extraordinarily high. See U.S. Bureau of the Census, *Statistical Abstract of the United States for 1976* (Washington: Government Printing Office, 1976), pp. 158–59.
65. *Territorial Enterprise,* September 24, 1871, and April 2, 1875.
66. Ibid., August 17, 1867, and June 22, 1876.
67. For notes on the respectable women see *Territorial Enterprise,* October 10, 1869, June 6, 1872, August 27, 1872, and August 31, 1872.
68. For notes on men's suicides see Doten Diaries, June 5, 1865, May 18, 1866, November 9, 1866, June 1, 1868, October 23, 1871, and December 8, 1874.
69. *Territorial Enterprise,* August 29, 1876, and August 31, 1876.
70. *Carson City Morning Appeal,* March 13, 1875. Shepperson, *Restless Strangers,* p. 103.
71. *Territorial Enterprise,* May 6, 1875; September 24, 1871; and November 13, 1875.

Chapter 7

1. Clifford Geertz, "Ideology as a Cultural System," in *Ideology and Discontent,* ed. David Apter (New York: Free Press, 1964), pp. 47–77.
2. Harold Garfinkel, *Studies in Ethnomethodology* (Englewood Cliffs, N.J.: Prentice-Hall, 1967).

3. For a thorough theoretical and empirical discussion of the social functions of deviance within a small community see Kai T. Erikson, *Wayward Puritans* (New York: John Wiley and Sons, 1966).

4. John S. Haller, Jr., and Robin M. Haller, *The Physician and Sexuality in Victorian America* (Urbana: University of Illinois Press, 1974), pp. 146–49.

5. *Virginia City Territorial Enterprise,* March 13, 1870.

6. Eleanor Flexner, *Century of Struggle* (New York: Atheneum, 1970), pp. 113–30.

7. Haller and Haller, *The Physician and Sexuality,* pp. 24–43.

8. *Territorial Enterprise,* June 26, 1869, August 26, 1871, December 21, 1871, and May 19, 1874.

9. Ibid., April 12, 1876; and Alfred Doten Diaries, Special Collections of the University of Nevada at Reno, December 21 and 22, 1871.

10. Russell R. Elliott, *History of Nevada* (Lincoln: University of Nebraska Press, 1973), pp. 246–47.

11. Doten Diaries, August 6, 1870.

12. *Territorial Enterprise,* February 9, 1871.

13. Ibid., May 25, 1869.

14. Ibid., July 29, 1869.

15. Ibid., August 27, 1871.

16. Ibid., September 10, 1879.

17. Ibid., August 11, 1877.

18. Ibid., August 29, 1871.

19. Hon. C. J. Hillyer, "Speech on Woman Suffrage," in Nevada Legislature, *Appendix to the Journal of 1869* (Carson City, Nevada: Henry R. Mighels State Printer, 1869), pp. 1–13.

20. *Territorial Enterprise,* May 21, 1880.

21. Ibid., July 20, 1879.

22. Haller and Haller, *The Physician and Sexuality,* pp. 97–102.

23. David J. Pivar, *Purity Crusade: Sexual Morality and Social Control, 1868–1900* (Westport, Conn.: Greenwood Press, 1973), pp. 50–73.

24. *Territorial Enterprise,* November 4, 1874.

25. Personal interview during four days of field study in Ely, Nevada in May, 1973. Not acknowledging customers is also a modern Peruvian custom. See Katherine Arnold, "The Whore in Peru," in *Tearing the Veil,* ed. Susan Lipshitz (London: Routledge and Kegan Paul, 1978), p. 65.

26. Louise M. Palmer, "How We Live in Nevada," *Overland Monthly* 2 (May 1869):462.

27. Mary McNair Mathews, *Ten Years in Nevada or Life on the Pacific Coast* (Buffalo: Baker, Jones and Co., 1880), p. 193.

28. *Territorial Enterprise,* April 26, 1868.

29. Ibid., February 8, 1878.

30. *Gold Hill News,* December 12, 1863.

31. Ibid.; see also March 30, 1864, and April 9, 1864; *Virginia Evening Bulletin,* December 12, 1863.

32. *Territorial Enterprise,* March 11, 1872.
33. Ibid., March 20, 1878.
34. Ibid., July 3, 1876.
35. Ibid., April 9, 1878, and April 12, 1878.
36. Ibid., November 30, 1870.
37. Ibid., July 7, 1868.
38. *Gold Hill News,* March 30, 1864.
39. *Territorial Enterprise,* October 22, 1867. For examples of news of special entertainment for ladies and children see March 14, 1868, and September 14, 1867.
40. Ibid., February 26, 1875.
41. *Gold Hill News,* January 1, 1867.
42. *Territorial Enterprise,* January 5, 1871.
43. Ibid., December 20, 1867.
44. Ibid., April 18, 1871.
45. Ibid., September 3, 1867, April 19, 1868, and April 26, 1868.
46. Ibid., April 26, 1868.
47. Ibid., August 8, 1879.
48. Mathews, *Ten Years in Nevada,* p. 212.
49. Ibid., p. 165.
50. Pivar, *Purity Crusade,* pp. 33–34.
51. For extensive discussion of the British Contagious Disease Acts and the campaigns against them see Glen Petrie, *A Singular Iniquity: The Campaigns of Josephine Butler* (London: Macmillan & Co., 1971); and Duncan Crow, *The Victorian Woman* (London: George Allen and Unwin, 1971).
52. Pivar, *Purity Crusade,* pp. 52–62.
53. State of Nevada, *Journal of the Senate of the Sixth Session of the Legislature of the State of Nevada* (Carson City, Nevada: State Printing Office, 1873), Bill 99, "An Act to Regulate the Social Evil in the State of Nevada."
54. *Territorial Enterprise,* March 4, 1873, and April 16, 1873.
55. Nevada Legislature, *Statutes of the State of Nevada Passed at the Eighth Session of the Legislature* (Carson City, Nevada: John J. Hill State Printer, 1877), pp. 181–84.
56. *Gold Hill News,* October 14, 1863.
57. *Virginia Evening Bulletin,* December 9, 1863.
58. *Territorial Enterprise,* July 7, 1867, and July 17, 1876.
59. Nellie's infamous saloon on the Barbary Coast provoked a number of citizen complaints. However, until she had been convicted of keeping a disorderly house there was no valid reason to revoke her license. See *Territorial Enterprise,* September 27, 1876, and June 7, 1877.
60. For records of formal and informal complaints see *Territorial Enterprise,* August 7, 1866, July 15, 1868, August 12, 1868, and July 11, 1877.
61. Ibid., February 3, 1878.
62. Myron Angel, ed., *Reproduction of Thompson and West's "History of Nevada, 1881"* (Berkeley: Howell North, 1958), p. 376.

63. William R. Gillis, comp., *The Nevada Directory for 1868–69* (San Francisco: M. D. Carr and Co., 1868), pp. 245 and 268.

64. Ibid., p. 268.

65. *Territorial Enterprise*, July 1, 1875.

66. Although most police and justice court records for Virginia City were destroyed by fires, a number of newspaper items described individual women's arrests. Also, newspapers sometimes published monthly arrest reports. For those reports see *Territorial Enterprise*, September 5, 1866, October 19, 1866, January 7, 1867, and September 6, 1876; *Virginia Evening Bulletin*, February 3, 1863, October 7, 1863, and May 4, 1864.

67. *Virginia Evening Bulletin*, August 14, 1863, and August 20, 1863.

68. Gillis, *Nevada Directory*, pp. 256–57.

69. *Territorial Enterprise*, March 17, 1875, March 31, 1875, and July 1, 1875.

70. Ibid., February 1, 1878.

71. For a discussion of the role of social control resources in shaping the amount of legal response to a public issue see Erikson, *Wayward Puritans*, pp. 22–23.

72. *Territorial Enterprise*, September 21, 1870.

73. Ibid.

74. For a list of signers of the petition against the Eureka see *Territorial Enterprise*, July 15, 1868.

75. *Gold Hill News*, April 26, 1867.

76. *Territorial Enterprise*, July 21, 1877.

77. Ibid., April 5, 1877, June 21, 1877, and July 22, 1877; see also the United States Census manuscripts for 1880 for Virginia City.

78. *Virginia Evening Chronicle*, February 22, 1877; and *Territorial Enterprise*, February 22, 1877.

79. *Territorial Enterprise*, July 10, 1878.

80. Ibid., August 1, 1869, February 25, 1874, and January 30, 1878; and *Virginia Evening Bulletin*, September 22, 1863.

81. Joseph Cusfield, *Symbolic Crusade* (Urbana: University of Illinois Press, 1963), pp. 1–35. This work discusses the importance of social dominance in the temperance movement in the United States.

Chapter 8

1. Harry Benjamin and R. E. L. Masters, *Prostitution and Morality* (New York: Julian Press, 1964), pp. 163–65; and Charles Winick and Paul M. Kinsie, *The Lively Commerce: Prostitution in the United States* (Chicago: Quadrangle Books, 1971), pp. 89–96.

2. These mechanisms for emotional distance in prostitution were first described sociologically in Kingsley Davis, "The Sociology of Prostitution," *American Sociological Review* 2 (October 1937):744–55. This landmark article provides the first serious sociological analysis of sexual commerce. It is flawed, however, by the author's assumptions that prostitution necessarily

involves female sellers and male buyers and that no social system can ever do without sexual commerce.

3. Travis Hirschi, "The Professional Prostitute," *Berkeley Journal of Sociology* 7 (Spring 1962):33.

4. The issue of prostitutes' existential choice is beautifully discussed by Ruth Rosen in her introduction to the collected letters of a turn-of-the-century prostitute. See Ruth Rosen and Sue Davidson, eds., *The Maimie Papers* (Old Westbury: Feminist Press, 1977), pp. xiii–xlviii.

5. The basis for any sociological discussion of self, interaction, and deviant identity is the theory of differential association in Edwin H. Sutherland, *The Professional Thief* (Chicago: University of Chicago Press, 1937).

6. Harold Garfinkel, "Conditions of Successful Degradation Ceremonies," *American Journal of Sociology* 61 (March 1956):420–24.

7. For an excellent discussion of the interaction of self-esteem with deviant behavior and social stratification see John P. Hewitt, *Social Stratification and Deviant Behavior* (New York: Random House, 1970).

8. Some examples of these social commentaries are Jane Addams, *A New Conscience and an Ancient Evil* (New York: Macmillan Co., 1913); and William W. Sanger, M.D. *The History of Prostitution: Its Extent, Causes, and Effects Throughout the World* (New York: Eugenics Publishing Co., 1937 [1897]).

9. Degradation of that objective exchange is examined in Georg Simmel, "Prostitution [1907]," in *Georg Simmel on Individuality and Social Forms* ed. Donald W. Levine (Chicago: University of Chicago Press, 1971), pp. 121–26.

10. The sociological construct of "dirty work" was introduced in Everett C. Hughes, "Good People and Dirty Work," in *The Other Side: Perspectives on Deviance* ed. Howard Becker (New York: Free Press, 1964), pp. 23–36.

11. For notes on the "toilet assumption" and Americans' fear of unwanted waste see Philip Slater, *The Pursuit of Loneliness* (Boston: Beacon Press, 1970), pp. 12–19.

12. The low status of dirty workers is indicated by the fact that three of the four lowest-rated occupations on the North-Hatt Occupational Prestige Scale administered in 1946 and 1963 were janitor, garbage collector, and street sweeper. Prostitution, needless to say, was not ranked. See Milton M. Gordon, "The Logic of Stratification Scales," in *Social Stratification in the United States* ed. Jack L. Roach, Llewellyn Gross, and Orville R. Grasslin (Englewood Cliffs, N.J.: Prentice-Hall, 1969), pp. 128–30.

13. Sigmund Freud, "Some Psychological Consequences of the Anatomical Distinction Between the Sexes [1925]," in *Freud: Sexuality and the Psychology of Love* ed. Phillip Reiff (New York: Collier Books, 1974), pp. 183–93.

14. Freud, "The Most Prevalent Form of Degradation in Erotic Life [1912]," in Reiff, *Freud,* p. 60.

15. For detailed case histories see Harold Greenwald, *The Elegant Prostitute: A Social and Psychoanalytic Study* (New York: Ballatine Books, 1970 [1958]).

For other specific psychoanalytic discussion of why women become prostitutes see Karl Abraham, *Selected Papers on Psychoanalysis* (New York: Basic Books, 1953); and Helene Deutsch, *The Psychology of Women,* vols. 1 and 2 (New York: Grune and Stratton, 1944 and 1945).

16. Freud, "A Special Type of Object Choice Made By Men [1910]," in Reiff, *Freud,* pp. 49–58.

17. Freud, "The Most Prevalent Form of Degradation in Erotic Life [1912]," in Reiff, *Freud,* p. 64.

18. The social construction of femininity is a much-debated topic, and a thorough discussion of it would take a book in itself. Fortunately that book has been written by Nancy Chodorow, *The Reproduction of Mothering: Psychoanalysis and the Sociology of Gender* (Berkeley: University of California Press, 1978). See especially chapters 7 and 8 on female oedipal construction and resolution.

19. Freud, "The Most Prevalent Form of Degradation in Erotic Life [1912]," in Reiff, *Freud,* pp. 65–66.

20. Chodorow, *The Reproduction of Mothering,* pp. 200–202.

Appendix 1

1. Richard E. Lingenfelter, *The Newspapers of Nevada: A History and Bibliography* (San Francisco: John Howell Books, 1964), pp. 84–96.

2. Mark Twain [Samuel Clemens], *Roughing It* (New York: Signet Classics, 1962 [1872]), pp. 223–27.

3. Advisory Committee on Problems of Census Enumeration of the Division of Behavioral Sciences in the National Research Council, *America's Uncounted People,* ed. Carole W. Parsons (Washington: National Academy of Sciences, 1972), pp. 25–39.

4. *Virginia City Territorial Enterprise,* February 7, 1880.

5. Mary Ellen Glass, "Nevada's Census Taker: A Vignette," *Nevada State Historical Quarterly* 9 (Winter 1966):1–12.

6. Theodore Hershbert, "A Method for the Computerized Study of Family and Household Structure Using the Manuscript Schedules of the U.S. Census of Population, 1850–1880," *The Family in Historical Perspective: An International Newsletter* 1 (Spring 1973):10–16.

Selected Bibliography

The Comstock Lode and the American Frontier

Angel, Myron, ed. *Reproduction of Thompson and West's History of Nevada, 1881*. Berkeley: Howell North, 1958.

Armstrong, Robert D. *A Preliminary Union Catalogue of Nevada Manuscripts*. Reno: University of Nevada Press, 1967.

Brown, Richard M. *Strain of Violence: Historical Studies of Violence and American Vigilantism*. New York: Oxford University Press, 1977.

Browne, J. Ross. "A Peep at the Washoe." In *Crusoe's Island*. New York: Harper Brothers, 1864.

Chirchill, Caroline M. *Little Sheaves*. San Francisco, 1874.

Curti, Merle. *The Making of an American Community*. Palo Alto, Calif.: Stanford University Press, 1959.

De Quille, Dan [William Wright]. *The Big Bonanza*. New York: Apollo Editions, 1969 [1876].

Drury, Wells. *An Editor on the Comstock Lode*. New York: Farrar and Rinehart, 1936.

Elliott, Russell R. *History of Nevada*. Lincoln: University of Nebraska Press, 1973.

Gillis, William R., comp. *The Nevada Directory for 1868-69*. San Francisco: M. D. Carr and Co., 1868.

Jeffrey, Julie Roy. *Frontier Women: The Trans-Mississippi West, 1840-1880*. New York: Hill and Wang, 1979.

Lamott, Kenneth. *Who Killed Mr. Crittenden?: Being a True Account of the Notorious Murder Trial that Stunned San Francisco, the Laura D. Fair Case.* New York: David McKay Co., 1963.

Lillard, Richard G. *Desert Challenge.* Lincoln: University of Nebraska Press, 1969 [1949].

Mathews, Mary McNair. *Ten Years in Nevada or Life on the Pacific Coast.* Buffalo: Baker, Jones and Co., 1880.

Palmer, Louise M. "How We Live in Nevada." *Overland Monthly* 2 (May 1869):457–62.

Shinn, Charles Howard. *The Story of the Mine.* New York: D. Appleton and Co., 1896.

Thernstorm, Stephen. *Poverty and Progress.* Cambridge: Harvard University Press, 1964.

Turner, Fredrick Jackson. "The Significance of the Frontier in American History." In *American Historical Association Report for the Year 1893.* Washington, D.C.: American Historical Association, 1893.

Twain, Mark [Samuel Clemens]. *Roughing It.* New York: Signet Classics, 1962 [1872].

Comstock Newspapers

Gold Hill Daily News
Virginia City Daily Territorial Enterprise
Virginia City Daily Trespass
Virginia City Evening Bulletin
Virginia City Evening Chronicle

Major Unpublished Sources on the Comstock

Doten, Alfred. Diaries. Special Collections of the University of Nevada at Reno.

Fair, James Graham. Biographical sketch and personal dictation. Bancroft Library of the University of California at Berkeley.

Kinnersley, Thomas Harold. "Virginia, Nevada, 1859–1890: A Study of Police, Water, and Fire Problems." Ph.D. dissertation, University of California at Los Angeles, 1974.

Nevada Legislature. Appendix to the Journals of the Senate and Assembly. Eighth Session, "Recapitulation of the Inhabitants of Storey, State of Nevada." Vol. 3. Carson City: John J. Hill State Printer, 1877.

Probates of prostitutes living in Storey County. Storey County Courthouse.

United States, Department of the Interior, Census Office. Manuscripts for the Eighth, Ninth, and Tenth Censuses of the United States. (1860, 1870, and 1880).

Nineteenth Century Prostitution in Great Britain and the United States

Acton, William. *Prostitution.* New York: Frederick E. Praeger, 1969 [1857].

Best, Joel. "Careers in Brothel Prostitution." Paper presented at the annual meeting of the American Sociological Association, New York City, 1980.

Finnegan, Frances. *Poverty and Prostitution: A Study of Victorian Prostitutes in York.* Cambridge: Cambridge University Press, 1979.

Gentry, Curt. *The Madams of San Francisco.* New York: Ballantine Books, 1971 [1964].

Gorham, Deborah. "The 'Maiden Tribute in Modern Babylon' Re-examined." *Victorian Studies* 21 (1978):353–79.

Hirata, Lucie Cheng. "Free, Indentured, Enslaved: Chinese Prostitutes in Nineteenth Century America." *Signs: A Journal of Women in Culture and Society* 5 (1979):3–29.

Johnson, C. D. "That Guilty Third Tier: Prostitution in Nineteenth-Century American Theaters." *American Quarterly* 27 (1975):575–84.

Sanger, William W. *The History of Prostitution: Its Extent, Causes, and Effects Throughout the World.* New York: Eugenics Publishing Company, 1937 [1897].

Walkowitz, Judith. "Notes on the History of Victorian Prostitution." *Feminist Studies* 1 (1972):105–14.

The Regulation of Prostitution and Morality

Degler, Carl N. "What Ought to Be and What Was: Women's Sexuality in the Nineteenth Century." *American Historical Review* 79 (1974):1467–90.

Goldman, Emma. *The Traffic in Women and Other Essays on Feminism.* New York: Times Change Press, 1970 [1900].

Gusfield, Joseph. *Symbolic Crusade.* Urbana: University of Illinois Press, 1963.

Haller, John S., and Haller, Robin M. *The Physician and Sexuality in Victorian America.* Urbana: University of Illinois Press, 1974.

Hart, H. L. A. *Law, Liberty, and Morality.* Palo Alto: Stanford University Press, 1963.

Petrie, Glen. *A Singular Iniquity: The Campaigns of Josephine Butler.* London: Macmillan & Co., 1971.

Pivar, David J. *Purity Crusade: Sexual Morality and Social Control, 1868–1900.* Westport, Conn.: Greenwood Press, 1973.

Roby, Pamela, and Kerr, Virginia. "The Politics of Prostitution." *Nation,* April 10, 1972, pp. 463–66.

Rugoff, Milton. *Prudery and Passion: Sexuality in Victorian America.* New York: G. P. Putnam's Sons, 1971.

Women Endorsing Decriminalization. "Prostitution: A Non-Victim Crime?" *Issues in Criminology* 7 (1973):137–62.

Wolfenden Report: Report of the Committee on Homosexual Offenses and Prostitution.
New York: Stein and Day, 1963.

Twentieth Century Prostitution in the United States

Addams, Jane. *A New Conscience and an Ancient Evil.* New York: Macmillan
   Co., 1913.
Benjamin, Harry, and Masters, R. E. L. *Prostitution and Morality.* New York:
   Julian Press, 1964.
Bryan, James H. "Apprenticeships in Prostitution." *Social Problems* 12
   (1965):287–97.
Cresse, Paul G. *The Taxi-Dance Hall.* Chicago: University of Chicago Press,
   1932.
Davis, Kingsley. "The Sociology of Prostitution." *American Sociological Review* 2
   (1937):744–55.
David, Nanette. "The Prostitute: Developing a Deviant Identity." In *Studies in
   the Sociology of Sex,* edited by James Henslin, pp. 297–322. New York:
   Appleton, 1971.
Goldman, Marion S. "The Ideology of Prostitution." In *Women on the Move: A
   Feminist Perspective,* edited by Jean R. Leppaluoto, pp. 145–53. Pittsburgh:
   KNOW, 1973.
Goldstein, Paul J. *Prostitution and Drugs.* Lexington, Mass.: Lexington Books,
   1979.
Gray, Diana. "Turning Out: A Study of Teen-age Prostitution." *Urban Life and
   Culture* 1 (1973):401–25.
Greenwald, Harold. *The Elegant Prostitute: A Social and Psychoanalytic Study.*
   New York: Ballantine Books, 1970.
Heyl, Barbara Sherman. *The Madams Entrepreneur.* New Brunswick, N.J.:
   Transaction Books, 1979.
Hirschi, Travis. "The Professional Prostitute." *Berkeley Journal of Sociology* 7
   (1962):33–50.
James, Jennifer, and Meyerding, Jane. "Early Sexual Experience and Prostitu-
   tion." *American Journal of Psychiatry* 34 (1977):1381–85.
Lemert, Edwin J. *Social Pathology.* New York: McGraw-Hill, 1951. Chapter 8,
   "Prostitution and the Prostitute," pp. 236–80.
Millett, Kate. *The Prostitution Papers: A Candid Dialogue.* New York: Avon
   Books, 1973.
Milner, Christina, and Milner, Richard. *Black Players: The Secret Life of Black
   Pimps.* Boston: Little, Brown and Co., 1972.
Reckless, Walter C. "The Distribution of Commercialized Vice in the City."
   American Journal of Sociology 32 (1926):164–76.
Rosen, Ruth, and Davidson, Sue, eds. *The Maimie Papers.* Old Westbury:
   Feminist Press, 1977.
Sheehy, Gail. "The Landlords of Hell's Bedroom." *New York Magazine* 6
   (1972):67–80.

————. *Hustling.* New York: Delacorte Press, 1971.

Thomas, William I. *The Unadjusted Girl.* Boston: Little, Brown and Co., 1923.

Winick, Charles, and Kinsie, Paul M. *The Lively Commerce: Prostitution in the United States.* Chicago: Quadrangle Books, 1971.

Social Theory

Blau, Peter M. *Exchange and Power in Social Life.* New York: John Wiley and Sons, 1964.

Chodorow, Nancy. *The Reproduction of Mothering: Psychoanalysis and the Sociology of Gender.* Berkeley: University of California Press, 1978.

Degler, Carl N. *At Odds: Women and the Family in America from the Revolution to the Present.* New York: Oxford University Press, 1980.

Durkheim, Emile. *The Division of Labor in Society.* Translated by George Simpson. Glencoe, Ill.: Free Press, 1958.

————. *The Rules of the Sociological Method.* Translated by J. H. Mueller and S. A. Solovay. Glencoe, Ill.: Free Press, 1958.

————. *Suicide.* Translated by John A. Spaulding and George Simpson. Glencoe, Ill.: Free Press, 1951.

Engels, Fredrich. *The Condition of the Working Class in England.* Moscow: Foreign Languages Publishing House, 1953.

Erikson, Kai T. *Wayward Puritans: A Study in the Sociology of Deviance.* John Wiley and Sons, 1966.

Freud, Sigmund. *Freud: Sexuality and the Psychology of Love.* Edited by Phillip Reiff. New York: Collier Books, 1974 [1910–1925].

Hughes, Everett C. "Good People and Dirty Work." In *The Other Side: Perspectives of Deviance,* edited by Howard Becker. New York: Free Press, 1964.

Marx, Karl. *The Economic and Philosophic Manuscripts of 1844.* New York: International Publishers, 1964.

————. *The Eighteenth Brumaire of Louis Bonaparte.* New York: New York Labor News Co., 1951 [1852].

Mitchell, Juliet. *Women's Estate.* New York: Pantheon Books, 1971.

Simmel, Georg. *Georg Simmel on Individuality and Social Forms.* Edited by Donald N. Levine. Chicago: University of Chicago Press, 1971.

Sutherland, Edwin H. *The Professional Thief.* Chicago: University of Chicago Press, 1937.

Weber, Max. *The Methodology of the Social Sciences.* Edited by Edward Shils and Henry Finch. New York: Free Press, 1959.

Index